Magic
Time

EDWIN WILSON

Magic Time

A MEMOIR

Notes on
Theatre & Other
Entertainments

S·K

A Smith and Kraus Book
PO BOX 564, Hanover, NH 03755
Editorial 603.643.6431 To Order 1.877.668.8680
www.smithandkraus.com

ISBN: 978-1-57525-947-5 (hardcover with jacket)
ISBN: 978-1-57525-942-0 (paperback)
Library of Congress Control Number: 2019952510

Typesetting and layout by Elizabeth E. Monteleone
Cover: Photo by ©Paul Kolnik
Cover: Design by Joan O'Connor

For information about custom editions, special sales, education and corporate purchases, please contact Smith and Kraus at editor@smithandkraus.com or 603.643.6431

To the memory of Chic

In the theatre when a performance is about to begin the actors who open the show stand in the wings, just behind the Stage Manager. When the latter, signaling the beginning of the performance, says into the microphone "House lights to half; house lights out," one performer will often turn to another and say: "It's Show Time," or simply "Magic Time."

This book is a memoir, mostly about my years teaching and writing about theatre. Occasionally it ventures into other areas: travel, encounters with interesting people, detours into film, and the like. For me, the entire journey has been a fascinating adventure, but like any journey, filled with ups and downs, twists and turns. On the whole, however, I feel I have been one of the most fortunate people on earth.

TABLE OF CONTENTS

CHAPTER ONE

The Early Years

In the winter and spring of 2018, I was putting the finishing touches on a revision of a college theatre textbook, *The Theatre Experience*, the 14th edition of which was to appear in January 2019. Chic, my wife of nearly 50 years, had died a year and a half prior to that time and like most survivors of a longtime marriage I discovered that the loss was far more devastating than I could ever have imagined. One thing that had kept me busy was preparing with my co-author, Alvin Goldfarb, the 10th edition of another text: *Theatre: The Lively Art* which appeared in January, 2018. Now I was putting the finishing touches on the book that had originally started my textbook career, knowing that it might be the last edition on which I worked.

The question arose: what was I going to do now? I lived in an apartment on Central Park West in Manhattan with friends nearby but I was facing endless days with little or nothing to do – a daunting challenge. My first thought was perhaps to write a murder mystery. I had written my first mystery three years before entitled *The Patron Murders*. It had been reasonably well received but was not successful commercially. Still, I had enjoyed working on it and had an idea for a sequel but I asked myself: "Was this what I really wanted to do?" Then I had another idea. Perhaps I could write about my experiences in the New York theatre over more than half a century. The idea was not to write an auto-biography – to quote Rodgers and Hart, that "never entered my mind" – but perhaps a recollection of sorts focusing on the experiences I had had with interesting and noteworthy people I'd worked with. That's how this began.

To say that I took a circuitous route to maturity, as well as to a career, would be the height of understatement. I took a painfully long time – some would say an inexcusably long time – to find myself and discover what I wanted to do, both in life and in the theatre. I was born and raised in Nashville, Tennessee. My father had grown up on a farm in southern Kentucky (in the same county from which the writer Robert Penn Warren had come) and had attended Vanderbilt University, graduating from both the college and the law school. He never practiced law, however, but went into business – a career he very much wanted me to take up as well.

To prepare me for a career that would mirror his he insisted from very early in life that I have a job each summer. I began when I was twelve working on a farm that belonged to a friend of his. Then at 13, I worked in a small, neighborhood clothing store – also owned by a friend of my father's. The only problem that second year was that after a few weeks officials from the state employment bureau showed up on a routine check and declared that I was underage to be employed in the shop and I was forced to quit. By the time I was 15, however, that was no longer a problem and for several summers I worked in the warehouse of a wholesale grocery operation, again a business owned by a friend of my father, a man named Charley Ragland, of whom more later. The pattern of summer work continued into college years with my working one summer in a coal mine in southern Kentucky – this time not because of a friend but because my father was in the coal business.

In terms of education, I went to a progressive grammar school in Nashville, and when the time came for me to go to high school my parents sent me away to a boarding school – the Episcopal High School (EHS) in Alexandria, Virginia. Though we never discussed it, I feel certain this was my mother's idea. At this point in time families in Nashville rarely sent their children away to prep school, but my mother wanted me and my sister to have the best education possible. My guess is that she reasoned that the well-known Eastern prep schools – Groton, St. Paul's, Exeter, Taft, Hotchkiss – would be a bridge too far for me, a 13-year old boy, particularly one who was not into football or basketball. So she settled on a Virginia school, and one that was close to Washington, where my parents had good friends.

In what was to be a pattern in my life, I almost did not get in to E.H.S. Rather, as the school year began my parents were told I was on a waiting list and so I was enrolled in high school in Nashville. Two weeks later we were notified that someone had withdrawn from E.H.S. and that I could attend if I wanted. My mother replied that of course I would come. As I have said, I was 13 at the time but despite a great deal of fear and trembling inside I went along with my parents' plans. Within a day or two they took me to the Union Station where I boarded a train to Chattanooga at which juncture I took another train headed to Washington. How I managed to do this all by myself, I will never know: changing trains with my luggage, not knowing how to go to meals or tip the porters. After sleeping in an upper birth overnight I got off the train, totally alone, in Alexandria, where I was relieved to find someone from the school who had come to meet me.

In those days the dorms for students at E.H.S. consisted not of rooms but "cubicles," with iron hooks on the walls on which to hang jackets and trousers and a not very wide piece of canvas at the opening to the hall. It was very primitive and utterly devoid of privacy. I was not yet 14, was two weeks late, and did not know a single person, boy or master, at the school. I felt that, without question, I was the most miserable person on earth. Throughout the fall I wrote letters home every day, with tears falling on the paper, explaining how unhappy I was and what a mistake this whole thing had been. Realizing how utterly and woefully unhappy I was, my parents understood that they must do something. And so at Thanksgiving my father came to Washington and took me into the city to be with him and to see my parents' friends.

Before coming, my father asked me what I would like to do so I looked at *The Washington Post* and saw that there was a musical at the Shubert Theatre starring Al Jolson (probably on his sixteenth farewell tour). Titled *Hold on to Your Hats,* it was set in Mexico and featured Jolson and his fellow performers dressed in sombreros with bandoliers across their chests. It was light-hearted and the audience enjoyed it, especially the double-entendres many of which went over my head completely but which all of the adults seemed to enjoy enormously. Finally, at the end, we saw what everyone had come for: Jolson came down to the front of the stage and took off his hat. Though still in the rest of his costume, he got down on his knees and sang "Mammy" and then, "Swanee."

I gradually discovered I could survive, though that first year the misery never went fully away. By the beginning of my second year I found things I could get involved in, particularly in the spring. Somewhere in the winter or early spring of the 1942-43 year, a fellow student, Bill Backer, who was a year ahead of me, sought me out. "I want to write a musical," he said, "and I want someone to help me do it." The idea would never have occurred to me and why Bill singled me out to join him I never knew. Besides which, at a school like E.H.S., the notion of something like an original musical was revolutionary, unheard of, and in fact, almost subversive. The school was 104 years old and in all that time nothing even approaching an entertainment like this had ever been contemplated, let alone presented. To me, however, it sounded like something I could latch on to and so, I signed up.

We set to work with Bill writing the music and the two of us creating the story and the lyrics. We enlisted fellow students and a few of the younger faculty members and their wives to become not only actors but stage managers and stage hands. We came up, as well, with crude scenery and costumes and began rehearsals. For a theatre we picked Liggett Hall, a venerable structure that had served as the school chapel for many years and whose stage was now used for declamation and debating contests. One of the oldest structures on the campus, in its long history nothing remotely like a musical comedy had darkened its stage.

I don't remember the title of that production but the plot was simplicity itself: a scandal had arisen at the school because the word was out that a girl was living in one of the dorms, a clear violation in any circumstance but particularly at what had been an all boys school for a hundred years. Bill and I stretched this as far as we could until we finally felt it necessary to introduce the denouement, which was that the female was not a young lady but a cat. Not a particularly original or sophisticated plot line, but in a school that had never had a musical of any kind whatsoever, it was enough, and the play was considered a great success, so much so that the next year we were allowed to present another musical.

The title of the second show I do remember. It was *A Cheer for the Team*, a gentle lampoon of several of the more visible and venerable faculty members and it proved to be even more successful than the production the year before. This was especially true since we were able to identify and enlist students who had a resemblance to or could emulate the mannerisms of the faculty members they were portraying.

Bill graduated and went to Yale and I did not attempt to write another show at EHS without him, especially since he was the one who wrote the music. In later life Bill became the premier writer in the U. S. of advertising jingles – the most successful composer in that field of all times. When I would visit him in his office in New York some twenty-five years later, the most prominent piece of furniture in the room was his upright piano; it went wherever he went. While with McCann-Ericson he wrote two extraordinary songs for Coca-Cola: "Things Go Better With Coke" and "I'd like to Teach the World to Sing in Perfect Harmony." In a famous TV commercial, the latter featured a group of fifty or more youngsters singing outdoors in a large open field on a hillside in Italy. For Miller Lite Beer Bill wrote: "Every Thing You Ever Wanted in a Beer, and Less."

After my four years at E. H. S. I returned to Nashville and enrolled in Vanderbilt to begin college in the fall of 1945. This was only a few months after the end of World War II and during my first year at college the military draft was still on – replacements were badly needed for the exhausted soldiers, sailors and marines who had been fighting in Europe and the Pacific. When an 18 month enlistment – six months shorter than any previous term – was instituted in the summer of 1946, I decided to enlist. And so, after four quarters at Vanderbilt I joined the army and was sent for basic training to Fort Bragg in Fayetteville, North Carolina.

When I was about to leave for the Army a number of

friends, knowing of my interest in entertainment, urged me to attempt to get into Special Services, the entertainment and recreation branch of the service. "Now that the war is over, no one will think you are joining Special Services to avoid combat," they said. After basic training, however, there was no opportunity to get into anything specific. I was sent immediately, just before Christmas, to Seattle, where, after three weeks, I joined other service men on a "Victory Ship" for a two week "slow boat" to Japan on a ship called the Central Falls Victory.

Travelling with an odd mixture of enlisted men and a few officers I did not relish the idea of a two week sail across the northern side of the Pacific in the dead of winter, especially since, like others, I was faced with endless hours of KP duty in the kitchens and deck swabbing in between. Searching around for a way to get out of this, I discovered aboard the ship a large locker with musical instruments in it. I had not joined a band in high school but in grammar school I had played a very questionable trumpet in the school orchestra. I searched out other musicians on the ship and found several excellent ones: a drummer, saxophone, trombone and guitar players, whom I recruited. There were about seven of us in all. I found they were all naturals. Because I was leading them I did not have to play that much. After a few rehearsals, we were ready to audition for the officers, which we did, and were engaged to present a jam session of sorts late every afternoon, just before evening chow. As a result, we were all relieved of all chores, KP or otherwise, and the arduous trip became considerably less punishing.

I did not disembark in Japan – where I might have searched for a Special Services unit – nor did I get off in Guam, our next port of call, where I might also have joined Special Services. No, I went with about a dozen other men to Iwo Jima, landing two years to the day after the first landing of the Marines that occurred on February 19, 1945. The battle for Iwo had been one of the costliest and toughest of the war. The island was less than ten square miles in size and had been originally created by a volcanic explosion. As a result its beaches consisted not of white sand but dark volcanic ash. The U. S. had wanted to take the island in order to create a landing strip for crippled airplanes returning from bombing raids on Japan.

This tiny space had been defended by 23,000 Japanese troops who, prior to the invasion, were subjected to weeks of merciless bombing. The landing force of U. S. troops numbered roughly 60,000, but the superiority in numbers mattered little in terms of the odds the invaders were facing, which consisted not only of rough terrain but eleven miles of underground tunnels the Japanese had dug. The island was finally conquered five weeks after the invasion, but at a heavy, heavy cost: the U. S. suffered casualties of nearly 6,000 dead and over 17,000 wounded.

One of the eeriest sights I have ever seen, before or since, was a swath of beach 50 or 60 feet wide reaching from the waters edge over the bare stretch of dark sand to the island undergrowth at the top, stretching some half a mile from end to end. On this dark, granular half-mile swath were spread the 6,000 white crosses and Stars of David, each about 2 1/2 feet high, set above the grave sites of the men who had lost their lives in the deadly, costly invasion. It was eerie in the extreme and deeply moving. In the center of this scene, at the water's edge – looking out to sea – was a white, open gate, with vertical poles at the sides, 25 to 30 feet tall, and a 20 foot cross piece at the top. It was, in effect, a gateway to the beyond and presented a scene, a vision, that was, quite literally, unforgettable.

On my arrival on Iwo I was immediately dispatched to the Port Director's office which consisted of a small Quonset hut near a beach where my superior and I intermittently did the paper work necessary, ironically, to send the scrap metal in the water just off shore back to Japan. We had time on our hands and one benefit to me was that I found a manual lying around that instructed the reader how to learn touch typing, something that was to prove invaluable to me for many years to come. The free time became helpful to me in another way. I discovered that the sole radio station on Iwo, a branch of the AFRS (Armed Forces Radio Service), was not too far away from us in two other Quonset huts at the foot of Mount Suribachi. Suribachi, it will be remembered, was the small mountain famous for the much-replicated flag raising. Those who worked there went back and forth in a jeep the five miles to headquarters for meals and lodging.) In slack times at the Port Directors – of which there were quite a few – I asked permission from my superior to go to the radio station where the friendly sergeant in charge was happy to have someone help him. Radio broadcasts, I discovered, were the only entertainment on the island, not only for the personnel in service, but also for the bored wives of lieutenants and other young officers serving on the island.

Two months after I started helping at the radio station, the sergeant in charge was suddenly re-assigned to the Philippines which meant that I, a lowly corporal, became the only man on the island who knew how to operate the station. I was asked to take charge and realized that finally I was in Special Services. Running the station was mostly a matter of following a routine. Power was supplied by two diesel generators and one of my chores was to run outside, while a 15 minute disk was playing, to refill the generators so we could continue operating. Basically, there were three types of programs: recordings on 16-inch vinyl, each side of which provided 15 minutes of entertainment making a total of 30 minutes when you played both sides. Whether a comedy, a drama, or music by Tommy Dorsey, Louis Armstrong or Benny Goodman – one of the greats – the trick was that after the first 15 minutes you had to lift the needle, flip the large disk, put it back on the turntable, and place the needle on the first groove. Each second was precious.

A second type of program was created from "slow news," which was dictation from AFRS to the stations of the latest news. It came in like this: "Today General MacArthur…Today General MacArthur…said in Tokyo…said in Tokyo…" The idea was that someone in the station wrote this all down so that an announcer could repeat the message as one uninterrupted newscast on the nightly news. The third type of program was an occasional live interview with someone who had done something newsworthy or with a visitor to the island. There was, as well, a fourth category: the serendipitous live program that fell in the station's lap – a virtually impossible occurrence but one that happened to me in the third week that I was in charge of the station.

I referred above to the nearly half-mile long, extraordinary "cemetery" along the shore where the troops that had lost their lives in the invasion had been put to rest. This was not a permanent resting place, however. That would be a cemetery in Hawaii and to dig up the caskets and send each of them to Hawaii was the task of a "grave-diggers" unit – an all African-American group – that had recently arrived on Iwo. It was at once a wrenching assignment but also an important and necessary one. Not too long after they had arrived – at a time when I had been in charge of the station for only three weeks – I received a surprise visit from three of the officers in charge of the unit. From their ranks, they told me they had assembled a choir that sang gospel songs and spirituals – was there any chance they could appear on the radio station? They invited me to visit their small assembly hall to hear the group, which I did the next day. What

I heard was an unforgettable performance: 30 men without a sign of sheet music, singing a cappella, in four-part harmony with amazing richness and subtlety. Needless to say, by the next Sunday afternoon they were on the radio presenting an hour-long program of their music, a program that continued long after I had left, and for as long as they remained on the island.

I reveled in playing the large 16" disks and flipping them over as quickly as possible when we were airing a 30 minute segment, which many of them were: programs by Glenn Miller, Duke Ellington, and Harry James. Also, laboriously taking down short wave slow news broadcasts and repeating it later in real time over the air. After two months of running the radio station, however, I was suddenly called to headquarters and asked to report to the commanding General. "Have you been in touch with your senator?" the general asked. Dumbfounded, I replied that I had not. "Your congressman then?" he continued. Still befuddled, I answered with a firm no. "Well," he said, "we have just received an order from headquarters in Tokyo like none we have ever received before. They've ordered us to send you to Guam – just you – and to do so immediately. Do you have any idea how this happened?" "No, sir, absolutely not; I swear." "Well," he declared, "we can't let you go. You're the only one who can run the radio station. On the other hand," he said, holding the order in his hand, "this seems unequivocal. We will have to work it out."

So we arrived at an arrangement where I would stay for an additional three weeks, train several replacements, and then leave for Guam. Very quickly three men showed up who I taught the intricacies of running the station and after which, I was on my way to Guam where I would spend the rest of my time in service, joining Headquarters Company, writing for the enlisted men's newspaper and making friends that I kept for the rest of my life. Guam is a beautiful island, verdant, luscious, with gorgeous white sand beaches. After a fairly short time on the island – living with colleagues in the enlisted men's dormitory – I was made aware by my colleagues that there was a serious inequity in treatment between officers and enlisted men and women. Not anything to do with official or personal mistreatment, but in our days off, namely, our lack of access to those wide, white sandy beaches.

On weekends, all of the officers, who had jeeps and the like available, would head off to those inviting beaches, while the enlisted folk remained back at headquarters with only a softball field and a bedraggled volley ball court at their disposal. I wrote an article about this that appeared in our enlisted personnel's newspaper. Not long after that the editor, the managing editor and I were ordered to appear at headquarters to meet with a stuffy, self-important, pretentious major who gave us a lecture on how tough things were for the higher ups; a lecture that concluded with a question which he considered final and definitive, a question I will never forget: "Do you have any idea," he asked, " how far we are from the nearest railhead?" Given the fact that Guam stood in the middle of the western Pacific Ocean, hundreds of miles from the Philippines to the west, of Australia to the south, and of Japan in the north, we said we thought we grasped the notion of just how far we were from a railhead. In any event, two weeks later the enlisted personnel were called together and told that trucks would be available the next weekend to take us north to the beaches, happily, a practice that continued from then on.

Many months later, after I had been out of the army and back in Nashville for a few weeks, I learned the story behind my transfer from Iwo Jima to Guam. My father's good friend and regular golf partner was Charley Ragland, the owner of the food warehouse where I had worked all those summers ago. When I first landed on Iwo Jima and was assigned to the Port Director's office in the Quonset hut, I had written my family about my frustration at being stuck in that job with little or nothing to do. It was, I wrote them, "a waste of time and a failure of the army to take advantage of my abilities and use me in the best way possible." Charley Ragland, it turned out, while playing golf with my father would ask him how I was doing. "He writes us that he is being wasted in his job on Iwo Jima," my father told him.

Charley grew up in Murfreesboro, Tennessee, where he was a close friend of Jean Faircloth. The two of them stayed in touch even when Jean became Mrs. Douglas MacArthur and went to the far corners of the world with the General. Charley wrote to his friend Jean in Tokyo telling her that a young man who used to work for him was on Iwo Jima, not being used to his potential. Some weeks later Charley received an answer: "I've spoken to the General about the Wilson boy," Jean wrote back. "We are having him moved to Guam and if he is not happy there, let us know and we will bring him to Tokyo." Some years later, at a reception at the Waldorf Astoria, my wife and I found ourselves standing near Mrs. MacArthur and went over to speak to her. I did not mention Iwo, but I did say that I grew up in Nashville and that when I was much younger I had worked for Charley Ragland. "Ah, Charley Horse," she said, using her nickname for him, "What a great time we had together; all those years ago."

Returning to Vanderbilt: by going year round I was able to finish only one year behind the time when I would have finished originally. In the spring of my senior year I saw a notice for a special, one-year graduate course at the University of Edinburgh in Scotland. It was a program, I was certain, created to take advantage of Americans with the G. I. Bill and when I arrived at my first class I knew that to be the case. Of the seven students in the Masters program, six were Americans and of those six, it turned out I was the only one who finished the course and earned a diploma. The year in Edinburgh was everything I had hoped it would be. As far as I am concerned, Edinburgh is one of the most enchanting towns in the British Isles. I lived in a boarding house in the Georgian section – homes that had been built between 1760 and 1840, many of which were still preserved. I could walk to school, across Princes Street, the main street that has on one side an enormous garden, then cross over the Royal Mile that runs from Edinburgh Castle to Holyroodhouse Palace and on to the University.

My teachers were venerable and first rate – the program, I should add, let us choose from an array of disciplines and professors. In the Graduate School dining hall I fell in with a group of five or six students in various disciplines with whom I had lunch several days a week and with whom I stayed in touch for a number years, especially Charles Waterston who eventually became the Director of the Royal Scottish Museum (and who, incidentally, was also the uncle of the actor Sam Waterston). Some 25 years later my wife and I had a chance to visit Charles and his wife who gave us a personal tour of the museum as well as a wonderful dinner.

The same year I was in Edinburgh my younger sister, Sue, was taking her Junior Year Abroad at the Sorbonne in Paris where she and a roommate were living with a French family in the 16th Arrondissement. I went across to Paris several times during that year to visit her and see Paris and in the spring to join our parents for a tour of Italy. In the summer my sister joined me when I revisited Edinburgh to attend the famous festival that had just begun four years before. Perhaps the thing I most enjoyed about my year in Edinburgh were my trips to London (during which I would sit up all night in a railway coach) in order to take in the British theatre. I saw virtually everything that was on that year: Laurence Olivier and Vivien Leigh in *Antony and Cleopatra* one night and *Caesar and Cleopatra* the next night, John Gielgud in Christopher Fry's *The Lady's Not for Burning,* virtually everything that was playing.

It just so happened that in the Fry play two young actors were making their stage debuts: Richard Burton and Claire Bloom. Some forty years later, when I was interviewing Claire for a television series, I told her I had seen that production. "Every night we were in that show," she said, "there was one scene where I could not resist looking at the audience. It was a scene in which John, in that sonorous, unmistakable voice, would be declaiming blank verse written by Fry, but the audience would be staring, not at Gielgud but at Richard silently scrubbing the floor."

After my year in Edinburgh I returned to Nashville; it was time to settle down. Charley Ragland, the man who had been my benefactor when I was on Iwo Jima and in whose warehouse I had worked as a teenager, had as part of his grocery operation a coffee company: purveyors of Colonial Coffee. It was a small operation – one man in charge, really, and a couple of more men in the roasting room. Mr. Ragland offered me a job as the assistant to the director of the coffee company. For one thing, he said, he wanted to beef up advertising and also expand our reach into west Tennessee. It sounded fine to me so I took the job.

I settled into life in Nashville as a young bachelor and into my work for Colonial Coffee. My parents, I could tell, were enormously pleased: at last I was in business, at last

I was settling down. I realized that of all the jobs I might have had, this one, along with the usual routine requirements of meeting deadlines and such, had its rewarding aspects. There was, for instance, advertising. In launching our new campaign into west Tennessee I had a free hand and one thing I wanted to introduce was a singing commercial. In this regard, it was fortunate that we were in Nashville. Known, of course, as the home of Country Music, the city was home to a range of other kinds of music as well. Owen Bradley, for instance, had a first-rate, live popular orchestra a la Glenn Miller or Tommy Dorsey and then there were the Anita Kerr singers. Anita had a close-harmony group who over time made dozens of successful records, first in Nashville, then Los Angeles and finally in London. Her singers really were the go-to back-up group for everyone. To create a singing commercial for Colonial Coffee I got in touch with Anita and together we created the words and music for – if I do say so myself – a smashing commercial.

Just when it looked as if I was on a predicable career path, however, something began to nag at me – theatre. Though it was clear that for my parents there was really only one choice of a vocation, they had unwittingly offered me an alternative. It turned out to be a miscalculation on their part that neither they nor I could have predicted. From the late 1930s through the early 1950s, once and sometimes twice a year, my parents took the train to New York where they loved to hear performers like Hildegarde or Jimmy Durante at the Empire Room in the Waldorf or the Persian Room at the Plaza. But they also very much enjoyed the theatre. At some point, they began to include me on these trips, with the result that I saw first-hand, theatre in its golden age: the original productions of *Streetcar Named Desire*, *Death of a Salesman*, *Oklahoma!* – you name it.

Toward the end of my second year at Colonial Coffee I began to have stirrings, feint yearnings, that I should perhaps attempt to carve out a career in the theatre. These feelings were extremely tentative and infrequent at first but the notion grew in my mind. I had no clear idea of what I wanted to do in the theatre; I knew I had no desire to be an actor and also was aware that I had no talent for the visual side of theatre: scenic, lighting or costume design. That pretty much left directing and playwriting. Of these two, although I had done a bit of directing in the theatre department at Vanderbilt and had never written a play in my life, not even a dramatic scene, I felt it would make more sense to begin with playwriting.

Having begun to think along these lines, I knew that there would be two large hurdles: breaking this idea to my parents and getting into a good drama school. Of those two, facing my parents would be the more difficult. As far as the school to which I would apply, I knew that Yale had perhaps the oldest and best-known drama school in the country. I also knew that Yale would be the most palatable and readily accepted school by my mother and father.

I let all these thoughts simmer for several weeks but finally decided that it was now or never and told my parents. It was also not easy to break the news to Charley Ragland who had been so kind to me through the years.

In addition, there was the not insignificant matter of getting accepted at Yale. The first requirement for admission was to write a play, which, as I say, I had never done before. I, therefore, set about writing a play. I don't even remember what it was about; I only recollect that it was a pretty frail reed in terms of drama. Also, because I was a coward, I had not taken a personal stand that I was going to change the course of my life no matter what, but rather let the final determination depend on whether or not I was accepted at the drama school. In the end, after several agonizing weeks, I was accepted. As I will explain later, that was not the end of the story, but for now we move on to this seismic shift in my life.

In the Fall of 1954, therefore, at the age of 26, I was starting all over – an extremely problematic situation. Unlike others of my age I was at ground zero, on the bottom rung of the ladder, in serious danger of becoming a drifter, even a ne'er do well – a person who would never make up his mind. I didn't think of myself this way, but I was quite aware that doubtless that would be the way everyone else would look at me.

CHAPTER TWO

New Haven

When I arrived in New Haven in the fall of 1954, I immediately had two strokes of good luck. The first was with Harold and Edith Whiteman. They were both from Nashville and although they were a few years older than me, I knew them both. They were a golden couple. Edith had been outstanding all through high school and college and at the end of her four years at Vandy was awarded the accolade of "Miss Vanderbilt." Harold, who had gone to Yale, had had an equally impressive career that included, among other things, serving as Captain of the Yale football team. After college they had gotten married and moved to New Haven where Harold was now Dean of Freshman.

I looked them up when I first arrived and Harold asked me where I was going to live. I said I hadn't really thought about it, whereupon he told me that if I wanted to sign on, he could recommend me to serve as a "freshman counselor." When I asked what that meant he explained that the position, usually held by someone in the graduate schools (law, medicine, arts and sciences, drama) who would agree to live on the freshman campus and be a shepherd and counselor for some 18 freshman would be afforded not only free board but meals as well. As you might imagine, this was a "no-brainer" and I agreed to take the position right away.

My 18 freshmen students turned out to be a diverse

group but none of them were difficult to communicate with or manage. I was naïve about these things and it was not until some point midway through the school year that I realized two of my charges came from quite well-known families. Joseph Verner Reed, Jr., who came from a social family and whose father, among other things, was a founder of the Shakespeare Theatre in Connecticut, would himself, later in life, become a diplomat as well as a U. S. ambassador. As for Robin Lehman, he was the son of the financier and art collector for whom a wing at the Metropolitan Museum is named. I became closer to Robin than most of my charges because he was quite shy as well as the one who I felt most needed reassuring.

And then in New Haven, there was Kay Angell, the widow of James Rowland Angell, a famous scientist and the legendary president of Yale from 1921 to 1937. My family has a summerhouse in the mountains of North Carolina where our next door neighbors were Major Stuart Cramer, a veteran of World War I, and his wife Julia. When the Major learned from my father that I was headed to Yale he remarked: "I must let my sister Kay know." None of us knew – it came as a complete surprise – that his sister had married the man who had been the august President of Yale from the early 1920s to the late 1930s. In any case, the Major was as good as his word and shortly after I got settled in New Haven I got in touch with Mrs. Angell, the late President's widow.

Kay Cramer Angell it turned out was the doyenne of New Haven. At her large, attractive home, just off Whitney Avenue she had receptions, part soiree and part salon, to which she invited the cream of New Haven society along with the most prestigious and entertaining faculty members at Yale. She also included attractive, up and coming junior faculty, as well as a few graduate students who she felt would add youth and energy to the mix. I was lucky enough to fall into this last category and ended up at her house every six weeks or so throughout my time at Yale. Kay Angell was the most engaging hostess I've ever encountered; gliding effortlessly from one group to another through her large living room and the dining room next to it, she addressed everyone by name, engaging them in conversation about their area of interest. Remarkably young at heart, she was grace itself, lively and fun. In addition to being the consummate hostess she was also an activist serving, among other things, as a co-founder of what later became the Culinary Institute of America. Because of Kay Angell I was able, in my time at Yale, to meet, and in certain cases get to know, some of the most interesting and engaging people at Yale and in New Haven.

Meanwhile, I threw myself into life at the Drama School, an immersion that was to last for the next four years. The MFA in Theatre at Yale is a three-year program in which the student majors in one of several areas: acting, directing, design, playwriting, the last being the one in which I was specializing. Through the next three years I met all the requirements in my specialty but was also able to include graduate courses in Yale College such as Shakespeare seminars and theatre history. I was also able to take a yearlong course given in his college quarters by author Robert Penn Warren. Though best known for his novels and poetry rather than playwriting, his native wisdom about the written word was timeless and memorable. I remember reading a couple of scenes from a play I was working on. When I finished, Warren singled out my heroine for particular notice. "She's the kind of woman," he said, "that when she speaks, butter melts and runs her way."

31

Purely by chance, the year I studied with Mr. Warren I became involved with him in quite a different matter. Occupying several buildings across the street from the Drama School are the quarters of the Graduate School of Art and Architecture. Shortly after I arrived at Yale, a friend from Nashville told me I should look up another Nashvillian, Jane Doggett, who was studying in the Art and Architecture program. Jane and I had not known each other in Nashville; I was older than she and our paths had never crossed. In any event, I looked her up and became fascinated with the work she was doing, especially her studies under the Chair of her department, the renowned artist Josef Albers who became famous not only for his teaching but also for his art, especially his "Squares" – a technique of overlaying squares and combining colors in an amazing manner.

Jane was in her last two years at Yale and we became good friends for those two years, in the second of which she expressed concern about her "Third Year Project," the final hurdle in getting her degree. This concluding assignment was to design and illustrate a small book and Jane said that she had no idea where to begin. She wanted to do something meaningful and original but had no idea of where or how to identify the text she would design. I recalled that once in our seminar, Warren mentioned that all his life he had been writing poetry, a practice he had continued, but that most of it had never appeared in book form. I asked Jane if she would like for me to approach Warren and see if he was open to the idea of having one or more of his poems appear in a small volume, privately designed. She was enthusiastic about the idea and so I approached Warren who readily agreed to meet her so they could talk about it. When the two met, they got along splendidly, after which Jane designed and produced the book.

It was a slim volume containing a single poem that

had been published in the periodical *The Partisan Review* but had never appeared in book form. Entitled *To a Little Girl, One Year Old, In a Ruined Fortress* it is a haunting, evocative poem about his three-year-old daughter, Rossana, to whom it was dedicated. Jane's illustrations – spread throughout the volume – were monochromatic abstracts: a dark, dark green, almost black color, with nonrepresentational swirls, sea foam and splashes. Recognizable figures were included in only two drawings: a swarm of butterflies in one and a lone bird in another. A part of the 3rd year final assignment was not only to design a book but to actually print it. On the last page of Jane's book, in the smallest of type, appear the words: "This book was designed, illustrated, and printed by Jane Doggett in the Department of Graphic Arts, School of Design, Yale University." Needless to say, both Warren and the Design Department at Yale were immensely pleased with the results.

Jane went on to have one of the most fascinating careers of any graphic designer in the 20th century. After graduation Jane – following three years of design assignments in the U. S. and abroad – was approached in 1959 by architect Roy Harrover who had been commissioned to design a new airport for Memphis, Tennessee. Roy, who knew Jane from Nashville and Yale, invited her to join his team in creating signage for the new airport. She readily accepted and discovered her life's work. Beginning with Memphis, Jane revolutionized airport signage and graphics to the point where she became the world's foremost creator in that field. In all she ended up designing over 40 major airports not only in the United States but in Asia and around the world.

Her innovations included everything from choosing the most legible font for signage, to the placement of signs, to color coding terminals. Jane invented the notion of giving each terminal its own identity: Terminal A would have red signage and coloring, Terminal B's color would be blue, Terminal C's, Green. As far as signs were concerned, she noticed that airports at the time placed them at eye level, meaning that passengers standing behind other people could not even see, let alone read, schedules, directions, and other information. Jane was the person who set signs up high, well over the heads of everyone standing in front of you. She developed signs for approaches to airports, placing them on highways two or three miles away to guide drivers into the airport itself and into the areas where they wanted to go.

Jane has a house in Maine and another in Jupiter Island, Florida, the latter a fascinating concrete creation she designed where, Chic and I, some twenty-five years later, visited her. I had not seen her from that visit until the spring of 2018, when someone produced a 30-minute documentary about her achievements and she was taking a victory lap, speaking to groups who were showing the film. I caught up with her at the Yale Club in New York where she appeared a few days after a rousingly successful visit to her alma mater, the Yale School of Art and Architecture. At the Yale Club appearance we had a long-delayed reunion. Seeing me across the room she said to the person next to her. "It's Ed, my old friend, the one who introduced me to Robert Penn Warren." Later she said that she had been told that the book she had designed was "now worth a great deal of money – if you could find one." Needless to say, my copy is not for sale.

Returning to my life at the Drama School, there were two more aspects of the school in the mid-1950's to note. One is the school itself. At that time Yale clearly had the strongest professional faculty of any drama school in the country, in every aspect of theatre: acting, directing, design, writing. Also, along with Carnegie Mellon, it attracted the most ambitious as well as the most talented students anywhere. As a result we often learned as much from our fellow students as from the faculty. I remember an occasion when an up-to-date, well-informed young director presented as a project one act of Samuel Beckett's *Waiting for Godot*. Like many of us present, I had never even heard of Beckett, let alone seen one of his plays. As the action – or should I say, lack of action – unfolded everyone was dumbfounded. It was a revelation; most of us had never seen a dramatic work based on such an abandonment of logic and realism and in its place, the shock and enlightenment of looking at the world from an entirely new perspective.

Another advantage of being at the Drama School at this time was the fact that it was in New Haven, home of the Shubert Theatre, the prime try-out spot for new Broadway shows. In those days, new plays coming to Broadway invariably went "out of town" before coming to Broadway so that mistakes could be corrected and new material added before the production faced the critics in New York. Though Boston and Philadelphia were popular try-out spots, New Haven was by far the favorite. Moreover, in those days there were many more new plays headed for Broadway.

One of the members of my playwriting class became extremely adept at sneaking into rehearsals at the Shubert and alerting the rest of us to a play or musical that looked promising. It did not hurt either that the Shubert was only a few blocks away and that ticket prices, especially in the balcony, were not nearly as expensive – even allowing for inflation – as they are today. As a result, during our years there most of us saw a trove of interesting new plays.

By far my most memorable experience I had along these lines was a night in early February 1956, the show being one our surreptitious class scout had sidled into and recommended. It was a Saturday night and in New Haven it had been snowing all day as part of a huge storm that continued into the night. I had an early dinner with friends that evening and headed for the Shubert where I got a single ticket in the second row of the balcony. The show, which was supposed to begin at 8:00 p.m. had still not begun 40 minutes later. Finally, at 8:45 the director, Moss Hart, came on stage and apologized for the delay, explaining that there were chandeliers in a ballroom scene that had not been functioning properly. A few minutes later the curtain finally went up on the first ever performance of the musical *My Fair Lady.*

Advanced word was that because the star, Rex Harrison, had never been in one before he was frightened to death of appearing in a musical; and it is true that during the musical numbers Harrison, his hands in the pockets of his cardigan, would drift, first to one side of the stage and then to the other, where a prompter was clearly giving him the next few lines in a song. Despite this it was clear that the audience was enjoying the show tremendously. This was underscored when, halfway through the first act, Rex as Henry Higgins, Julie Andrews as Eliza, and Robert Coote as Pickering sang "The Rain in Spain Stays Mainly in the Plain."

When the number was over the three of them sank back on a sofa while the audience broke into a thunderous burst of applause. Shortly, the three singers rose and tried to continue – it was obvious that they expected this to be a "throw-away" number about elocution and nothing more, and that they should move ahead. Clearly, they had been wrong. Several times the performers stood up to continue but the audience would not let them. Finally the problem was solved, not by the two veterans, but by the newcomer, Miss Andrews. She was in the middle and took the two older gentlemen by the hand and led them in a deep bow. When the performers finally acknowledged the appreciation of the audience, the latter let them continue.

It later turned out that the long delay at the beginning had nothing to do with chandeliers, but only with Rex Harrison and his almost pathological fear of appearing in a musical. He had been extremely difficult in rehearsal, especially with regard to Miss Andrews, but the final straw was the final Saturday afternoon rehearsal that, for the first time ever, involved the full 26-piece orchestra. Hearing this sonorous sound coming from the pit, Harrison was petrified and fled to his dressing room, locking the door and swearing never to come out and never to go on. When it appeared that Harrison was firm in his decision, Moss Hart let the entire cast and crew go, saying there would be no performance that night and so everyone fled from the theatre into the snowstorm.

Management, however, would have none of this and explained to Harrison that because of the storm they were not going to cancel the show but have everyone come and when they were seated, go on stage and say there would be no performance because Rex Harrison was too afraid to perform. In addition, his agent told Harrison that if he did not appear that night he would never work in New York again. Faced with the prospect of this humiliation, Harrison finally agreed to continue, whereupon both cast and crew had to be summoned from the far reaches of the city: cafes, gyms, movie theatres. This took time, which was the real cause of the delay, not, as I say, the chandeliers, but at long last the show began. In the end the audience did not get out until well after midnight, but no one was complaining.

As for my activities at the Drama School, I had a production of a full-length play in my third year. It was part comedy, part homespun character study, and part fantasy.

The title came from an old-time Southern hymn *In the Sweet Bye and Bye.* In the play – laid in the South, naturally – a young man has promised his father, a farmer, that he would get a job "close to the land" but had been unable to find one because of hard times. At the same time, his girlfriend's father – the town's mayor – would not let the two marry unless the young man had a job. Finally the boy finds a position that meets the requirements: with the local mortician, burying people in a local cemetery.

All of this is background (known in the theatre as exposition). The action begins when a would-be doctor-scientist comes to town and convinces the mayor that he has a pill that will let people live forever and that the mayor's small town is the perfect place to prove the efficacy of the drug. If this happened it would, of course, ruin the business of the undertaker. Everything leads up to a town meeting to vote on whether or not to take the drug, with an impassioned plea by the mortician that if people lived forever they would never get to that land in the "sweet bye and bye" where they could reunite with their loved ones. Not surprisingly it is discovered at the last moment that the doctor/scientist is a fake and the drug would never work. The whole thing, one might say, was the height of naiveté. Amazingly, however, the play had a future life as a musical.

Just down the block from the Drama School was the local Jewish Community Center where a spring musical was put on each year. The composer of the shows at the Center had heard about my play and decided it would be an ideal libretto for his show that year. I thought it was the most far-fetched notion I had every heard of. What I had not reckoned with is that the mothers of small girls at the community center wanted a production each year that would showcase their daughters who had been studying ballet. The composer understood this, and so, headed by a Yale director, a full-scale musical actually took place and no one seemed to be bothered in the least by the fact that the libretto on which it was based depicted the ultimate in a small-town Protestant milieu. It may have been one of the most incongruous theatrical pieces of all time, not only because of the two religions involved but even more because of the juxtaposition of young ladies wearing ballet tutus alongside the young hayseeds of the rural south. No one, however, seemed to mind.

During my four years in New Haven my focus was quite naturally on my work at the Drama School, but my friendships and interests reached into other spheres, especially the law school and Art and Architecture. In that first year as a freshman counselor I became close friends with a law school student, Jim Proud, the Head Freshman Counselor and we remained close friends the rest of our lives, with Jim serving as my lawyer for many years and the lawyer for my wife after she and I were married.

There turned out to be a number of other students in the law school with whom I became friends. A few of them even asked me to take part in mock trials in the school playing the role of a witness or an "expert." Otis Pearsall, another good friend in the law school, ended up living in Brooklyn Heights with his wife Nancy and we remained good friends through my years living near them in the Heights and into the years of my marriage. It was also through friends at the law school that I met J. W. Moore and his wife, Etta. The Moores were from Bozeman, Montana, but J. W., whose full name was James William Moore, had for some years been on the faculty of the law school after having distinguished himself as a student there and gone on to become recognized as the greatest authority in the United States on Federal Practice, a subject on which he had written some 34 volumes.

After I finished my year on the Freshman campus and was looking for a place to live, it turned out that the Moores, to whom I had been introduced, had a third floor apartment at their home in Hamden, a suburb of New Haven where a number of faculty lived. This apartment, which had an outside stairway allowing its occupant to enter and leave without disturbing the Moores, had usually been rented by a law student, but it turned out that no one had taken it for the year to come, and so I signed on to stay there and for the next two years the Moores became my second family.

Another person living in Hamden with whom I had become friendly was Virginia Dean, the widow of Alexander Dean who had been head of the directing program at the Drama School during its first 12 years. Virginia, herself an outgoing, engaging personality who had worked at the Drama School as well, had in turn, introduced me to a neighbor, Isabel Wilder, the sister of the playwright Thornton Wilder. At the end of my second year Isabel was giving a birthday party for her brother at her home where a colleague of mine was to serve as bartender. When the friend found he could not be there he asked me to take his place and so, on the appointed day, I found myself alone in the living room with Mr. Wilder before the other guests had arrived. I had recently seen a wonderful production of his play *The Merchant of Yonkers* in New York. (The play on which, some years later, the musical *Hello Dolly* was based.) Looking for a topic of conversation, I asked about a moment in the play when three actors stood around a table in Dolly's living room and after putting their finger tips on the table, sang an old Civil War song "Tenting Tonight." It was so moving, I said, that everyone in the audience was longing for one more verse. "There's an old saying," he said, "always leave them asking for more."

Returning to my work at the Drama School, in pursuing playwriting it slowly became obvious to me that though I might possibly make a go of it as a dramatist and that though I understood the principles and techniques of writing well enough, my work was really not sufficiently idiosyncratic, inventive, or off-the-wall to the degree one finds in a truly original talent. At the same time, I continued to improve in the fields of dramatic analysis and criticism. The one class everyone who entered the Drama School was required to take was Alois Nagler's History of Theatre, a subject about which he had written the definitive book. Known to his colleagues as "Ahlie," he grew up in Austria, where he became a widely recognized theatre historian as well as a literary editor and critic for a newspaper in Vienna. In the late 1930s, he visited the United States as a guest lecturer at several universities. Given the situation in Europe with war on the horizon, he decided to remain in the U. S. and shortly thereafter his wife, who had remained in Europe, joined him here. He was not only widely recognized but held important posts in international theatre history organizations. Needless to say, I took every course Ali offered.

Sometime in the beginning of my third year it was announced that the Drama School was going to institute an additional new degree: a Doctor of Fine Arts. It would be the only such degree offered at Yale. There were several reasons for initiating this degree. The MFA was a three-year program meaning that, except for writing a thesis, those obtaining this degree had completed as much class work as a PhD student everywhere else. The result was that graduates of the masters program at Yale who became teachers and had completed three years of class work were often at an unfair advantage vis-à-vis rivals from elsewhere when it came to questions of promotion and tenure. Instituting a DFA could, among other things, equalize this situation. Just as with the

41

PhD, the new degree was referred to as a "terminal degree," meaning you could go no higher, though to me it always seemed a rather morbid label.

For me personally the new degree seemed ideal and I signed up for it at once. During that final year, knowing I was going to continue in the program, one faculty member strongly urged me for forego the MFA degree I was due to receive in June, arguing that I was continuing my studies and the masters degree was superfluous. I said, "No way. I've completed the work, I want the degree – who knows what might happen a year from now?" In going for the DFA, a student, having completed all the course work and now writing his or her dissertation, could either stay at Yale or move elsewhere – to teach or begin working at a theatre. I, however, had been offered a job at the Drama School teaching one of the playwriting classes and given an office, so I stayed.

Both the office and the position were courtesy of John Gassner who, at the beginning of the 1956-57 school year, had become the Sterling Professor of Theatre at the school. The Sterling Professorship, by the way, was Yale's highest ranking among professors. John's position was in playwriting although his real forte was as an author. No one before or since has written as prodigiously about theatre as John did, turning out one or two books a year on the subject in addition to editing countless play anthologies.

John's wife Molly was indispensable in these endeavors, serving in any number of capacities to aid him. Both John and Molly took a great interest in my work and were extremely helpful to me not only for the last two years I was at Yale but for some time after. John also became, along with Ali Nagler, my dissertation advisor, which brings us to the dissertation itself. The chief requirements for dissertations were that they be full length (my dissertation ended up being 345 type-written pages) and, most difficult of all, that they be wholly "original," meaning that you must research and write on a subject no one had ever covered before. Under this stricture, many students spent months, even years, finding an acceptable subject.

As I began the task of identifying the topic for my doctoral dissertation, I recalled that in one of my classes I had come across the Shakespearean criticism of George Bernard Shaw. To most people Shaw's criticism of Shakespeare was an enigma. On the one hand he was perhaps the most artful, perceptive and original theatre analyst of all time. On the other hand, when it came to Shakespeare he was, possibly, the most excessive, scathing, censorious critic the Bard has ever had. Shaw called *Othello* nothing but melodrama, said that *Cymbeline* was "for the most part stagey trash of the lowest melodramatic order," and argued that Shakespeare "never thought a noble life worth living or a great work worth doing" and furthermore, that he was "for an afternoon and not 'for all time'."

Because of such diatribes Shaw had been utterly dismissed as a serious critic of Shakespeare. This judgment was shared by Eric Bentley, perhaps America's most highly regarded theatre critic at the time who, on the other hand, had praised Shaw's music criticism and written a book about it. In the volume about music Bentley observed that because of Shaw's extreme prejudices and excessive judgments one would never be able to write a book about his Shakespeare criticism. Despite this virtually universal judgment about the intractability of Shaw's criticism of Shakespeare I decided to dig a bit deeper into the subject. In doing so I discovered that the way to discover exactly what Shaw had in mind was to approach the whole matter from a different perspective. Shaw himself gave me the clue on how

43

to go about this. In a number of his comments, not only about Shakespeare but about other dramatists as well, he always separated form from content. Put another way, he made a distinction between what was said, and how it was said. Shaw reiterates this notion time and time again. A devoted Socialist, Shaw was not just a theoretical believer, he participated in a number of Socialist clubs and activities. In his criticism of Shakespeare he rails ceaselessly at the Bard for not having the socialist ideas and the forward-looking theories of Shaw's contemporary Henrik Ibsen. This is what Shaw felt that drama should be about: advancing a radical political agenda. It is an absurd criterion to apply to Shakespeare but the fact that the Bard wrote in the late 17th century and Ibsen three hundred years later was of no consequence to Shaw, as ridiculous as that seems.

Because of his attitude Shaw said there were times when he would like to "dig Shakespeare up and throw stones at him." Having said this, however, Shaw immediately adds "but I am bound to add that I pity the man who cannot enjoy Shakespeare. He has outlasted a thousand thinkers and will outlast a thousand more." Among the many things for which Shaw heaped unbounded praise on Shakespeare was his ability to create fascinating and believable characters and what Shaw called his "word music," by which he meant the rhythm and sheer sounds and timbre of his language.

Having decided that, thanks to Shaw himself, I had found the key to how one should read and interpret his Shakespearean criticism I felt that I then had to determine whether the negative criticism so far outweighed the positive that it would not justify a full-length project. It shortly became clear, however, that there was more than enough on the positive side of the ledger to move ahead. I presented my proposal to Professors Nagler and Gassner and, after receiving their approval, moved full speed ahead.

The next step was to locate the material: all of Shaw's Shakespearian criticism that could be found. Part of this was easy and another part was devilishly difficult, in fact, almost impossible. The easy part arose from the fact that from January 1895, until May, 1898, Shaw wrote weekly theatre reviews for the magazine *The Saturday Review*, all of which were later published in three volumes under the name *Our Theatres in the Nineties*. The other sources, however, were not reviews but random items: letters to actors, actresses, directors, producers and the like. Also, off-hand comments in unexpected and random places – in a musical review, perhaps, or a letter to a friend.

I spent most of the fall of 1957, searching for and collecting every possible comment by Shaw about Shakespeare that I could find. In the late fall of 1957, I wrote a first draft of the dissertation and in winter of '58, I wrote a second draft. In early spring I began to type the final version. During that spring I also had to deal with two disturbing things that occurred. I was perhaps a third of the way through typing that final version when I found myself beginning to feel panicky, fearing that I might not finish in time or something might go wrong and I would be unable to graduate in June. My apprehension built to the point where, having been invited to dinner by Mr. and Mrs. Moore, I was sitting with them in Mory's restaurant when I became panicky, afraid that I was seriously ill. I told them I didn't feel well: something was wrong, and I needed to see a doctor.

Alarmed, we left dinner and they took me to the emergency room at Yale-New Haven Hospital where the Resident Physician on duty took me in hand and put me through a series of tests. While he was doing this he began to ask questions. When he learned I was typing my doctoral dissertation he asked how far along I was. "About half way through," I answered. "And this is the middle of March," he said; "When do you have to be finished?" he asked. "Late May," I said. "Ah," he said knowingly, "That's it." "What do you mean?" I asked. "There's nothing wrong with you," he said, "You've had an anxiety attack. It happens to people in your situation all the time," whereupon he began writing a prescription for valium. "Take one of these every day. Pace yourself; take off at least one day a week; figure out how many pages a day you need to type in order to finish in plenty of time. You'll be fine."

The Moores, who had stayed with me, were not at all surprised to learn what the problem was and offered great moral support. When they took me back to my apartment they urged me to call them regularly and to come see them any time I wanted. I didn't think it would be as simple as the doctor had suggested, and it wasn't. I never really relaxed and the anxiety did not disappear entirely, but I took it one day at a time and managed to keep it under control. As everyone around me knew I would, I finished my typing with a week or so to spare.

A brief postscript on my dissertation at Yale: three years after I graduated, E. P. Dutton published a volume called *Shaw on Shakespeare* consisting of the Shavian Shakespearian criticism that I had assembled, along with a lengthy introduction I wrote.

The other episode that pulled me up short was of a different order. The office I occupied and in which I was typing my dissertation was the one formerly used by the professor who had been in charge of playwriting when I first came to Yale. His name was Bunny Essler, a former screen writer; why a screen writer had been hired to teach playwriting none of us could quite understand. We soon discovered, however, that we could learn enough from each other not to feel deprived. In any event, I was sitting in Bunny's old office, taking a break from my typing, when I glanced at a bookcase along one wall of the office. On the bottom shelf I noticed a pile of scripts. Picking them up, I soon discovered that they were old submission scripts. Leafing through them I came upon mine. And then came the shock; the unbelievable revelation. Scribbled across the cover were the words "Not sure – we should wait."

It took me a moment to realize precisely what this meant. Here I was, occupying a professor's office, teaching a playwriting course, when there had been a good chance, a strong chance, that I might never have been admitted to the school in the first place. Across the cover of my submission script (admittedly an ad hoc play written without any prior experience) were words that indicated I had at best a 50/50 chance, but more likely a 30/70 chance of being accepted. After the shock of that realization there came a deeper, more troubling thought: what if, five years earlier, I had not been accepted at the Drama School? What would I have done? I had gambled my whole life on getting into Yale but could easily have been refused. Would I have been afraid to turn elsewhere and continued in the coffee business? Would I have been miserable for the rest of my life? It was too much to fathom. What saved me from total despair was the realization that I had better get back on schedule with my typing or I really would fail to finish in time.

Commencement that year was on the 5th of June, a day on which a steady rain was falling. As a result, the venue of graduation had to be moved from a splendid outdoor setting to Woolsey Hall, an equally splendid but smaller space that was safely indoors. After the ceremony the faculty, MFA graduates, and I – along with families – returned to the Drama School for our own celebration. In addition to the usual frivolity and congratulations, a bit of a fuss was made over the fact that I was the first DFA graduate at Yale, including a laurel wreath placed on my head that one of the faculty had thoughtfully commissioned.

Many years later my wife and I learned that there was an amazing coincidence regarding my graduation ceremony. Purely by chance she had been invited by a neighbor to attend the ceremony and had seen me receive my diploma, although neither one of us realized this connection until many years later. My wife's name at this time was Catherine (Chic) Leavenworth. Born in Durham, North Carolina, she grew up there, and was given the nickname Chick by her grandfather who referred to her as his "little chickadee." As she grew older she kept the name, still pronouncing it as her Grandfather had, but dispensing with the final "k" when spelling it. In her freshman year at Peace College in Durham she met Robert Leavenworth, a senior at the Duke Law School. When he graduated they were married and moved to his hometown, New Haven, Connecticut, where he joined a law firm and later became a judge. Unfortunately for Chic, her husband died when he was very young. While living in New Haven she had made many friends, including Edith and Harold Whiteman and the lady who had invited her to my graduation, but a year or two after her husband had died she moved to New York where she found a job with a large firm and moved into an apartment on East 68th Street.

CHAPTER THREE

Brooklyn Heights and Broadway

My first job after Yale, in the fall of 1958, was teaching at Hofstra College, the largest private university on Long Island. The college had an excellent theatre department, partly because it was very active in awarding scholarships to talented students but also because of its excellent faculty and a first-rate chairman, Bernard Beckerman, an engaging gentleman and well-known Shakespearian scholar. Added to this was the fact that the president of Hofstra was also a Shakespeare enthusiast. It proved to be a heady atmosphere, not only because of Bernie and the rest of the faculty, but also because of the scholarship students who that year included Lainie Kazan, later a very successful film and television performer, and Francis Ford Coppola of *Godfather* fame as well as many other highly successful films. Interestingly enough, at Hofstra it was not film that engaged Francis but directing stage musicals. (As an aside I should add that Bernie, who I came to admire more and more, in later years became the Brander Matthews Professor of Dramatic Arts at Columbia University.)

As much as I was enjoying Hofstra and teaching, after two years I once more felt the wander lust, this time with my eyes set on the place I think I had always been aiming for: New York. In a move that I have never understood and probably will never fathom I decided that in New York I wanted to live in Brooklyn Heights, a place which I had never seen nor in which I had ever set foot. Nevertheless that is where I began looking and in a relatively short time found an apartment at 28 Remsen Street. It was a garden apartment in the basement of an old brownstone, only eight houses away from the Esplanade, the marvelous walkway in Brooklyn Heights that overlooks the East River and Lower Manhattan.

The apartment, which had been the large kitchen in the original brownstone, was one sizeable room with a bathroom, a miniscule kitchen, and an alcove for a bedroom. It opened out on a small back garden area with several Ailanthus trees, known as "the tree of heaven" featured in the title of Betty Smith's novel as *The Tree that Grows in Brooklyn*. What had been the large fireplace in the original kitchen had been bricked in, creating an enclosed space that was an exact fit for a small, 68-key, painted piano I found on Atlantic Avenue in Brooklyn. The piano turned out to be a magnet for a number of friends from drama school days including Gib Leibinger, who had written a musical with Pete Gurney at Yale and Gib's wife, Jinx, a singer on the Perry Como show.

The apartment was my home for the next six years. I kept my small car in a garage nearby and found it easy to drive to Manhattan and find a parking place for a date, for the theatre, or a meal with friends. As for the Heights itself, I quickly re-connected with my friends from the Yale Law School, Otis Pearsall and his wife Nancy who lived in a marvelous town house only a few blocks away, a brownstone with which the Heights is filled. In fact, it was while I was living there that Otis, Nancy and their friend Clay Lancaster, who had published a book about the homes in Brooklyn Heights, were successful in having the area declared a "historic district," the first such designation in New York

City. To this day the Heights has the greatest concentration of 19th century brownstone homes in the United States.

Fortunately, the Heights Casino, a small club with two indoor tennis courts, was only two blocks away and I was able to enjoy tennis there regularly during my years in the area. In my second year of playing, the pro put me together with another member who was free on the odd Tuesday and Thursday morning. It turned out to be the actor Rod Steiger who at that time was living nearby with his then wife, Claire Bloom, and Rod and I played every couple of weeks for two or three years. Needless to say, the one thing I did not bring up but always let him initiate, was anything to do with his career.

At almost the same time I moved to Brooklyn Heights so did my friends from Nashville and Yale, Edith and Harold Whiteman. Jim Hester who, with his wife Janet were to become Chic's and my closest friends some years later, was President of NYU and had invited Harold to become Vice-Chancellor of Student Affairs at the university. Once the Whitemans arrived in Brooklyn Heights not only did I see a great deal of them, Harold and I became frequent partners in Casino tennis tournaments.

As for the theatre, my first employment in the fall of 1960 was reading play scripts for Robert Whitehead, unquestionably the most urbane, tasteful, gentlemanly producer the Broadway theatre has ever seen. Bob, who shared an office with his partner, Roger Stevens, a businessman who at the time was also the greatest philanthropist in American theatre, was in the penthouse of 165 West 46th Street in the heart of the theatre district. I got the job through Lewis Allen who had graduated from Episcopal High School five years ahead of me. Lew and Bob had met while they were serving in the American Field Service in North Africa and Southern Italy in World War II. Someone who knew both Lew and me suggested I get in touch with him and he, in turn, arranged an interview for me with Bob. Needless to say, although the pay was extremely modest, the position was one I could hardly have expected to land so early in my move to NYC.

The job did not last too long, however, because Lew had decided that he wanted to begin producing on his own and had rented a small, two room office on a lower floor in the same building. When he asked me if I would like to work for him as his assistant I accepted immediately. Again, the pay was minimal but unlike play reading, it was a full-time position, besides which Lew already had a couple of projects in mind. The first was an independent film, *The Connection*. It was the story of druggies, people desperate for a fix, who were trying to make a "connection." Based on a play by Jack Gelber, the film was being directed by Shirley Clarke, who was near the end of shooting but short of the money needed to finish editing and other expenses. Lew felt he could raise the money in order for Shirley to complete the project and thereby become the "producer."

Lew was a great idea man and utterly charming, but his idea of office management fell short of the mark. My first job, therefore, was to take the scraps of paper and backs of envelopes on which his investors in the film had scribbled their names and indicated the amount they would invest and make some sense of them. We finally pulled all that together and the film was finished. Being controversial, even by standards of the day, the film never made its money back but it launched Lew as a daring producer.

Lew's next project was a Broadway production, a play titled *Big Fish, Little Fish*. This time Lew did not come in at the end and back some small-scale effort, but was there from the beginning and went all out on talent and everything else: top-flight actors, designers and a world-famous director, Sir

John Gielgud. The cast included Jason Robards, Hume Cronyn, George Grizzard, Ruth White, Elizabeth Wilson and Martin Gabel. If, however, Lew went for glamour and fame in his choice of the director, actors and designers, he remained faithful to his commitment to daring, controversial, cutting-edge material in the subject matter of the play. Hugh Wheeler, a mystery story author, was making his debut as a playwright with *Big Fish*. The plot concerned a former college professor who, though dismissed from his position because of an accusation of homosexuality, remained the center of attention of a loyal group of friends. Jason played the role of the ex-professor and his circle of friends was portrayed by the actors mentioned above.

The play began rehearsals in New York in late January and opened for an out-of-town try-out in Philadelphia. The Broadway opening was in mid-March. The play received mixed to good reviews, played for 101 performances and received two Tony Awards, one to John Gielgud for best direction and another to Martin Gabel for best supporting actor. (It should be noted as well that Hugh Wheeler, the playwright, later won acclaim as the writer of librettos of such musicals as *A Little Night Music, Sweeney Todd,* and *Candide*.) For me, the entire experience was invaluable. I got to see first hand the entire process of mounting a Broadway play, from casting and hiring the actors and staff, through rehearsals, the out of town try-out and the run in New York. I was involved in one way or another in many aspects of the production: finance, publicity, rehearsals and performances. In addition I got to know people with whom I would cross paths more than once in the future: Jason, Liz Wilson and Hume Cronyn.

In the late fall of 1961, the British director Peter Brook began showing up in Lew's office. Peter was a wunderkind, a prodigy, an infant-terrible. At the age of 22 he had been made Director of Productions at the Royal Opera House in London; when he was 25 he had directed three major Shake-spearian productions for the Royal Shakespeare Company; in 1958, at the age of 33, he directed Alfred Lunt and Lynn Fontaine, the most famous husband and wife team in the history of the American theatre in a landmark production of *The Visit*. I had seen both *The Visit* and a 1960 production he directed of a delightful musical farce called *Irma La Duce*. By the time he showed up at Lew's office he was indeed a legend.

The purpose of Peter's visit was to begin work on a film version of *Lord of the Flies*, a novel by William Golding embraced by critics and readers who favored dark, nihilistic material. The book tells the story of a group of English boys who had been flown out of Britain to escape a war taking place. They were headed to the Far East but their plane crashed near an island in the Pacific Ocean. Half the group were school boys and the other half were choir boys. Turned loose on this rugged island covered with trees, rugged hills and thick underbrush but no adults, the boys break into rival gangs and revert to anarchy, primitivism and hostility. Both Lew and Peter were drawn to the material but they arrived at their interest by very different routes. Peter, as I have said, had proved himself in the English-speaking world to be something of a genius as a stage director. Lew came from a very different background. Born in Berryville, Virginia, he was a son of old Virginia. Berryville was hunt country: the hunt breakfast, the loving cup, riding to the hounds, hurdling over brush fences. Lew attended the required educational institutions: Episcopal High School and the University of Virginia in Charlottesville. But then World War II came along and while serving in the American Field Service in North Africa and Europe he had met Bob Whitehead. After he finished wartime service and college, Lew went to New York where he got a job in Bob's office. Lew's wife said he had gone to work for Bob, not because he had to but "to prove to his mother he had a job."

As close as he was to Bob, however, Lew had his own ideas about the material to which he was attracted. Bob was a traditionalist, albeit a truly outstanding one, but Lew had other ideas. As I have said, he was drawn to cutting-edge material, the daring, the challenging and offbeat, hence the drug culture in his first film and homosexuality in his first play. A novel like *Lord of the Flies* was right up his alley and hence, he and Peter were made for each other because, as will become clear, Peter had visions of approaching film-making in a way no one else had before and he felt this was a good story with which to begin.

In early 1962, the project began in earnest. There were many tasks ahead: finding 33 young English boys for the cast as well as hiring the necessary staff – cameramen, lighting experts, an assistant director, people to handle day-to-day financial and other administrative matters. There was also the daunting task of finding the appropriate shooting locations and after locating them, getting permission to film there. On a scouting trip to the Caribbean, Lew and Peter discovered the island of Vieques, 75 miles east of Puerto Rico, with expansive, uncluttered, pure white beaches and rugged interior hills thick with underbrush and sometimes impenetrable foliage. It seemed to be ideal and Peter realized that they could actually film on three beaches that, in editing, could be combined into one beach.

It was during this time that we added another person, Elinor Jones, to work with me in Lew's office. Ellie had been married to Tom Jones, the writer with Harvey Schmidt of the long-running musical The Fantasticks. After her divorce she and Tom had remained friends and some years later Ellie wrote several successful off-Broadway plays, one of which was *Collette* about the famed French writer, a play she also produced, Needless to say, it was a great help to have someone working alongside me in the office, especially someone as capable and refreshing as Ellie. While speaking of the office I should mention Lew's wife Jay Presson Allen, a well-known and successful Broadway playwright and screenwriter, responsible for such stage plays as *Tru* and *The Prime of Miss Jane Brodie* and whose screen plays included *40 Carats, Travels with my Aunt, Cabaret, Funny Lady, Death Trap,* and *La Cage aux Folles.* Jay, who had been introduced to Lew by Bob Whitehead in the mid 1950s when the two got married, would from time to time show up in the office and was a no-nonsense, sharp, perceptive lady, always quick with a cutting remark or a bit of risible repartee.

Meanwhile Lew's staff was preparing for and went to work finding the 33 boys needed for *The Lord of the Flies* cast. They must all be young – between the ages of 11 and 14 – and English. We dispatched a young man, Mike Mac-Donald, the son of Dwight MacDonald, a well-known literary critic of the time, to scout likely places where he might find the sons of English families living in or posted to New York or Washington – the Embassies, the Old Etonian Club – and the New York docks where transatlantic ocean liners arrived. On one occasion while roaming around this last location, Mike was questioned by authorities who thought he might be soliciting young boys for illicit purposes. For the character of Ralph, leader of one of the rival gangs, a young man named James Aubrey was discovered in a swimming pool in Jamaica only a few days before shooting began. The only young man signed up from England was Hugh Edwards for the role of Piggy, who had to be overweight. Hugh, a youngster from the small town of Camberley in

England, had answered a notice in a newspaper sending along a photograph that featured precisely the image Peter had been looking for in the character.

In the spring of 1962, I suddenly came to realize that, except for Peter, everyone we were hiring, whether part of the film-making team or the behind-the-scenes personnel, not a single person, not one, had ever held the position for which he or she was being hired.Peter had made a few films previously, including a version of *The Beggar's Opera* with Laurence Olivier, and *Moderato Cantabile* with Jeanne Moreau and Belmondo. Everyone else, however, was a total novice. The so-called Executive Producer, the man responsible for keeping tabs on daily expenses and looking ahead to future budgets was Al Hine, a writer friend of Lew's. Al, who wrote offbeat, humorous material such as his novel *Lord Love a Duck*, had never been near a spreadsheet or a calculator in his life. Gerry Feil, credited with being Associate Producer but actually the Second Cameraman and later the Assistant Editor with Peter, at that point had no experience in either cinematography or editing.

The head photographer was to be Tom Holliman, a distinguished still photographer. Among other iconic photographs for which Tom was responsible was a shot of the famous cellist Pablo Casals walking down a white sand beach along the shore in Puerto Rico with a black umbrella over his head. Although Tom had taken many such still photographs, he had never taken a single shot with a movie camera. I remember Lew and Peter handing Tom an 8-millimeter film camera and sending him off to Central Park to see what it was like to handle such an instrument. Except for Peter, the list of neophytes working in one capacity or another on *Lord of the Flies* would include everyone, even Lew himself.

Peter, it turned out, had very strong views on just how he wanted to make this film and he got Lew to agree to his conditions before he would proceed. Lew, of course, agreed to all of them; artistically this was to be Peter's film. Most of these items, I might add, ran quite contrary to accepted filmmaking practices. The conditions were as follows:

a) The film would be made without a script: Peter would use the novel itself for sequence, actions, and all the speeches.

b) The film would be shot in sequence, moving though time with no back and forth the way virtually every movie is filmed. Ordinarily a filmmaker shoots all the scenes in a single location at one time. For example if the script calls for several scenes on a beach, say scenes 3, 7, 10 and 14, they are shot all at one time and introduced at their proper place during editing.

c) The film would be presented without background music of any kind.

d) There would be no limit to how many scenes were photographed or how much film was required.

Each one of these was completely unheard of in film-making, from the lowest low budget effort to the most expensive extravaganza. Virtually every film ever made was shot with some kind of script. Without a script the actors have no lines to learn and they must make them up as they go along. In *Lord of the Flies* we had 11 year old boys making up the words. Moreover, there is no sense of how the sequence of scenes should unfold. The same was true for shooting out of sequence: when one shot was set up – the interior of a room in a palace or in a college dorm or on a mountain top and such a setting was the site of scenes 3, 8, 17, 24, etc. – it made sense economically to shoot them at one time, one after another before moving to a different location.

Meanwhile, on Vieques plans had been made for places where the staff would be housed as well as the young boys in the cast. In the case of the boys an abandoned pineapple factory, deemed satisfactory as a dorm, was located near the beaches. In addition, three mothers of boys in the cast had been signed up to serve as chaperones and "house mothers." After everyone departed for Vieques – cast, crew, and staff – I was the only one left to mind the office in New York, although I was to join them ten days later. There was another reason for me to remain in New York. As I have said, Hugh Edwards, the young man who was to play the key role of Piggy, was the one cast member coming from London and he would not arrive until the day after the others had departed for Vieques. I was to meet Hugh at JFK airport in New York, take care of him for the night, and send him on his way to Puerto Rico the next day.

Once on Vieques, the crew and the cast took a day or two to settle in and then shooting was to begin. During the morning filming at one of the beach locations everything went well. The afternoon that first day was a different story. About 30 minutes after shooting began a squadron of Navy fighter planes suddenly appeared, flying low over the beaches in wave after wave. It turned out that, unknown to Lew and Peter, not far from the beaches was a Naval Air Station that carried out daily exercises along the shore. Shooting had to be halted and the cast and crew dismissed while Lew and Al Hine, after determining the location of the Naval Air Station, rushed there to locate those in charge. After working out a schedule with the Naval authorities of when planes would suspend their exercises, two days later shooting began again.

About three days after shooting resumed, another problem arose. After only a few days of filming Peter realized that shooting in sequence might not work so well after all, in consequence of which I received an urgent call back in New York. Would I please go to Brooks Brothers and buy 33 boys dark blue blazers and then go to a make-up supply shop and purchase several gallons of tan body paint and send both items post haste to Vieques. Upon arrival one set of blazers would be "distressed," that is torn and slightly slashed, so that there would be one set for scenes taking place later in the film and another set of clean blazers for earlier scenes. As for the body make-up, it would be applied for scenes that took place later in the story. A third dictum from Peter, that there would be no background music was discarded much later in the process. Thus, at the end only one of Peter's "innovations," the one calling for no script, remained in place.

For reasons that I will explain later, I left the project at the end of shooting in Vieques, but I kept very much in touch with Ellie and Lew as well as with what was happening on the film. In the end Peter ended up with 60 hours of material, a ratio of forty-to-one of raw footage to finished product, a ratio virtually unheard of, that must have rivaled the most prodigal ratio of raw film to finished product, perhaps, in the history of filmmaking. Peter and Gerry Feil took all the material to Paris where they rented an apartment and began editing, putting the pieces together to make a narrative. Nine months later they had a rough cut to show Lew. Several of us, Lew, his wife, Jay, Ellie and I, as well as a few others, sat in a screening room and saw the results.

At the end most of us sat in stunned silence. After a time, Jay who as far as cinema was concerned, was the adult in the room, began to speak. "First," she said, "there has to be music. There is a boy's choir in the story; why can't we at least have some remnants of church music? Also, there are places where the film makes no sense; where I have no idea of what is happening." Jay had friends in Hollywood

– writers, directors, editors – she told Lew that at the very least they should have an editor friend of hers take a look at it and let them know what he thought.

I remember seeing a later version – not the final cut – in which the opening scene was a long shot, taken from the top of a hill covered with tropical trees and plants, that looked down on a long line of boys in black choir robes walking single file on a wide, white sand beach while in the background were the strains of a Kyrie Eleison sung by boy sopranos. It was a haunting, unforgettable scene. But it never appeared again. Instead, the opening scene in the final version consisted of five minutes of still photographs, providing the exposition before the story began: a boys school, a study hall, a cricket match and the like, then air craft and the bombs of war, and after that the plane that flew the boys to the Pacific followed by the crash of the plane into the sea near a beach. Behind this were ominous explosions and drumbeats: laborious and dull.

Before I leave *The Lord of the Flies* I feel it is important to say a few words about what Peter was doing here: the philosophy and approach behind his idea of how the film should be made. Peter's work in the theatre had been extraordinary; he could take a classic and breath new life as well as new meaning into it. In his later years, heading his experimental theatre in Paris, he stretched the boundaries of traditional theatre, challenging long-held concepts in his staging and in the way his performers inter-acted with one another. Whatever the final results, his work for the stage was always challenging. But film is not theatre. There are fundamental differences that somehow Peter was tone deaf to, oblivious of, or defiant toward, probably the last. The stage has parameters and givens that film does not and vice versa.

A theatre performance always involves a physical site where the event takes place: there is a space for the performers and a space for the audience; there is a script, words that have been memorized by the actors (even where improvisation is called for there is a pre-determined outline or sequence of events); there is a time limit to the event, a beginning and an end (it may be one hour or six hours, but the time span is clearly understood by both performers and audience). None of this applies to film, which is made over an extended period of time and involves many locales, a multitude of scenes not limited by time or space, an alternation of "shots" – long shots of actors, close ups, landscapes, moving trains or planes – an extensive editing process, and finally, distribution to thousands of movie theatres and television sets.

The end result, the finished product, could not present more of a contrast: a film presentation in a movie theatre or on TV is constant, immutable, unchanging. Shown a thousand times or ten thousand times a film will always be precisely the same. In the theatre, no two performances are ever exactly the same: from night to night they vary in small ways and large every single time the curtain goes up. Both theatre and film involve actors, locations and a story, but the differences between the dynamics and the circumstances of stage and film – the way they are created and put together and the way they are exhibited and presented – are so extensive and profound that to attempt to apply the approach or the methods of production of one to the other is suicidal if not impossible.

Early in the summer, after buying and shipping the boys' blazers, I had returned to Vieques and remained there until filming was completed. In the final days on the island, however, I received a call from Professor John Gassner at Yale

– which could not have been easy for him to arrange given the remoteness of Vieques. He explained that he was going to take a sabbatical leave in the upcoming school year and would like for me to take his place teaching the playwriting courses at the Drama School in the 1962-63 academic year. The proposal took me completely by surprise and I had to collect my thoughts before I could give him an answer. After I had caught my breath I thanked him profusely and told him that I was honored but would like a day or two to think it over. I told him that I would give him an answer possibly the next day but no later than the day after.

The more I thought about it the more I began to believe it was the thing to do. The shooting of the film was virtually over; after we returned to New York there would be things to clear up but I was certain I could take care of them in the weeks before school began. Besides, Ellie would be there to take care of things and with my teaching schedule at Yale, which I knew would be confined to three days a week, I could put in an odd day here and there at Lew's office if I was needed. There was another factor I considered: although we got along well, I knew that I sometimes got on Lew's nerves by my insistence on our keeping up-to-date on our finances and correspondence. I was just trying to keep a semblance of order in the operation but Lew had always been a free spirit. I had the feeling that although he knew I was doing the right thing, it sometimes bothered him. Putting all this together I decided I should accept the offer to teach the coming year at Yale. When I told Lew the next day he acted as if he was disappointed but I'm certain that he was actually relieved. Needless to say, when I left a few weeks later, we parted on the best of terms.

(One last note about Lew. Although, as I have pointed out, he had a penchant, even a passion for producing cutting edge, challenging, avant-garde material, it was the height of irony when fifteen years later he attained fame and fortune not with something daring but with the ultimate in safe, feel-good, family entertainment: the musical *Annie* which opened in 1977, ran for six years on Broadway, won a Tony Award, and toured forever.)

In September, 1962, I began my year of teaching at the Drama School with anticipation as well as a certain apprehension: this was a huge responsibility. I could not have been more pleased, however, with the arrangements awaiting me. John Gassner, whose classes I was to teach, had set for himself a schedule consisting of three straight days clustered in the middle of the week: Tuesday, Wednesday and Thursday. This meant that I could go to New Haven early Tuesday morning, stay two nights, and return to New York on Thursday evening. Meanwhile, Harold Whiteman had arranged for me to stay those two nights in the Yale Alumni House which at that time was a historic three-story white clapboard home near the center of the campus, only a short walk from the Drama School.

The three-year curriculum in playwriting was well established – the first year students began writing scenes: a confrontation between two family members, a comic encounter between two strangers, a love scene. During the school year they would progress to one-act plays. In the second year, they would expand and consolidate their work on one-acts and begin tackling the full-length form, with outlines, scenarios and the like. The third year they would move on to full-length scripts. In beginning my duties I had the advantage of having recently completed this three-year program in playwriting, plus having taught one of the courses during the year when I was writing my dissertation.

Though he was a first-rate historian and critic, I realized that when it came to playwriting, John had limitations. To begin with, he himself was not a playwright. With a person of wide-ranging understanding and imagination this was not an insuperable barrier, but it made it that much more difficult to understand and apprehend the process. The truth is: you cannot teach playwriting, any more than you can teach someone to compose a tuneful melody or create a breathtaking sculpture or paint a striking portrait or landscape. Technique will only go so far; it is when inventiveness, insight, inspiration, even quirkiness enters the equation that art results.

With playwriting there are added hurdles. Bill Zinsser, a Renaissance man and a long-time friend of mine, wrote the definitive volume on prose writing: *On Writing Well*, which became a bible of sorts and has sold over a million and a half copies. I don't believe, however, that even if there was a large enough market for such a volume on playwriting it could have a similar impact. Bill's book is a guide to specific kinds of writing: *The Interview; The Memoir; Criticism of the Arts*. Playwriting does not fall so neatly into categories. The playwright must not only have a way with words, but an almost limitless imagination; he or she must envision situations, confrontations, actions that take place in a limited time and space. The imagination, the invention, must run free. In a way, a play is a blueprint of a production, but it must also contain the seeds, the cues for the promise and possibilities of action, ideas, and feelings.

You can challenge and encourage a playwright, question him or her, give an informed reaction or guidance, but the heart and soul of the matter must come from the individual composing the piece. John Guare, a highly imaginative writer who went on to pen such plays as *The House of Blue Leaves* and *Six Degrees of Separation* was a student in my third year class at Yale. Such a person, such a "free spirit," who thinks and imagines outside the box, needs to be encouraged when his fancy takes flight. I think John always felt hemmed in by Professor Gassner and when I gave him free reign, telling him more than once to "go for it," he felt liberated, a feeling for which, through the years, he has expressed his appreciation.

That same year there was a student in my class who was unlike any playwriting student probably in the long history of the Drama School. I don't know how he found his way there, but I was always grateful that I was the one teaching him. His name is Billy Edd Wheeler and happily he is still with us. He was born in West Virginia and lived most of his life in the environs of southeast West Virginia, southwest Virginia and the mountains of western North Carolina. It was in a Yale classroom, however, that I encountered him. By the time he arrived at Yale he was already a master of the guitar and a successful song writer, providing songs that had been recorded by everyone from Johnny Cash and June Carter to Judy Collins, Bobby Darin, Kenny Rogers, Nancy Sinatra and Elvis Presley, among others. Eventually Billy Edd was inducted into several Music Halls of Fame, awarded two honorary college doctorates, and received 13 awards from ASCAP.

Billy Edd had come to Yale because he wanted to learn how to write plays, musicals, and outdoor historical dramas, which he succeeded in doing quite successfully in later years. He was one of those refreshing, original talents on his own wavelength. I remember a scene he wrote about three people preparing and eating a batch of collard greens that had his classmates laughing until the tears ran down their cheeks. Since I was from Nashville and furthermore, appreciated his talent, he and I became closer than the average teacher and pupil. We would steal off, find an empty room, and he would play a few of his songs for me. I can't remember too many of the titles, but there was one I can never forget: the title was "She's a T-Bone Talking Woman, but She has a Hot-Dog Heart."

CHAPTER FOUR

Directing and Producing

During the school year of 1962-63 the fact that I was in New York half of every week meant I could keep up with my friends there, including those active in the theatre. As a result, in the Spring I met with John Holmes, the producer of the Theatre-By-The-Sea in Matunuck, Rhode Island, a well- established, upscale summer theatre. I don't remember who arranged for me to meet him; the meeting may have been set up by Ellie Jones with whom I had stayed in touch. In any case, he and I agreed that I would direct two plays for him in the coming summer. I mention Ellie because one of the plays I was to direct was *The Fantasticks* the book and lyrics of which Tom Jones, Ellie's ex-husband, had written. In any case, I was happy to get the job.

The second play I was to direct at Matunuck was a staged version of the poem *John Brown's Body* by Stephen Vincent Benet which ten years before had been a hit on Broadway. As with many summer theatres, the actors, designers and technicians had been engaged by the management. If the theatre had a resident director, he or she would have a great deal to do with the hiring (particularly of the performers) but many times the directors were brought in to do only a portion of the season. At a first-rate summer theatre, when directors arrived, fortunately they found topnotch performers already hired. A good example during the season I was directing at Theatre-by-the-Sea was Estelle Parsons who was appearing at the theatre in a play called *Hey You, Light Man* written by a recent Yale Drama graduate, Oliver Hailey. The play was an imaginative tale of an actor who, when the performance is over, remains on the set, living back stage rather than returning home to his dysfunctional, unhappy family. One night a lady audience member, who had fallen asleep during the performance, awakes and sees the man on stage, whereupon she joins him after which a very unconventional romance ensues. Estelle, who was marvelous in the role of the woman (an extremely ditsy but surprisingly intelligent lady) went on to have a 60-year career on the stage and in film and television, winning numerous honors along the way, including an Oscar for her role in the film *Bonnie and Clyde*.

When I began rehearsals of *The Fantasticks* I discovered that I had a first-rate cast. Playing the young girl was an actress-singer whom the pianist and music director had recommended to the producer and who proved to be ideal. When it opened, Tom and Harvey, the creators of the show, attended the production, not only because they were friends but mostly, I think, to see how the show fared at the Theatre-By-The-Sea which featured a proscenium, picture frame stage; this was to be the first time the play, which had opened in New York three years earlier, had been done on such a stage. Happily, the production came off exceedingly well and they, as well as the audience and theatre management, were quite pleased. After the performance Tom had a lengthy talk with the actress playing the young girl after which he spoke with me, saying how pleased he was and remarking that the ingénue was quite good, but adding: "of course, we would never be able to use her in the production in New York." I was silently amused some six months later when this same young lady took over the part in the production at the Sullivan Street Theatre in Manhattan and remained in the show for months to come.

Early in the fall of 1963, I decided to move into producing myself. I had been headed in this direction for two or three years, but now I took steps to do something about it. My ideas about producing were high-minded – in retrospect, much too high-minded. Like Lewis Allen, I wanted to do something meaningful and purposeful, but whereas Lew was fascinated by the daring, the outré, and controversial, as far from the mainstream as possible, I wanted to do something that in my mind was probing. substantive, and serious.

A playwriting agent, Cindy Degener, fixed me in her cross-hairs and introduced me to one of her clients, Wallace Hamilton. Wallace had written a somber, probing play entitled *The Burning of the Lepers* that had been produced in the Spring of 1962 at the Arena Stage in Washington D.C., mounted by a well-known director, Alan Schneider, so it came with a good provenance. To say that it was serious would be an understatement. Set in 14th Century France, it dramatized the history of a group of lepers who had been segregated from their neighbors and blamed for a series of local catastrophes – a charge of which of which they were completely innocent. Giving in to hysteria, their accusers gathered them together to be burned. It was based on historical fact and was about as shocking and downbeat as one could imagine, but it was skillfully written and extremely powerful, even moving.

I set about raising money, hiring the director and other creative personnel and renting a theatre. For the last I went to Warner LeRoy's apartment in the Dakota apartment house on the West Side to sign papers for the use of the York Theatre, which he owned and was one of the best off-Broadway theatres in the City. (Warner later turned the theatre into a

71

swinging restaurant called Maxwell's Plum.) I had a strong director and an "A" team of designers that included Robin Wagner, who designed the scenery and lighting and later became one of the most highly regarded designers in the Broadway theatre. In planning our advertising we decided to drop the final three words of the original title and call the play simply *The Burning*, assuming that the audience would become aware of the target of the flames soon enough.

We were set to open the second week in December, 1963, which we did. In the meantime, however, life intervened. A bare three weeks before we were scheduled to open, on November 22, 1963, President John F. Kennedy was assassinated in Dallas, Texas, the most tragic event in our country's history in nearly 100 years. We would never have scheduled our opening three weeks after a National tragedy if we had had any idea it might occur; absolutely no one, of course, saw this coming. As a result, we were put in an almost impossible position but for financial and other reasons we had no choice but to proceed. When we did open we received respectful reviews from virtually everyone, and laudatory notices from a few. But the combination of the seriousness of our subject matter and the continuing shock and sorrow of the assassination was too much to overcome. We had respectful audiences but not sufficiently large ones and, not surprisingly, were forced to close a few weeks after we opened.

In the fall of 1964 I began teaching a graduate seminar in playwriting at Hunter College. During my earlier years in New York I had gotten to know several of the faculty members of the Drama Department at Hunter. Located at 68th Street and Lexington Avenue in Manhattan, Hunter was at the center of things, including a subway stop that announced the College on its signs. I will be saying much more about Hunter later on; in the meantime, it is worth pointing out that because it was in Manhattan, its Theatre Department was particularly strong, staffed with a combination of former or future industry figures, in such areas as design, and scholars who had a particular fondness for live theatre and enjoyed the fact that they were teaching where the action was.

The Graduate course in playwriting had been taught by a well-known playwright who unexpectedly and unfortunately died suddenly and much too young. The Chair of the Theatre Department, Marvin Seiger, knowing that I had taught several such courses at Yale, asked me if I would be interested in taking over the course. Needless to say, I was extremely happy to do so – it was not as if I was overburdened with employment. And so I happily began what was going to turn out to be a 45-year relationship with the Department and Hunter College. Our class met two nights as week – scheduled this way so that older students who already had jobs would be able to attend. Later, as I will explain in due time, I expanded the course to include a theatre workshop which produced the plays developed in the course.

In the summer of 1965, I obtained a position as the resident director at the Barter Theatre in Abingdon, Virginia. The Barter was the stuff of legends. Located in furthest Southwest corner of Virginia where the State comes together with North Carolina, Tennessee, and West Virginia, Abingdon still has a population of only 8,000 people. Robert Porterfield, born in 1905 on a farm in nearby Glade Springs, Virginia, decided in his early teens that he wanted to be an actor, something that probably never crossed the mind of anyone in that area before or since. Tall, personable and with a deep voice, he attempted several times to gain admission to the American Academy of Dramatic Arts in New York and finally succeeded.

While studying at the Academy, he secured the occasional acting job while also becoming friendly with a number of fellow performers. When his father died in the early 1930s, Bob had to return home to run the family farm. In the meantime, the Depression had hit and changed the lives of almost everyone, including actors in New York. It was at this point that Bob had a vision. One newspaper account described what happened: "When theatres went dark, actors found themselves out of work. Meanwhile, back in Porterfield's part of Virginia, farmers were stuck with crops they could not sell. That was when Porterfield came up with his genius of an idea: bring actors to Abingdon to barter their performances for farm goods." Another newspaper continued the story: "Bringing some twenty of his fellow actors who came from New York, Bob offered admission to plays by letting local people pay with farm products or produce in lieu of money. In Porterfield's words: 'With vegetables you cannot sell, you can buy a good laugh'." When the actors arrived they took on all sorts of additional duties: building and painting scenery, making costumes, locating furniture and props, serving as stage managers. In July of 1939, *Life* magazine published an article that included the line: "What sounded like the craziest idea in the history of the American theatre is now a booming success."

The actors who took part in Bob's plan ended up including a who's who of well-known performers: Gregory Peck, Ernest Borgnine, Patricia Neal, Hume Cronyn, and Gary Collins among them. The theatre survived World War II, and continued to thrive in the post-war period. At the same time, Bob continued to come up with ideas. In 1953, when he heard that the Empire Theatre in New York was closing down, he made a deal with the outgoing owners to gain possession of all of its theatre seats as well as the theatre's paintings, lighting fixtures, and the electrical control system if he could remove them in a few days' time. Organizing a fleet of trucks from nearby farms and towns, Bob got them all to New York and within the required time stripped the inside of the Empire and moved everything to Abingdon. Within a matter days, he had the whole kit and caboodle – seats included – installed in the Barter. In time, the practice of audience members bringing products or produce as a ticket faded away, although it was reported that for many years some practical joker would arrive with a bushel of corn or a basket of tomatoes and demand entry.

When I arrived at the Barter in the late spring of 1964 I discovered an astonishing thing: 30 years after the theatre had begun Bob was still attracting top-flight performers, designers and technicians for his summer season. I discovered, for instance, that Liz Wilson, who had gotten her start at the Barter, was going to play the lead in the clever, madcap, ingenious *Oh Dad, Poor Dad, Mama's Hung You in the Closet and I'm Feeling So Sad* by Arthur Kopit – the opening play of the season and the first one I was going to direct. Arthur was and is one of the most talented playwrights of his time: off-beat, clever, thoughtful, and highly imaginative. As for Liz, I had first met her when she appeared in Lew Allen's production of *Big Fish, Little Fish* and she would go on to have a distinguished lifetime career in theatre and film. At the Barter she proved to be wonderful to work with and terrific in the roll of the mother. Because of its originality and humor, the play was a signal success. Another performer, hired for the season and appearing in three of the plays I directed, was Ned Beatty who became one of Hollywood's most reliable and frequently used supporting actors over a period of 60 years. A third actor, John Glover, became a fixture on the Broadway stage for the next half century.

Early in the summer Bob had a mild heart attack, not life threatening, but severe enough to require him to retire temporarily from running the theatre. As a result I was asked to take on some of his managerial duties in addition to my directing tasks. Before his attack Bob two or three times invited me to go with him to his family's farm in Glade Springs, where he delighted in making supper for us, including his special dish: wilted lettuce. It was on such trips that I learned, not only to know the man but also to be the beneficiary of his worldly wisdom. As for the directing, the summer proved to be the best possible tutorial and training ground particularly in what I learned from the actors. Out of the harsh light of New York and environs it was a marvelous place to work, to experiment a bit, and to develop a strong ensemble among the performers. It proved to be an invigorating, refreshing and immensely instructive experiment.

In the Fall of 1965, I became involved as an Associate Producer with an off-Broadway production of *Rooms*, a combination of two one-act plays by a well-known screen writer, Stanley Mann. It was being produced by Gene Persson whose wife, the actress Shirley Knight, was starring in both plays. Opening at the Cherry Lane Theatre, as off-Broadway productions go it was a classy affair. Though it received favorable reviews and ran for a respectable two months, I fear that it fell into the category of a success d'estime where my off-Broadway producing ventures seemed to land. Gene himself, who continued to produce both in New York and in London, had his biggest success when he later mounted the musical *You're a Good Man Charlie Brown*, a long running off-Broadway hit.

In the late summer of 1966, someone I knew phoned me and told me I should get in touch with a friend of hers, a person she had spoken to about me. "Concerning what?"

I asked. "You should speak to her yourself," she replied, "let her tell you." It turned out that the friend was Judy Abbott, daughter of the legendary director George Abbott – in the Broadway theatre, the most important single figure of 20th century. Born in 1887, Mr. Abbott first wanted to be a writer and attended George Pierce Baker's famous theatre class, Drama 47, at Harvard, the starting point of all early 20th century playwriting hopefuls such as Philip Barry, S. N. Behrman, Sidney Howard, and Eugene O'Neill. Mr. Abbott, as everyone called him, did plenty of writing during his career but when he came to New York in 1915, it was as an actor that he first found employment. Ten years later, in 1925, he made his debut as a director and continued to direct, write and produce for most of the 20th century. All in all, Mr. Abbott was involved in a staggering 120 Broadway productions. (As a footnote, in addition to his theatre credits, he was involved in some 30 major motion pictures.)

Tall (6'2"), statuesque, always standing fully erect, Mr. Abbott was imposing not only because of his reputation but because of his calm, authoritative presence. To say that he was a nonpareil, a legend in his own time, would be an understatement. And so, when someone said that she thought I ought to speak with Judy, his daughter, I said absolutely. Judy and I were introduced and immediately felt comfortable with one another. We talked about a number of things, many of them having nothing to do with theatre. In time, she let me know what was afoot. Her father, George, wanted to mount a play, a comedy written by Abe Einhorn, entitled *Agatha Sue, I Love You.* The novelty of the situation was that Abe had worked as a stage hand on several Abbott productions, and here he was, the author of a Broadway play. George's notion was that although the play was slight, it had a solid chance of becoming successful. (A sideline to all of this: because of the novelty of the situation Jim Stevenson wrote a "Talk of the Town" article about Abe that appeared in *The New Yorker* magazine. Jim, in addition to writing "Talk of the Town" pieces for the magazine was one of the most prodigious cartoonists in *New Yorker* history. By coincidence, a few years later, Jim and I met and became close friends, but more about that later.)

Judy, who was set to be the producer of the play, said that she was looking for a Co-Producer, not just an Associate Producer, George had already lined up a couple of those, but a bona fide Co-Producer. Obviously, she was asking her partner to raise a certain amount of money but it was a fairly modest sum. My theory, though I never asked her, was that neither George nor Judy wanted the production to appear to be too nepotistic an affair and that someone else, in addition to a family member, should also be involved. As far as raising money was concerned, I reasoned that with the legendary George Abbott involved it would not be too difficult to do, which proved to be the case. The next step was to meet her father. I knew the legend: no one ever, ever called him "George," it was always Mr. Abbott. There was a familiar story: when Hal Prince and Robert Griffith, both protégé's of Abbott, produced their first Broadway show, *Pajama Game,* and asked Mr. Abbott to direct it, Abbott said to Griffith: "Bobby, please call me George." Whereupon, Griffith replied: "I certainly will, Mr. Abbott."

The day Judy was going to introduce me to her father, I decided to call him George. He was very much my senior, being 79 when I was 39, and there was the weight of the legend. But I decided that since I was the co-producer of the play he was directing I might as well take the plunge. This was not something I felt strongly about, not a matter or principle, but rather more of a whim. I would be respectful of him and if, when I called him "George" he reacted negatively, I would abandon it immediately. Judy and I entered his office, he and I were introduced, we shook hands and I told him how honored I was to be a part of the production and how much I was looking forward to working with Judy and him. Somewhere early in the conversation I called him "George" and nothing happened: the earth did not shake; his expression did not change. And so, for the next, almost 30 years of our relationship, until his death, I addressed him as George.

I enjoyed tremendously observing him at rehearsals and learned a number of invaluable lessons – his quiet but firm command of the actors, his sense of pace, his awareness of everything that was happening at the center of the action but also on the periphery, his sense of when it was propitious to interrupt the actors and when to leave them alone. Rounding out the extremely talented team designing the show were people George had worked with before: Bill and Jean Eckart responsible for both scenery and lighting and Patton Campbell, the costume designer. We went to Boston for previews and it was then that I learned two things: One was how truly talented George was at taking the rough draft of a show and polishing it to the point where it reached its full potential; the other, unfortunately, was a let-down of major proportions – the realization of how woefully inept our two stars were.

While we were in Boston I discovered that one of the secrets of George's genius was what happened when he first observed a performance in front of an audience. He listened to the audience in a way I had never seen before; in essence, he and they became collaborators. After each performance he knew exactly which lines to cut; which scenes were too long and which were too short; which scenes needed to be completely rewritten or replaced. His sensitivity to these things was extraordinary and to me a revelation. The problem, in our case, was that his two lead actors, for different reasons, were incapable of accepting and making the changes George knew needed to be made: changes that his previous casts, going back 30 years, had the talent and the wherewithal to make.

The story of the play had to do with two not very savvy horseplayers who thought they had an idea of how to strike it rich, with the aid of a young, innocent girl. Playing the leader of the gang of two was Ray Walston, an actor with whom eight years earlier George had worked very successfully on the musical *Damn Yankees*. The problem was that in the intervening period Ray had gone to Hollywood to star in a TV show called *My Favorite Martian*. The show ran from September 1963 until May 1966. Television was made in those days by having crewmembers just out of camera range hold up cue cards on which, in four-inch high letters, the next few speeches were printed. It turned out that, because of this routine, Ray had utterly and completely lost the ability to memorize lines, relying instead on his cue cards. In the course of rehearsals I noticed that he carried around a tape recorder; it became obvious that at night he read his lines in the recorder and played them back to himself just before a scene was to take place. A man in that condition had zero ability to incorporate the kind of changes that George's directing required.

Throughout his career George had worked with actors who responded to his methods with alacrity – performers who were accustomed to taking changes in stride, learning new lines every day: "quick studies" they were called; actors to whom he could give 12 or 15 pages of new material one night knowing they would have it down pat, ready for a 10 a.m. rehearsal the next day. How was George to know about the 180 degree turn Ray had taken. In all his years he had never run into an actor in this condition. To make matters worse, Ray's co-star was a man named Corbett Monica, not an actor at all – I don't think he had ever been on a stage before – but a raffish nightclub comedian. I think the idea had been that the veteran, the reliable stage stalwart, Ray Walston would be able to prop him up. Talk about irony.

In any case I think all of us – George, Judy, the author, Abe, the other actors, everyone – knew in Boston that we were headed for failure in New York. Instead of a vessel arriving at the dock in full sail, we were limping into port with our sails torn to shreds and our ship taking on water.

And that is what happened. We opened, and not to our surprise, received mixed to negative reviews. One tabloid had as its headline over the review: "Agatha Sue Won't Do." George was never one to linger over failure and we closed in three days. The only redeeming moments were an extremely lively, festive opening night party on the second floor of Sardi's restaurant during which my backers from Nashville and New York mingled pleasantly with the performers, designers and crew. For my parents, there was also the pleasure the next day of the four of us – my mother, my father, George and me – having a lively, congenial lunch together.

Piano players in a theatre or a night club in the early years of the 20th century were accustomed to the phrase "vamp until ready." It meant to continue to play randomly until the singer or comedian is ready to begin his or her act. If I had been retrospective in the days following the closing of *Agatha Sue* – which I was not – I would have realized that I had been vamping for 15 years. If I had taken an honest look at myself I would have realized that, in truth, I was a wandering minstrel, a vagabond, a rootless parvenu, who had no focus, and in fact, no career. I had been moving through life like a sphere in a pin-ball machine, bouncing from one post to another, with no clear sense of direction:

the coffee business, drama school, teaching some, directing some, producing some.

There was no real pattern to it; the only constant was the fact that once I began studying at Yale, everything I did centered around theatre, but in the most random, haphazard way. Where was I headed; what possible goal could I pursue? I was not like anyone around me; on all sides I saw doctors, lawyers, investment bankers, teachers, scientists, artists. Even in the field I was closest to, everyone my age had long since settled on a specialty: acting, directing, designing, teaching, writing, producing. I was all over the place.

Though I seemed totally oblivious to the facts; looking back on it, I realize that I was totally unaware that, in truth, I was a lost soul, a "poor little lamb" as the line in the Whiffenpoof song goes. Anyone honestly looking at me would say: "Get a grip on yourself; stop fooling around, ricocheting from pillar to post, decide what you want to do and do it." At one point in *Death of a Salesman*, Arthur Miller has Willy say: "I feel kind of temporary." With me "temporary" was a permanent condition. I was avoiding the facts, refusing to face the truth and then within a very short time, the answer came, not because I suddenly became decisive and faced the truth – far from it – but strictly because of outside events.

It was Washington's birthday, February 22, 1967, when I received a call early in the morning from Edith Whiteman. Edith and Harold Whiteman, it will be recalled, had been helpful to me when I first arrived at Yale. In the meantime, Harold had been brought to NYU to be a Vice-Chancellor and he and Edith had lived first in Brooklyn Heights, where I re-united with them, and then moved on to the Washington Mews across from the NYU campus. The Mews had originally been a lane for horses and carriages behind the grand private homes facing the north side of Washington Square, but it had gradually been taken over by NYU and turned into charming faculty homes.

Edith informed me that she was giving a small dinner party that night – including several people she and Harold had known in New Haven – but that a man she had counted on, and who was supposedly leaving his wife, had called to say he was going back to the wife and could not come. She needed a man, a body, to round out the table and I must come. I told her I had a date. "Get out of it," she said, commandingly. I acquiesced – after all the Whitemans had been wonderful to me for a dozen years, first in New Haven and then in Brooklyn Heights – and arrived at their home to find that I was placed beside a young widow, a friend of the Whiteman's from New Haven, who, as I have mentioned, had moved to New York when her husband had died when he was quite young. I later learned that Edith had told several friends that she had corralled me not as a date for this lady – there was no thought of that – but to even up the numbers. In Edith's mind her other guest and I would be quite incompatible. "After tonight," she explained to several friends, "these two will never see each other again."

I had been dating for the past twenty years, a series of lovely, intelligent, attractive ladies, some of whom I escorted for as long as a year or more, but never reaching a point with any of them where I wanted to get married. I met Catherine Stuart Leavenworth, Chic (pronounced "Chick", as I have explained previously), and despite Edith's disclaimer, began dating her in a way I had never dated anyone before. After all those prolonged liaisons through so many years that never resulted in a conclusion, this was dramatically different. Within three months of meeting Chic I had asked her to marry me and within five months, we were actually married. I need not elaborate on how incredible, how lovely, how lively I found her to be and how much I wanted to spend the rest of my life with her.

We married in July of 1967, in the chapel of St. Bartholomew's Church on Park Avenue and honeymooned in Bermuda, a place where neither of us had been before. When we returned I moved from my apartment in Brooklyn Heights to her apartment on East 68th Street in Manhattan. In the meantime, I realized that this was a whole new ball game – being married, that is. I began to focus in a way I never had before. I realized I needed a full-time job, with security, retirement benefits, and all the rest. I had a wife to support. Fortunately, I knew exactly where I wanted to turn. For the last three years I had been teaching the Graduate Playwriting Seminar at Hunter College. During that time I had gotten to know the theatre faculty quite well and they had come to know me. In the spring of 1967, after I became engaged to Chic, I approached the Chairman of the theatre department, Marvin Seiger, about taking a full-time job and as luck would have it, a long-time faculty member was retiring at the end of the 1966-67 school year so there was an opening. Thus, I became a full-time faculty member where I was to remain either at Hunter or its affiliate, the City University Graduate Center, for the next 40 or more years.

I felt I was fortunate to be at Hunter. Founded in 1870, as a woman's college, its chief mission was to prepare young women to be teachers in the colleges, high schools and grade schools of New York City. Tuition was free and admission was strictly on merit. Located on Park Avenue between 68th and 69th Streets, for 100 years it remained true to that mission and had an extraordinary record of success. Hunter students were the best and brightest the City had to offer. With the exception of Radcliffe (the women's college at Harvard) more graduates of Hunter went on to earn their PhD Degree than any women's college in the United States.

In January and February of 1967, just after *Agatha Sue* closed Judy and I stayed in touch. One of the things she spoke to me about was Merriewold, a summer retreat in the Catskill mountains. It had become an informal artists enclave and she thought I might enjoy spending time there in the summers. It sounded attractive to me. Judy had a place there, as did her father, George. So did the choreographer Agnes DeMille and her husband, as well as Richard Rodgers' daughter Mary Rodgers Guettel and her husband Hank. It sounded like an ideal place to relax and be with interesting, talented people. Judy offered to help me find a house to rent for the summer of '67 and I readily endorsed the idea. Then fate intervened in the person of Chic.

I think Judy had in mind the notion that it is always handy to have an extra man in the wings for cocktail parties, picnics, etc. I also believe that she was not a little upset when she learned later in the spring that I would not be coming to Merriewold as a single man but as a married one. The temperature appeared to go down noticeably when I told her about my forthcoming marriage. Nevertheless, we both put a good face on things and in mid-June, three weeks before our marriage, Chic and I went to Merriewold. The house I had rented, but never seen, belonged to a well-known socialite who apparently never came there. The shocking thing was that it proved to be a rather crude cabin in the midst of the woods. It was barely livable, but Chic and I knew we would be spending very little time there. In contrast to the house, however, the people in Merriewold, the ones I mentioned above, were extremely welcoming to Chic and me, including an invitation to attend George's 80th birthday party at his home on June 25th. The party was a low-key but extremely congenial affair and Chic had an opportunity to visit with George and explain to him that she and her brother, when they were teenagers in Durham, N.C., had a tap dance routine which they performed at Rotary and country clubs. (I think in the back of her head may have been a distant day-dream that George might invite her to audition for him.)

In the Fall of 1967, I began teaching full time at Hunter. Chic's apartment, where we were living until we could find a larger place, was a mere three block walk from the college – a fortuitous situation, to say the least. I threw myself into teaching, adding three undergraduate courses to my graduate seminar in playwriting. One of these new courses was the large Introduction to Theatre lecture course. In some ways I was well prepared to teach and lecture. My grammar school had been a progressive institution: the Peabody Demonstration School in Nashville. It offered a solid academic curriculum but there were departures. Each class, for example, had a year-long project that was shared with the rest of the school at the end of the year. The fifth grade, for instance, planted a garden on a large plot of land set aside on the school grounds. Each year the class would plant flowers and shrubs in the fall that would bloom in the spring. The eighth grade project was a circus on which the class worked throughout the school year and in the late spring presented to the entire school – I will let the reader guess who the Ring Master was.

At the same time I continued to expand my Graduate Playwriting course. I had initiated a project for the class called Hunter Playwrights, the idea of which was to let aspiring dramatists see their work performed on a stage, in a workshop project if not in a finished production. I traipsed all over town tracking down viable spaces, finding church basements, making a deal for a small theatre at the West Side YMCA, as well as recruiting actors and directors. All the while my wife was assisting with finding props: old telephones, electric razors, coffee makers. (This program continued to expand under me and my successors and continues to this day with every student in the class having the opportunity to see his or her work performed by actors on a stage.)

Early in the fall of 1967, Chic began looking for an apartment for us. She looked mostly on the Upper East Side, and we made bids on two apartments, which with hindsight, I am glad we did not get. In the meantime, a friend of hers from New Haven told her about an apartment on the West Side where her daughter and the daughter's husband lived – 55 Central Park West, at the corner of 66th Street. We began looking there and found an apartment for sale. The owner was a widower who was extremely proud of the decorations that had the 1930's motif of a Joan Crawford film (the sofa attached to a chair which was attached to an end table, and so on around the room with every piece connected to the next one, all of them in the same fading blue hue.) Because he was so proud of the décor, he only wanted to sell it furnished and was mystified by the fact that no one seemed to want it the way it was. We made it clear that we wished to be first in line if he decided to sell it unfurnished, which eventually he did. It was perfect for us. On the 12th floor – spacious, every room with an incredible view of the Park – it was situated on the 66th Street transverse from 5th Avenue to the West Side. In the fall and spring I could walk across the Park to Hunter College, and at night the Number 10 bus took us directly to and from the apartment to the Theatre District. We lived in the apartment for the forty-nine plus years we were married, and I have remained there to this day.

One of the advantages of teaching is that you have the summer off. In 1968, the first summer after we had married, Chic and I were the fortunate recipients of good friends of hers who lived in a house on the shore in Greenwich, Connecticut. She had met this couple when living in New Haven – Paul and Louise Adams. Paul was an inveterate sailor, you might almost say, a fanatical one, who owned a sailboat that he kept in Sweden where he and Louise, often with visiting friends, sailed every summer. As a sort of delayed wedding present they invited us to stay in their Greenwich home while they were away. It was a grand place to spend our first summer, and Paul and Louise compounded it the next summer when they invited us to come to Sweden to sail with them for two weeks. Since we were already in Europe that summer we reasoned, we might as well add London and Paris to our itinerary, which we did.

CHAPTER FIVE

Quogue / The Coffee House / Trips Abroad

In the winter and spring of 1970 we began to investigate the idea of a place nearby where we would go for the summer. We had seen several small, low-key spots in lower New York State and southern Connecticut that appealed to us. In the meantime, good friends of ours, Hunt and Liza Taylor, had other ideas for us. I had met the two through mutual friends when I first arrived in New York. Hunt was in the family furniture business in an office building across 49th Street from Saks Fifth Avenue, and he and Liza lived in Westfield, New Jersey. They were friends we saw frequently and when we told them of our search for a summer home, they became great advocates of an area we had never visited: Long Island. Liza's aunt and uncle had a home in a small town, Quogue, on the South Shore, where the Taylors had been visiting ever since they got married. We had never heard of Quogue. Liza said she had a close friend, Peggy Jackson, who lived there and was in the real estate business; Chic should visit her. Quogue – the name comes from an Indian word – was located between Westhampton Beach and Southampton.

The day Chic went to meet Peggy she thought she was going to visit several places on the South Shore: Southampton, Water Mill and Bridgehampton. Not on your life. Peggy had always lived in Quogue and as far as she was concerned there was no reason to look elsewhere. In any event, after a full day of looking Chic saw a home near both the Beach Club and the Quogue Field Club that she felt, pending my approval, would be fine. I saw it a week later, approved, and we signed it up for the summer of 1970. We ended up spending our summers – and part of our winters – in Quogue for the next 45 years. We rented a variety of homes for the next 12 years and in 1982 built our own home, which is when we began to go out for occasional weekends in the winter as well as for most of every summer. Happily, that first summer in Quogue we met a number of people who became close, lasting friends for the rest of the time we were there.

Quogue was and is the most understated, low-key, unostentatious of all the Hamptons. It is small: with only three or four stores, a fire department and a post office in the center of the village. Young people ride their bikes everywhere in the village: to the beach, the tiny yacht club, the tennis courts, and most of all, Junior Sports, which boasts probably the best and longest-running summer day camp for the young in all of Long Island. The beech has one of the most gorgeous stretches of pure white sand to be found anywhere; and the Field Club (over 120 years old) has 15 tennis courts, paddle courts and a nine-hole golf course. (Originally the course was 18 holes but the back nine got blown away by the 1938 hurricane which did major damage not only to the golf course but destroyed as well the only two bridges connecting the mainland to the beech.) As for golf, there is no problem for aficionados: only a 20 minute drive from Quogue are two of the oldest and finest links courses in the U.S.: The National and Shinnecock, the latter a frequent site of the U. S. Open. Avid golfers choose one or the other and enjoy one of the finest courses the game has to offer.

I had played golf as a youngster, but the game I really enjoyed was tennis. During the week I played at the Field Club, but on weekends I began playing in a regular game at the home of Gardner Botsford. How this started I cannot recall but it was a stroke of enormous good fortune for me. Gardner and his wife, Tassie, lived in an old farmhouse that looked out on a bay. In the front yard was a weather-beaten hard-surface tennis court. Alongside the court was a time-worn rowboat, turned upside down, on which we sat between sets. Gardner, of whom more later, was the stepson of Raoul Fleischmann who, among other things, bankrolled *The New Yorker* magazine.

One of the other members of our group was Henry Gardiner, a direct descendent of the family to whom King Charles, the first, had bequeathed the ownership charter of Gardiner's Island in 1639. (Gardiner's Island lies between the two peninsulas at the East End of Long Island.) Despite this lineage, Hank, as he was called was as down to earth as anyone I have ever known. He and his wife Winnie lived in what had been, since the 1890s, a large boarding house on Quogue Street owned by his family. Henry himself was the chief designer of the exhibits in the Museum of Natural History where he had revolutionized the way artifacts were displayed, an approach that was later duplicated by natural history museums worldwide.

Gardner was born in Quincy, Illinois, the grandson of a man who had invented the mechanism for brakes on trains, so that going down a steep incline, the train could be slowed down and controlled. The family, in other words, was comfortable, but when Gardner and his brother, Steve, were relatively young, their mother divorced his father and took the boys with her to New York. In later life, Gardner wrote an autobiography entitled *A Life of Privilege, Mostly* which is divided into three parts. The early part (which his publisher insisted become the middle section in the printed book) was about his life in New York in the 1930s after his mother – clearly an extremely attractive lady – had married Raul Fleischmann and the family was living luxuriously in an elegant town house with five in-house servants and several others outside, including the family chauffeur. In the summers the Fleischmanns would decamp to the North Shore of Long Island where they had a home with a living room 42 feet long and a croquet court where they played with the likes of Groucho Marx and Wolcott Gibbs.

The second section of Gardner's book took place during World War II when he served in the Army. There was a famous photograph on the cover of *Life* magazine of a landing craft about to hit Omaha Beach on D-Day. In the center is the back of a soldier standing in bow of the boat facing the beach – the man is Gardner. Fluent in French, after the landing Gardner was charged with making contact with members of the French Resistance. He did and went with the invasion troops all the way to Paris; later he was awarded a Bronze Star and the Croix de Guerre. The third chapter consisted of Gardner's years as the chief non-fiction editor at *The New Yorker* magazine, shaping the work of such features as the "Letters from London and Paris."

In 1972 Gardner introduced me to the Coffee House, a low-key men's lunch club on 45th Street between 5th and 6th Avenues in Manhattan, very near the theatre district. It had remained exactly the same kind of informal, unpretentious organization its founders had in mind when they formed the club sixty years earlier. The guiding spirit behind the original idea was Frank Crowninshield, a blue-blood aristocrat who nevertheless had the idea of forming a small, intimate club that would afford the informality not available in larger, prestigious clubs such as the Knickerbocker or Union Clubs to which he also belonged. (Crowninshield was the editor of the magazine *Vanity Fair* that he had transformed from a fashion publication to a trend-setting, highly regarded literary magazine.)

In 1915 Crowninshield had gathered a group of like-minded friends and taken over the second floor of the Seymour Hotel at 70 West 45th Street where the club was to remain until 1982, nearly three-quarters of a century later. The ambience and liveliness of the Club was strengthened ten years after its founding when a brash young magazine called *The New Yorker* came on the scene occupying offices only a block away. (*The New Yorker* was to remain at the same offices – in two buildings in the West 40's between 5th and 6th – for the next 90 years.) In virtually every respect the Coffee House and *The New Yorker* were made for each other. The writers, editors and cartoonists of *The New Yorker* were precisely the type of people Crowninshield and his friends had in mind when they formed the Coffee House in the first place – smart, sophisticated, low-key, free-for-all, spirited individuals.

In the early 70s, when Gardner introduced me to the Club, it was still in the midst of what might be termed its Golden Age – a congregation of lively, well-informed, spirited, sometimes even loquacious, conversationalists. Gardner's personal favorite raconteur was Monroe Wheeler, a major figure at the Museum of Modern Art who, quite literally, knew everybody in New York at the apex of both the social and art worlds – the moneyed elite who were lovers of the arts, and everyone else who counted, not just in the visual arts, but opera, ballet, and theatre as well. It was a heady mixture and Monroe seemed to be at the nexus of it all. Moreover, he was a master storyteller describing the foibles of an artistic genius, as well as the peccadilloes and pretensions of their patrons. In his book Gardner describes how – after a lunch with Monroe – he would hasten back to his office at *The New Yorker* to write down, word for word, the anecdotes he has just heard from Monroe.

When I first began going to the Coffee House – in the early 1970s – the regulars included Herman Levin, the producer of *My Fair Lady*, Gordon Manning, the most entertaining and inventive TV news producer of all time, Sidney Offit, author, teacher, and the moving spirit behind the PEN American Center, Paul Greenberg, the behind-the-scenes producer of practically every important news anchor of the day (Huntley and Brinkley, John Chancellor, Walter Cronkite, Tom Brokaw); the actor, director and writer Garson Kanin, (in the early years with his famous actress wife, Ruth Gordon, and later with his second wife, the inimitable actress Marian Seldes). Added to this were *The New Yorker* stalwarts such as Roger Angell, the legendary baseball writer.

In terms of abiding friendships, however, my closest friends from the early Coffee House days were two *New Yorker* cartoonists, Jim Stevenson and Frank Modell. Both men were exceptional, contributing to the magazine, in Frank's case 1,400 cartoons and in Jim's, nearly 2,000 (1,989 to be exact). The latter, however, was not just exceptional but truly remarkable. Along with his drawings, Jim contributed frequent "Talk of the Town" articles to *The New Yorker.* Separately he wrote and illustrated over 100 children's books published chiefly by Greenwillow Books. Jim got his start at *The New Yorker* in an anonymous role. It is not widely known that frequently the most arresting cartoonists for the magazine, who were brilliant at the visual aspects of their craft, did not have the aptitude for creating clever captions. Jim was a master at this and his first job at *The New Yorker*, for which he was sworn to total secrecy, was to provide inventive, savvy captions to accompany the cartoons. One day, during my early years attending the Coffee House, a guest who came to the club was introduced as having just written a biography of the famous Peter Arno, a provocative, witty cartoonist who began at the magazine in the 1930s. The guest was completely taken aback when someone at the table asked him: "Do you know who wrote most of Arno's captions in his later years?" "He wrote them himself, of course," the man replied. "Sorry," said the questioner, pointing to Jim: "It was the man sitting across from you."

In the mid-1990s Jim ventured into the field of musical theatre. Collaborating with Dick Roberts, who wrote the music, Jim wrote the book and lyrics for *Rolling In Dough*, based on a book about a group of ladies in an Ohio town who formed an investment club that, against all odds, became successful. Jim's first wife, Jane, with whom he had nine children, had died in 1982. Eleven years later Jim married Josie Merck, an amazing person on her own. An accomplished artist, she also contributed generously, both with time and money, to any number of important environmental causes not just in the U. S. but around the world. Among Josie's innumerable friends was the lady who ran the Granbury Opera House, a small but elegant theatre on the square in Granbury, Texas, a town of 9,000 located 35 miles southwest of Fort Worth.

Chic and I planned to attend the premiere of *Rolling in Dough* and had decided to go by the way of Nashville, spending a few days with my family on the way to Granbury. The second night we were there we had a call from Josie – would we like to go the rest of the way by bus? She had arranged for a bus to take her, Jim and Josie's mother Betty by bus from Nashville to Granbury and would love for us to join them. This was, as they say, a "no brainer." Josie, Jim and Betty had just arrived in Nashville and would be spending the night at what had been the old Union Railway Station on Broad Street: a building that had been converted into a hotel. Chic and I appeared at 9:00 the next morning to be greeted by our friends standing beside a 40 foot silver and blue bus, the kind that carry Country Music stars from one engagement to the next. The bus had two small living rooms, one at the front and the other at the rear, 12 bunk beds and a small kitchen. The routine was that when a star and his or her band finished an evening engagement in one town, they would board the bus and head for the next. The five of us, however, were just along for the ride.

The plan was to take one day to get to Little Rock, where we would spend the night in a hotel and go on the next day to Granbury. Along the way we stopped for meals or coffee at such places as Dinah's Diner, The Roadside Rest Stop, Carl's Café and Ham & Biscuit Heaven. At each stop, as we pulled up, people in the parking lot and some from inside the diner would come rushing up to the bus, assuming we were famous country music stars. "What's the name of your band?" they would ask, or "Whose the star you play for?" We disappointed any number of would-be fans once they discovered we were nothing but interlopers.

When we finally arrived at Granbury we joined a large contingent from New York and southern Connecticut who had come for the premiere. The show went beautifully; everyone had a marvelous time; but unfortunately – like several musicals I have undertaken – the beginning of the line was also the end. As an adventure with the best possible friends, however, it was an adventure not to be forgotten.

It was the good fortune of my wife, Chic, and me to see a great deal of Josie and Jim over the final two decades of Jim's life. The four of us had lunch together at least once a month at a favorite West Side restaurant near their New York apartment; we visited them at their summer home on Block Island; and we were together at a number of events in the city, such as jazz concerts that Josie particularly enjoys. Invariably Jim was the same congenial, modest, unassuming person he had always been: a masterful, ingenious artist and writer masquerading as a person just like the rest of us.

I began the discussion of my relationship with Jim Stevenson with reference to the Coffee House Club. Before I leave the subject of the Club I should say a brief word about its neighborhood. The club began its life in 1915 on West 45th Street between 5th and 6th Avenues. Later in the century it was forced to leave that location but was able to find congenial accommodations just down the block. Later, a few years into the 21st century, it was forced to move once again and found a home one block South – on 44th Street between 5th and 6th Avenues. On 44th Street it was on the same block as the Harvard Club, the Yacht Club, The Penn Club (occupying the same building that until 1915 had been the home of the Yale Club), and the Algonquin Hotel, the home of the famous Roundtable of literary and theatrical fame. One block south of that, on 43rd, is the Princeton Club situated next to the Century Association, often referred to as the Century Club. (I was fortunate a few years after joining the Coffee House, to be invited also to join the Century.) This grouping of literary, arts, and academic clubs in three adjacent blocks in Manhattan is a remarkable phenomenon that has now endured for well over a century.

CHAPTER SIX

The Accidental Author, Part I

Moving back in time to our second summer in Quogue, in late August 1971, I was invited by Alfred Malabre to play golf at the National golf course. Over our first two summers in Quogue, Chic and I had become friends with Alfred and his wife, Pat. Alfred was a first-rate golfer and a long-time member of the National links and nice enough to invite me to play from time to time. Alfred was also the financial editor and a long-time writer for the *Wall Street Journal* who for many years wrote a featured column on the front page every Monday. He was, as well, the author of several very well-received books on economics. This particular day, playing golf at the National, as he and I walked up the 16th fairway, he casually asked me if I had ever done any theatre reviewing. I replied that, of course, I had written a great deal about theatre but not reviews, though, as a matter of fact, when I was living in Brooklyn and the famous 19th and early 20th century newspaper, *The Brooklyn Eagle*, was revived for a short period, I had written reviews for them. Alfred said that it was not imminent but that sometime in the future he understood the *Journal* might be looking for a theatre critic. By that time we had reached the 16th green and no more was said on the subject.

I was busy teaching and dealing with departmental chores at Hunter so throughout the following fall I thought no more about it. In late November, out of the blue, I had a phone call from a gentleman named George Melloan. It turned out that he was one of the editors of the *Journal's* Op Ed page, the one just opposite the editorial page, where "think pieces" as well as art, music and theatre reviews appeared. "Alfred Malabre says you might be interested in writing about the theatre for us," George said, and continued, "Is that so?" As I had not heard anything in three months and had a full plate at Hunter, I had quite honestly forgotten about Al's and my conversation on the golf course. After a pause, I finally replied yes. "Thank you," George said and hung up.

Again I heard nothing for another three months and assumed these people were not in the least serious. In late March, again quite out of the blue, George called again. "Are you still interested?" George asked me. Since "I had not heard anything in several months – twice," I said," I assumed it was the *Journal* that was not interested." "No point in going over what's been happening here," he said. "But if you want to give this a try here is what I plan to do. I'm sending you tickets to a play that opens next week. Write a review of it – of course, we will never print it – but we will see where we go from there." I said OK and a few days later received the tickets in the mail.

I wrote the review, sent it in and never heard a word. But shortly after that George called to say he was sending me tickets; I should write a review and if it was OK, this time they would print it. And that is what happened. The play was *Don't Bother Me, I Can't Cope* by a young, African-American woman playwright. I gave it a good review that appeared on April 21, 1972, with a headline (written as always by someone else) that read "Miss Grant Can Cope." From then on, for the next 23 years, I was the drama reviewer for the *Journal*, covering theatre in New York, around the United States and abroad, particularly in London where Chic and I would go at least once a year and sometimes more often. There was no contract between me and the *Journal*, nothing written down – all my benefits, etc. were covered by Hunter College and the City University. The *Journal* paid me by the piece and always covered my travel expenses, but that was it. After that first review we followed the same procedure: I would receive the tickets in the mail, see the show, write a review that would be picked up the next morning by a messenger and taken to the *Journal*. (A short time later, computers became ubiquitous and rather than using messengers I sent my reviews via email.)

Gradually, things settled down. The press agents acknowledged that I was the theatre critic for the *Journal* long before the paper itself did and after a short time, instead of receiving tickets by mail from George, I received them from the publicist in the theatre lobby on press night. In the midst of all this George proved to be a most pleasant fellow as well as an excellent editor, really first-rate, though he often remained as low-key as anyone I believe I have ever known. In the spring of 1973 I called George. "George," I asked, "am I the theatre critic for the *Wall Street Journal*?" "Well, er..." George responded hesitantly. "The reason I ask," I said, "is that someone from the New York Drama Critics Circle just called and invited me to join the Circle." George hesitated: "Well," he finally said, "I suppose." I told him I took his "suppose" as a yes and joined the Circle.

In the spring of 1978, I took a sabbatical from teaching at Hunter and Chic and I rented a flat in London for six months. Our landlords were Leonard and Sally Miall, a couple with whom we became quite friendly during our stay in London. The flat was in Queen's Gate Gardens, just off the Cromwell Road in Kensington, near The Royal Albert Hall, several museums, and the southwest corner of Hyde Park. The flat itself was ideal: two bedrooms and a living room that looked over a garden that was a full square block with lovely homes on all four sides. Leonard, though retired, remained a legend at the BBC where he had worked for many years. One day he invited Chic and me to spend the day at BBC-TV with him. We had lunch in the Executive Dining Room and were able to observe several of those famous BBC television dramas being filmed. (One we saw, I recall, was a memorable version of Rebecca that came out a year later.)

Chic and I took full advantage of our six months in London. In the late spring, we rendezvoused with my mother, my sister and her husband in Italy and France after Chic and I had spent some time visiting theatre sites in Greece. Back in London I stood in line at St. James's Palace to secure tickets for two days in the Royal Enclosure at Ascot. After that, through the good graces of a long-time friend in TV broadcasting, we were guests at the NBC tent at Wimbledon where we not only took advantage of a more than ample supply of strawberries, cream and champagne, but enjoyed excellent seats for the tennis matches.

As for covering the London theatre, whenever we were there I got in the habit of visiting the *Journal's* London offices in the financial district and over time I came to know well several journalists in the bureau who became good friends. My writing routine in London, the morning after we had seen a play, was to go to the stately, formidable Reform Club on Pall Mall with which the Century Association in New York had a reciprocal arrangement. With notebook in hand I would go to the high-vaulted library to write my review in long hand. I would then take the subway (known as the Tube) to the financial district and the offices of the *Wall Street Journal* where I would forward the review to the office in New York.

In the late spring our landlords, Leonard and Sally, invited us for lunch one Sunday to their country home near Windsor, the place where they were living while we were in their flat. When inviting us they had mentioned that there would be a third couple coming as well. When we arrived we discovered that the third couple was Julia Child and her husband Paul. After half an hour of drinks and pleasantries, Sally excused herself and headed for the kitchen to begin serving lunch and Chic went with her. Once out of earshot Chic asked Sally: "How in the world can you be so calm: preparing lunch for Julia Child?" "Not to worry," Sally assured her, "she will eat anything." Although Julia was clearly the most visible member of the Child family, thanks to her TV appearances, Paul turned out to be a lively, warm, engaging conversationalist. So pleasant was the lunch and the company that two hours turned into four when Chic and I suddenly realized we might be in danger of overstaying our welcome and expeditiously expressed our thanks and said goodbye.

Twice during this period of travel Chic and I went in a totally opposite direction from Britain or Europe, namely, to Japan, where I was sent, not by the *Journal* but by others. Once it was the Milwaukee Repertory Theatre that had a grant for an exchange program with a Japanese theatre and part of the grant was for the theatre to send a critic to Japan to write an article about their theatre. Chic and I went to Tokyo in late October, 1978. Fortunately, we were provided with an indispensable translator, Mrs. Kagigahari who had perfect English, having studied for two years at a college in Pennsylvania. Before each of the performances we attended she wrote a synopsis of the play we were to see, and at the performance sat between Chic and me to quietly, almost silently, explain what was happening. We saw half a dozen avant-garde productions, the avant-garde being surprisingly popular at that juncture in Japan, in addition to the traditional theatres of Kabuki and Noh as well as the most surprising one of all, the opening of the sixth revival of the Japanese version of the musical, *Fiddler on the Roof.*

How, we asked each other, could *Fiddler* be far and away the most popular modern musical of all time in Japan? The opening night was a sight to behold: a sloping bank, eight feet wide, that ran an entire block next to the theatre was covered by hundreds of flowers – maybe thousands – put there by fans in tribute to their favorite performers; Tevya, the lead role, was being played by Japan's most popular actor and anticipation of a special evening was palpable. The theatre seated 1,800 people and the production was lavish. Then, as the show unfolded, when the song "Tradition" appeared, a realization hit us. This was the secret of the musical's appeal to the Japanese audience: as much as any advanced nation in the world, Japan is a country bound by tradition, hence the connection. Though I had not been sent by the *Journal*, upon our return I wrote a lengthy piece on our trip that was published in the *Journal* in early November.

By a fluke, Chic and I were back in Tokyo a year later. Again, I was not sent by the *Journal* but was asked to join a delegation of representative theatre people being sent as part of an exchange program. Our group consisted of a cross-section of the New York theatre world at that time, among them two people from the Shubert organization, the immensely talented playwright Arthur Kopit, author of *Oh Dad, Poor Dad*, the play that I had directed at the Barter Theatre, and Ellen Stewart, the African-American fashion designer and theatre director who in 1961 had founded the La Mama Theatre in Greenwich Village, an experimental theatre that is still going today. It was a mixed bag if ever there was one: the two Shubert men in suits fit for stock brokers or corporate lawyers, the ever clever and delightful Arthur, and Ellen, the queen of the off-beat and avant-garde. We met with our theatre counterparts in Tokyo and Kyoto, saw a cross-section of their theatre, and had a number of lively, informative exchanges. Often, after a day of visits and conferences, we would be at our final performance of the day and I would look over at Ellen only to see her sitting, or perhaps lying down, fast asleep.

One bonus for Chic and me in visiting Tokyo was that Jim and Janet Hester were in residence both years and we were able to see a great deal of them both years we were in Tokyo. (Jim, as I mentioned earlier, had been the president of NYU in New York and was the one who had hired our friend Harold Whiteman away from Yale. It was through the Whitemans that we had met the Jim and Janet who became close friends from then on. The Hesters were in Tokyo because Jim had concluded his illustrious career at NYU and was currently the head of the United Nations University that had its headquarters there.)

There was one other trip Chic and I took while I was at the *Journal*, this one much less pleasant and entertaining than the two trips to Japan and various trips to Europe. In the early 1980s I was surprised to get a call from the USIA – The United States Information Agency. The agency was founded in 1953 by President Eisenhower, "to understand, inform, and influence foreign publics in promotion of the national interest and to broaden the dialogue between Americans and U. S. Institutions and their counterparts abroad." In 1999, the USIA was terminated and some of its duties turned over to other government agencies; prior to that, however, its budget was roughly 2 billion dollars a year. I knew nothing about the agency and am not certain I had even heard of it. Nevertheless, in the early 1980s I was asked by the USIA to go on its behalf to Romania and East Germany to meet with theatre and other arts leaders on behalf of the U.S. The plan was that my wife and I would fly to Bucharest, where I would have meetings and then, while there, we would be driven to a few other cities in Romania. We would then fly to Vienna, where Chic would join a friend while I went on to East Berlin and Dresden to meet with theatre leaders there before returning to West Berlin and Vienna.

At that time Romania and East Berlin were still very much under the control of the Soviet Union and would remain so for the rest of the decade. Moreover, Romania was ruled by a cruel, oppressive, ruthless dictator, Nicolae Caucescu. In the meantime, Chic and I were given all kinds of advice both by the USIA and friends who had travelled behind the Iron Curtain. We were told, for example, that the one thing we must carry was at least two cartons of Kent cigarettes, which we could parcel out, one or two cigarettes at a time as tips or the like. We were also urged to wear sensible clothes.

We had a taste of what we were in for when we landed at the airport in Bucharest. The airfield was completely surrounded – on all sides – by tanks with machine guns mounted on them. It was late afternoon when we arrived and we were taken to hotel: a shabby affair in downtown Bucharest. After unpacking we went down to the dining room where we were one of only three couples, and had as bland a dinner as we could manage to order. After dinner it was still light outside so we decided to take a short walk to see a bit of downtown Bucharest. It was eerie. We walked a few blocks, looking in shop windows, and suddenly realized that we were all alone; we had not seen a single person since we left the hotel. In a 25 minutes walk we saw four, maybe five, people. We were in a ghost town.

The next morning we made our way to the U. S. Embassy to meet with the Cultural Attaché who was to be our contact. He turned out to be a strange man indeed. In the first place, although he was the Cultural representative, he seemed to know little or nothing about the arts in Bucharest or Romania at large.I had done a bit of research and knew that one place I must visit was the National Theatre to speak with its Director, Radu Beligan, a man who I had learned was extremely proud of his Western contacts, especially in London. I had found on a map where the theatre was: two blocks south of the Intercontinental Hotel at University Square, only a few blocks from where we were. When I asked the Attaché, however, about visiting the theatre and meeting the director, it turned out that he had no idea where it was. Did I hear him correctly? It turns out I did.

Chic and I left the Embassy and quite easily found the National Theatre – an imposing building that had recently been constructed to replace the theatre that had been leveled by the Luftwaffe in 1944. It was also not difficult to meet the Artistic Director, who welcomed us warmly. He wasted no time in letting us know how friendly he was with Laurence Olivier and John Gielgud who, he said, he knew extremely well. From him I learned a great deal about theatre in Romania generally and in Bucharest in particular. Among other things he made it abundantly clear how tightly controlled the theatre was by the authorities. After two days of visiting smaller theatres and meeting with playwrights and directors, we were scheduled to be driven to the town of Timisoara in the far northwest corner of Romania with stops in several other towns along the way.

It turned out that our transportation was a very small van carrying, in addition to Chic and me, various household goods such as paper towels, pampers, and Kleenex to be

107

distributed to various destinations such as small towns on our route. The driver was a young man who, we were told, would certainly be an informer for the government. And so we set off, stopping along the way to make deliveries and in some cases, being held up by local celebrations – a wedding or a seasonal festival – that took up the entire roadway. When we reached our destination, in mid-afternoon, we went first to our lodgings and then I was led to a meeting with local theatre and arts officials – about a dozen in number – of whom, I was told, at least one would be a spy reporting to authorities.

The groups I met with were invariably courteous as well as extremely curious. I explained that theatre in the U. S. and Europe was divided into government sponsored theatre and privately financed productions – information of that sort – and attempted to answer their questions as helpfully as I could. Invariably, when one of these meetings broke up someone at the end would walk close to my side as we left and attempt to ask, as secretly as he could, how he might come to the U. S. and teach at a place like Hunter College. Sadly, of course, I could be of no help to them. The productions we saw in the provinces and Timisoara were often the classics and I discovered both by observation and in conversation that the way theatre producers and directors often got around censorship was to present a classic such as a Shakespearean play, a seemingly harmless choice, but to introduce some subversive element – change the narrative slightly or introduce a character or episode that the locals would immediately recognize as a critique of the regime or of some local authority figure.

Before we left Bucharest, Chic and I had inquired about hotels in the capital and identified one that we thought would be infinitely better than the one the Attaché had sent us to and when we returned to the capital, that is where we asked to be taken and indeed it was a considerable improvement. The attaché, not surprisingly, was upset that we had not returned to the second-rate hotel he had chosen. Once back in Bucharest I was taken the next morning by an official to meet someone in the cultural ministry while Chic, who remained in the hotel lobby was cautioned by the official not to let anyone attempt to wrest dollars from her. When we returned we discovered that she had been accosted and found refuge in retreating to a spot near the check-in desk where a friendly clerk helped her fend off anyone who approached.

We went for our last visit with the Cultural Attaché with whom we were to have lunch in the Embassy cafeteria just prior to departing. Before leaving on our road trip, we had learned that he was divorced and that his young, six-year-old daughter lived with him in the Embassy. In Timisoara, Chic had purchased a small doll to give the daughter as a present when we returned. It was raining lightly that morning and Chic carried the doll, gift wrapped, under her raincoat. She told the Attaché that she would like to give the present to his daughter but he assured her that he would take care of it and she should simply leave it on his desk along with her raincoat. After lunch, when Chic went to retrieve her raincoat, she saw the doll there, torn to shreds, eviscerated to make certain there was nothing lethal or explosive inside. Unfortunately, this was a sad reminder of the mental state of the man supposedly there to represent the best of his country: a harmless gesture destroyed by this paranoid official.

(Before leaving the subject of Romania it should be noted that Nicolae Ceausescu, the dictator of the country, was perhaps the most brutal and oppressive of all the leaders of iron curtain countries, so brutal, in fact, that when he and his wife attempted to leave the country on the heels of the revolution they were captured on December 25, 1989, and executed by a firing squad.)

We flew to Vienna where Chic joined our friend Peggy Joyce while I continued on to the Embassy in West Berlin where a USIA official took me in hand, giving me necessary information, instructions, and warnings. I was driven to Checkpoint Charlie, the Western side of the infamous bridge and crossing point into East Berlin, where I showed my passport and other papers and was patted down to make certain I was not concealing a weapon. I crossed the space between West and East and was met on the other side by another USIA person from East Berlin who helped me into a car and proceeded to drive me to Dresden.

Dresden, it will be recalled, is an ancient city in Saxony situated on the banks of the Elbe River. Among other things, it has a long, impressive history as a seat of culture, education and the arts, but in the closing days of World War II, in a highly controversial move, the city was bombed mercilessly by the Allies, with incendiary bombs added to regular bombs in order to kill fleeing German troops. It is estimated that 25,000 civilians lost their lives. In addition, many ancient cultural sites were destroyed. After the war it was occupied by the Soviet Union and though re-building had begun it was far from being restored to its former glory. Quite simply, the bombing had destroyed the heart of Dresden's history, its art, and its culture not to mention its churches, museums, and government buildings. I realized that even a 40-year interval would not have come close to erasing such a horrific memory.

It was against this background that both sides – the U. S. side represented by me and my USIA companion and their side represented by German citizens currently active in theatre and the arts – were aware that the arts have a way of transcending the ugliest of memories and realities. The atmosphere was much more congenial than that in Bucharest thanks to the fact that the background and education of the

USIA personnel in Dresden far exceeded that of their counterparts in Romania. As a result, we had a series of open, informative and cordial meetings, and I only hoped that I was able in some small way to contribute to a much desired and much needed healing process.

After our meetings I was driven back to East Berlin, repeated the Checkpoint Charlie crossing and rendezvoused with Chic in Vienna and we made our way home. Shortly after we returned to New York, I went to Washington to report to the USIA in a series of de-briefings what I had observed behind the Iron Curtain. I tried to give as full and accurate an account as I could of both the constructive and questionable steps being taken to open up communication between East and West. Though I was tempted not to, I could not avoid giving a full report concerning the incompetence and paranoid behavior of the USIA representative in Bucharest. For Chic and me, however, the entire experience was eye-opening – a first-hand experience of the tyranny of the East and the deep divide between our two cultures at that point in our history.

CHAPTER SEVEN

The Accidental Author, Part 2

Writing instead of my experiences that grew out of my affiliation with the *Wall Street Journal* but I would like to turn now to my work at Hunter College where, after all, I was teaching full time. Following nearly a century of its outstanding record as a women's college, in the aftermath of World War II significant changes to the institution began to occur. In 1964 men were admitted for the first and from then on Hunter became a co-ed college. The second change took place over several years, but by 1970 was in full force, namely, a program known as "Open Enrollment" or "Open Admissions." The background for the program was the emergence and emphasis after World War II of feminist causes and minority rights. Hunter had no reason to be concerned about women's rights as it was preeminent in that area from the beginning. Minority rights were another story and in this regard the spotlight was turned on all of the City University colleges: Brooklyn, Queens, CCNY and Hunter.

The problem was that graduates from second tier public high schools in the five boroughs of New York City, the leading students–the top five, for example – in such schools in Queens, Brooklyn, The Bronx and Staten Island often did not have the SAT scores to get into one of the senior colleges. It was this situation that was seized on and amplified to the point where those in authority determined they must make it possible for the very top graduates from any high school to be admitted to one of the senior colleges, hence Open Enrollment. In the case of Hunter this meant that total enrollment doubled in five years. In fact, it meant expansion in all areas. Remedial classes had to be provided for many of the incoming students and the physical plant had to be vastly enlarged. The High School building, located on the Lexington Avenue side of the college, was taken over and new buildings were constructed on the Southeast and Southwest corners of Lexington Avenue and 68th Street. (The Hunter High School, one of the finest public high schools in the country, was moved north on Park Avenue to the 90s, to a space that formerly housed a military armory; moreover, unlike the college, it was able continue its strict admissions policy and maintain its standards.)

Since the fall of 1967 I had been lecturing to a large class of 40 students in the Introduction to Theatre class at Hunter. With the onset of Open Enrollment the class size doubled and was moved to the former High School auditorium. Even before the expanded class size, however, and the influx of minority students, I had been wrestling with the question of what theatre textbook to use for the class. The textbooks then available took one of two approaches. One was the historical approach: theatre as practiced by the Greeks, the Romans, the Elizabethans, etc. The other approach stressed the elements of theatre: dramatic structure, acting, directing, design, etc. For an introduction to theatre class, I was not happy with either approach. To me, both approaches were too formal, too remote, too ex cathedra: handing down received wisdom rather than challenging the students and opening their eyes to what it meant to attend a theatre performance.

I determined that the Intro to Theatre course needed to be turned upside down, approached not as some formal rubric – a sacred text – whether historical or in terms of components. Rather, I felt it should be approached from the audience's point of view. Ninety per cent of the students in this or any other Introduction to Theatre class are potential audience members, not potential actors, directors or playwrights. What is crucial to students and non-professionals alike is the audience point of view. What is it like to go to the theatre, to sit and watch a performance, to experience a theatre event? With minority students or students who had rarely seen theatre this question was even more important. As a matter of fact, even before Open Enrollment I had eliminated a published text and was handing out mimeographed sheets with each lecture emphasizing what I felt was important at that point in the course. With the new influx of students who had such a wide range of past experiences, I felt this approach was more important than ever.

Put another way, I felt it was important for students not to be overwhelmed or bewildered by the information being thrown at them. As far as theatre was concerned, they needed to be reassured that whatever they see or feel at a performance is equally as important as what happens to others around them. Especially they need to be aware of the immediacy of the experience and its visceral quality fully as much as any aesthetic or intellectual elements. In a theatre seat, everyone is equal: some may understand more than others, some may have more background than others, some may be thrilled more by spectacle or movement, or understand music, or speech, or dance more than others. But each audience member should feel entitled to enjoy or absorb in his or her own way what occurs on stage.

Before continuing with my approach to teaching theatre I would like to point out that the subject matter – live theatre – has never lost its appeal despite the overwhelming threat of electronic and cinematic competition ranging from visual extravaganzas filling huge screens to the portability of scenes shown on a hand-held device. No, strangely enough it is as popular as it has ever been, perhaps more so. In addition to the presence of Broadway type theatres in every large city in America, as well as regional and off-Broadway theatres spread across the country, there is an enormous network of community and semi-professional theatres in virtually every town of any size in the U. S. Their official organization, the American Association of Community Theatres, states that there are 7,000 such theaters in Canada and the U.S. that produce over 45,000 productions each year to audiences numbering 7.5 million people. That is astonishing. At every level, we can say, there remains an unbelievable appetite for live theatre.

The reason is that it is live and not a picture on a screen. And because it is live, it offers us something that no screen, no matter how large, can ever provide: the experience of human contact. This is why theatre today, at every level from amateur to school and college productions to the most sophisticated Broadway shows remain so much in demand. It is this feeling and hunger that I wanted to address and explain in my theatre classes and later in my text books. The title of this book, *Magic Time*, is a term used by actors to describe a performance, but it also refers to the magic that occurs between actors and their audience.

Returning to my teaching at Hunter College, after a few years I felt I was getting such encouraging feedback from my students on my approach to teaching theatre and my use of mimeograph study sheets that in the fall of 1971, I began to wonder if it might not be the basis of a new kind of theatre text. I had never in my life had any notion of writing a text book; the idea had never dawned on me. It was as remote in my thinking as becoming an astrophysicist or an astronaut. But now, after preparing all my ubiquitous mimeographed sheets, I realized it might not be as far fetched as I had assumed. Consequently, I began to do a little research. At that time Barnes and Noble was not the behemoth it later became as a bookstore franchise – that is, even before the threat of Amazon came along. No, it was an academic bookstore featuring textbooks located in New York at lower Broadway and 18th Street. I made my way down there one day to see what the situation was with theatre textbooks and discovered that all the major academic publishers had a theatre text, except one: McGraw Hill.

After several tries, I got in touch with the appropriate person in the college arts division at McGraw-Hill and arranged a meeting. The upshot of that was that I was asked to write a sample chapter, which I did. We never used that chapter but in December of 1971 I did sign a contract to write an intro to theatre text. The next summer, the summer of 1972, Chic and I had rented a three-room white frame cottage in Quogue that overlooked a small body of water known as Ogden Pond. In the upstairs of the cottage was a small room I turned into an office and it was there that I spent the entire summer working on the first draft of the book, which I planned to call *The Theatre Experience*. I was particularly aware that the book should speak to people who have rarely, if ever, been to the theatre or who come from a different culture. The book would begin by discussing what a person might be aware of before attending a theatre performance: perhaps the play had been discussed and analyzed in a class, or the prospective audience member had been told about it by a friend or had read a review. Is the play going to be a classic or a new work; a serious play or a comedy; a long play or a short one? What, in other words, are the audience member's expectations before the event.

Next, what happens when a person actually goes to the

performance? What is the theatre building like on the outside: large or small, formal or informal, ornate or simple? Once inside, on what kind of stage will the play be performed: a proscenium or picture-frame stage; a thrust stage protruding into the audience; or a theatre-in-the-round space with the audience on all sides? Once the play starts what does one see: in the scenery, in the lighting; in the actors in their costumes; in the opening scene and the initial action? How does the action unfold; are there twists and turns; surprises? After discussing these initial ideas, impressions and reactions, I turn to another subject to be covered in the early stages of the book: the contrast between stage and screen.

This is one of the most helpful tools imaginable in explaining how theatre is a live event and how fundamentally this differentiates it from film. On first glance theatre and film appear to be very much alike: a physical theatre, an audience, a stage, a story being told. But there is the fundamental, primal, quintessential difference. Theatre is live; it requires, it demands that both performers and audience members be present and alive at the time of the performance. A film is set in stone: it can be shown 100,000 times in 5,000 theatres and each showing will be identical to all the others. In contrast (as I pointed out in discussing the film *Lord of the Flies*) it can truthfully be said that no two theatre performances, even one of a long-running hit such as *The Phantom of the Opera*, will ever be precisely or exactly the same: a new actor might replace a previous one, an actress might not be feeling well, the audience might be predominantly from out of town or elderly, in the winter, certain actors or members of the audience might have a cold. This list of variables could go on and on. This is because the audience is different every single night, in both large and small ways, but also because the actors, too, are live every night and, given the human quotient, no two performances by an individual, let alone an entire company of actors will ever be precisely the same.

Once prospective audience members accept the concept that a performance is a joint venture, that they are silent partners and co-conspirators with the actors, you have won half the battle of explaining the role of the audience in any performance. Having introduced and explained these concepts, I next turned to the elements that most texts plunge into without having explained the concepts described above. I begin to discuss acting, directing, playwriting, design and so forth, always putting the viewpoint of the audience member first, not that of the artists.

That first summer I did not finish the entire book, but I made a good beginning and was able to complete the manuscript shortly thereafter at which point I submitted it to McGraw-Hill. Upon reading it they were ready to proceed, which was welcome news indeed, and so the work of preparing it for publication began. It was at this point that I came to realize the importance, no, the absolute necessity, for a writer to have a first-rate and if possible, an exceptional, editor. Right out of the box I had the extreme good fortune of being assigned just such a person. Her name is Alison Meersschaert and without her the book would never have seen the light of day. Not only is she one of the sharpest, and most entertaining people I have ever known, her editing skills are nonpareil. The words of that first edition were mine but without her I could never have shaped them or put them together in the same way. In fact, the entire team was exceptional, even extraordinary.

Joan O'Connor, the designer, was given awards for her designs for the book. And then there was Inge King, the photo editor–researcher, of whom I will say more later. When Alison and I felt we had a solid manuscript and the book's many photographs had been selected it was shown to higher ups in McGraw-Hill and they moved ahead with publishing it. From the beginning neither the publisher nor I had the slightest idea of how the book would fare. One thing we knew was that being different from other intro books in the market meant it would take some getting used to by the teachers of theatre around the U.S., with whom current available texts were popular and entrenched. In the world of text publishing, books were often written by revered scholars with solid reputations whose work had become close to gospel in their particular field. In theatre, for example, Oscar Brockett was such a figure. After teaching at the University of Indiana he moved to the University of Texas in Austin where he became chairman of the theatre department, a position he held for nearly 40 years. Both his history book and his introduction to theatre seemed untouchable for many years.

Added to this was the fact that my book would be a sharp departure from the norm that led to additional concerns as to how the book would be received. Our best guess was that if it appealed to any group it would be the teachers of minority students like those in New York – in places like Chicago, Boston and Los Angeles. And so we launched. Obviously, no matter what happened it would not occur overnight. The first year sales were modest but acceptable. Gradually, however, sales began to improve. By the third year it became clear that the book would have a broader appeal than we first thought. Ivy League schools as well as large State universities began to adopt it. Two or three years out – at the time when McGraw-Hill needed to decide whether to publish a second edition or not – sales were encouraging enough for them to move forward. The first edition came out in 1975 and the second edition in 1979. By the fourth edition the book was the best selling volume in its field and remained so until it was taken over in the early 21st century by another one of my textbooks that I will discuss shortly. In the meantime, the book has appeared in 14 editions, the most recent being one published in January 2019 – in all a 45 year run.

Briefly I should mention what occurs when one prepares a new edition. I would say that roughly 25 to 30 percent of the book is revised extensively. Out of date material is eliminated, recent developments are added. New or first-time performers, directors or playwrights are discussed and explained. As for style, inevitably a previous text can always be made smoother, cleaner or shorter. Also, the photo program is refreshed, which leads to a further word about photographs: from the beginning, the book was heavily illustrated with photos, line drawings and charts. Each book originally had roughly 250 photographs. In the first two editions they were black and white. The 3rd edition had a 16-page color section, the 4th through the 8th editions had more and more color photo sections, and from the 9th edition on, the book was illustrated throughout with full color photographs. It did not hurt the appeal of the book that no other Intro volume had as many color illustrations introduced as quickly in new editions. In new editions of my books roughly 25% to 30% of the text and photographs are replaced with more recent or better material.

Before I turn to my collaboration with Inge King in creating our extensive photography program, I would like to mention the 6th edition of *The Theatre Experience* that featured the incomparable drawings of Al Hirschfeld. For seven decades in the 20th century, when his drawings were featured in the *New York Times*, Al was far and away the greatest artist chronicling the American theatre in his depictions of actors and other theatre artists as well as the miseen-scene of productions, drawings that were far too artistic and original to ever be described as cartoons or caricatures. And his deft touch, his unbelievable eye, his ability to capture the essence of a face or the body of a dancer was incomparable. His work was so original, so distinctive, one might even say, so inspired, that when he turned his pen to Carol Channing, Jason Robards, Eugene O'Neill, Lynn Fontaine or whomever, one knew immediately the person he was depicting. It was always at the same time both an amazingly accurate description as well as a commentary.

I had gotten to know Al and Dolly, his wife of 50 years, and visited them from time to time in their brownstone in the 90s on the Upper East Side of Manhattan. Many years earlier Al had decided that the most comfortable seat for his work at his easel was an old-fashioned barber chair and he had found one in Brooklyn, purchased it, and had it ensconced in his studio on the top floor of his home. He sat in it virtually every working day where he drew for the rest of his life. (Al lived to be 99 years old.) As we were preparing for the 6th edition of my intro book I asked Al if we might feature some of his drawings to illustrate the new edition. He readily agreed and the book was adorned with his drawings throughout. The text was divided into five sections and each section opened with a two-page montage of his drawings. In addition, the cover featured two incredible linear drawings, one of Chita Rivera and the other of Tommy Tune, which framed the title. Thanks to Al no theatre text book had ever had anything like it.

Returning to the photography side of the illustrations, as I suggested, this brings me to Inge King. By pure coincidence Inge was in the McGraw-Hill offices the day in late 1971 that I signed my first contract for *The Theatre Experience*, and served as the witness to the signing. At that time Inge was involved in the Child Development section of the company but she had always wanted to be a photo researcher and when the time came to pick a person for that position for my first book Alison Meersschaert chose Inge – the beginning of her career as a photo editor and an amazing stroke of luck for me. This began the collaboration between the two of us that was to last for 45 years and cover 30 editions of my three books, each one of which featured approximately 200 to 250 photos. Early on Inge and I developed a routine for picking the photos for each first edition as well as the replacement and new photos for subsequent editions. On Inge's part the process called for an immense amount of research and ingenuity. For photos of actual stage productions, she contacted the photographer who controlled the rights and in time came to know all of the top theatre photographers in New York and around the country – Chicago, Boston, Washington, Minneapolis, Los Angeles – as well as those in London and Paris.

Once she had the rights she would come to my apartment on Central Park West where we would spread them out on the dining room table and look at five or six photo possibilities for each space. For the first edition of any of our three text books this meant well over 1,000 photos to choose from. For later editions, the number would be roughly 330 photos. We would look at the five or six for each position and make our selection. After the first few editions, computers became ubiquitous and Inge would arrive with her laptop where we went through the same process. Inge's diligence, persistence, taste and judgment were impeccable and one of my great joys through all those years was working with her.

A marvelous personal story about Inge: in all of the first 40 years I knew her and worked with her she was single. I knew nothing about her private life, but she seemed not unhappy, rather she appeared quite contented with her life. A few years ago there was a fascinating change, however. As she tells it a number of years ago she attended the 25th reunion of her high school in Columbus, Ohio, where she saw Randolph Reynolds whom she had known when they were schoolmates. On the occasion of their 25th reunion, Randy, as she calls him, showed an interest in her and wished to pursue her romantically, but she demurred. Fast forward another 25 years and the two see each other again at their 50th high school reunion, whereupon not only does Randolph pursue her but after all this time she reciprocates. Following that, Randolph comes with her to New York and eventually the two are living together like husband and wife. My curiosity about what happened knew no bounds. When I asked her what happened, what changed over the 50 years, she responded: "He grew up."

With the early success of *The Theatre Experience*, my publishers at McGraw-Hill and I began thinking about publishing a theatre history text. If Professor Oscar Brockett and a half dozen others offered strong competition in the intro field it was nothing to the world of theatre history where competing with Prof. Brockett was the equivalent of climbing Mount Everest. His hold on the field was formidable. There was one thing, however, that everyone agreed on, namely, that his history volume was perhaps too "encyclopedic," meaning that it was too comprehensive and went into greater detail than was necessary. One fact or one detail after another lent itself to a certain ennui to the point where a repetitive rhythm set in.

I knew from my work on my first text that this can be avoided; you can get the same facts across but with variety and changes of emphasis. My publishers agreed that despite the odds against us, we should give it a try. From the beginning, however, I was aware that I should not attempt this on my own: I needed a collaborator. There were two reasons for this: first, I was not a theatre historian, per se. I had taught the subject but it was not my specialty. I needed the expertise of someone who was a true theatre historian. In the second place, I felt it would be good to have someone younger at my side. If these books were going to continue into the future, I needed someone to take over after I felt it was time to bow out.

Once again luck was on my side. My closest colleague in the doctoral theatre program at the CUNY Graduate Center was Dan Gerould, an eminent theatre theorist and historian. The CUNY Graduate Center served as the home of doctoral programs in all disciplines for the entire CUNY system: Hunter, Queens, Brooklyn, CCNY to name the major ones. It was located on 42nd street between 5th and 6th Avenues in a building that went through the block to 43rd Street and interestingly enough, had once been the home of the Aeolian Hall which among other distinctions had been the site where Paul Whiteman and his orchestra debuted George Gershwin's *Rhapsody in Blue*, featuring the composer at the piano. I began to split my time between the Hunter College and the Graduate Center and had gotten to know the theatre faculty at the latter. When I asked Dan to recommend a recent doctoral graduate who might be a good choice as a collaborator in writing a theatre history text he did not hesitate: Alvin Goldfarb. From my perspective it proved to be an inspired choice.

I had known Al when he was a graduate assistant in my Intro to Theatre class at Hunter and a student in the Masters Program at Hunter, a degree he completed in record time, just as he did with his PhD at the Graduate Center. Al had a frightening and impressive heritage. Both his parents had been victims of the holocaust during World War II. His father had been placed early in the war in Flossenburg, a

125

concentration camp near Dachau. His mother had hidden in a forest in the Ukraine with her family for the final two years of the war. After the war they were both moved to a Displaced Persons camp where they met and later married. In 1949 they made their way to Brooklyn. A short time later Al's father was able to buy a small store in Queens that sold candy, newspapers and other items and where they lived on the floor above the store. Both Al and his brother graduated from Queens College and Al went on to receive the graduate degrees mentioned above.

When PhD students in theatre completed their work at the Graduate Center most of them tried to find a job in the City: it was, after all, the center of the American theatre. I always advised them, however, to go elsewhere first. It would be much easier to get a good academic post outside NYC where they could make their mark and then return to New York if they still wanted to. Whether from my advice or others, Al took the latter route and it proved to be perfect for him. He and his wife, Elaine, went to Bloomington, Illinois, where he joined the theatre faculty at Illinois State University. For various reasons, some happenstance, but mostly because of Al's talent and temperament, he enjoyed a meteoric rise, from Assistant Professor, to Chairman of Theatre, to Dean of the Arts, to Provost of the University. Later, he was tapped by Western Illinois University to be its President when he was barely in middle age.

Al and I set about writing the history text entitled *Living Theatre* that came out in 1982. It was never destined to sell as well as an intro book because upper class courses are always smaller than freshman courses. Partly because of this, none of us really focused on its sales. Al, however, who watched the figures more closely than I did, pointed out, both to me and the publisher, that though not a runaway best seller, there had continued to be a steady demand for the book. Because of this, nine years later we came out with a second edition of *Living Theatre* that we watched more closely. When it continued to improve we came out more quickly with a third edition, at which point we had finally overtaken the leader, Oscar Brockett. Since then the editions have continued to appear, the most recent one being the 7th edition that debuted in the summer of 2017.

In the meantime we contemplated a third text book: an introduction to theatre for junior colleges and smaller universities. When I first came out with *The Theatre Experience*, I was writing for programs similar to the one at Hunter College, where we had a robust theatre curriculum that included upper level, two-semester courses in theatre history. Because history was so thoroughly covered later on there was no need to include much history in my initial volume. Smaller colleges or two-year programs, however, had no room for specialized, upper-class courses in theatre history: the intro course was it. Thus, we saw a need for an intro book that included a good deal of theatre history and so was born *Theatre: The Lively Art*, over half of which was a survey of history. In preparing the book, though Alison had moved into the upper echelons of corporate McGraw-Hill, Inge King, our photo edition, and Joan O'Connor, our designer were still with us and the first edition came out in 1990. It caught on almost immediately and by 2017 had appeared in 10 editions. Meanwhile, in the early years of the 21st century it overtook *The Theatre Experience* as number one in its field.

Over the past forty years Al and I have had a personal and a working relationship that has been as ideal as one could ever hope for with a colleague. We speak with each other almost daily; our talents complement each other in a remarkable way: he tends to be more practical and detail oriented than I am while I like to think that I bring to

127

our collaboration certain writing and visionary talents that complement his strengths. As the years have gone on, and I move into my 90s, I depend on him more and more.

With 31 editions of three text books over a 40 year period and nearly a quarter of a century of reviews for the *Journal* I asked myself: "How did this happen?" I had first raised the question with myself in the late 70s when my first book had come out and was doing reasonably well and I had been reviewing for the *Journal* for half a dozen years. The point is I never had any ambition to be a writer, in fact, had never given it a single thought. I had never, ever, thought of myself as a writer: I never took a writing course, I never submitted pieces of any kind – fiction or non-fiction – to a publisher; I never thought for a moment of being a reporter or writing a column for a newspaper. In fact, I wasn't even that interested in writing. Faulkner, Scott Fitzgerald, Updike, Roth, Bellow: none of these excited me as people to emulate. Neither did non-fiction writers: historians, biographers, philosophers, science writers. As a matter of fact, I was not even an avid reader. Fiction or non-fiction, I did not rush to read the latest bestseller or an acknowledged classic. This was true up to the point in my early forties when I actually did start writing.

A good example of my cavalier – one might even say, careless – approach to writing was my final exam in English my senior year at Vanderbilt. It was a four-hour written exam and the grade for the whole year depended on it. I did what I usually did: I put down everything I knew about the question on the exam in random fashion, helter-skelter, with no organization whatsoever. The theory was that I would let the professor pick out from my agglomeration of words the proper answer to the questions. It was like throwing mud at a brick wall and hoping some of it would stick. This cavalier attitude continued through the next ten years while I taught and tried my hand at various aspects of theatre: directing, producing, playwriting. Playwriting, by the way, is entirely separate, fundamentally different, from the kind of writing of which we are speaking.

To go a step further: when I began my writing career it certainly did not occur by design or ambition; it happened in each case by chance, by accident. My reviewing grew out of an off-hand remark on the golf course by a friend. My textbook writing occurred because I had prepared a semester's worth of mimeographed hand-outs for my students. So the question became: when my opportunities came to write, how was I prepared to do so? I pondered this: how in heaven's name did I learn to write? I had never taken a course in the subject, never been in a workshop, never read a manual, so where did it come from? And then it struck me – it was George Bernard Shaw.

Shaw was perhaps the greatest non-fiction stylist of all time in the English language and when I was preparing my doctoral dissertation I had been engaged for an entire year reading every thing he wrote about Shakespeare – all 270 pages. His reviews, essays, letters to actors and actresses: I had read each one of them three or four times, analyzed and probed them. Somehow, through this intensive study, by osmosis or some such process, I must have learned how to write prose: how to use a semi-colon, how to alternate short sentences with long ones, how not to repeat myself, how to phrase things clearly and concisely, when to ask a question and when to make a pronouncement, when to be abrupt and when to go with the flow. It must have entered my subconscious without my knowing it and when challenged much later to write, it had found its way to the surface.

Some time later I recognized another aspect of writing skills, one that does not originate with the author, namely editing. When I began writing seriously I had been blessed

129

with two exceptional editors: George Melloan at the *Journal* and Alison Meersschaert at McGraw-Hill. They helped me trim, clarify, round off rough corners and come up with readable prose. Later, I realized that this happened to be a talent I had a bit of myself. From the beginning I wrote and re-wrote, going over the draft of an article ruthlessly with a red pencil. Putting it all together, I was able to come up with decent prose. I carried this over to work on the text books, reviewing and attempting to clarify or improve material written by either Al or me.

During the first half of the 1980s my academic life was still marked by my immersion with the theatre program at Hunter College. In the decade before, in the 1970s, one of my proudest achievements had been to bring Harold Clurman to Hunter as a Visiting Professor, lecturing weekly to seniors and graduate students, a practice he continued through the spring of 1980, a few months before his death. (Harold's connection to Hunter was personal as well as professional. In his profession as a critic he was famous for always arriving at the theatre with a beautiful lady on his arm – Kim Stanley, Jackie Onassis, etc. – but for the last seven years of his time reviewing his most frequent companion was a young lady who had been a student of his at Hunter: Joan Ungaro.) Brilliant, demonstrative, flamboyant: Harold was legendary not just in one field of theatre but in three. In the 1930s he was one of the three founders of the Group Theatre, the organization that brought to the USA the Stanislavski approach to realistic acting. Putting the group theatre on the map were two stunning dramas by Clifford Odets, *Awake* and *Sing* and *Golden Boy*, both directed by Harold. In later years Harold distinguished himself not only as a director but as a critic and author as well. It would be an amazing achievement to become outstanding in any one of these areas; Harold was preeminent in all three.

In the fall of 1980, Donna Shalala became President of Hunter College. (Later, Donna was to become the President of two other universities: Wisconsin and Miami, and after that the Secretary of Health and Human Services in the Clinton Administration. In 2018 she was elected to Congress.) When we got to know one another one of the first things I brought up with her was the idea of honoring Harold, who had died in September of that year. She was enthusiastic about it and we set about planning a Memorial that occurred a year later, in the fall of 1981, in the Hunter Playhouse. It was an impressive, celebratory occasion with many of Harold's former colleagues or friends in attendance: the composer Aaron Copeland (a life-long friend and Harold's roommate when they spent a year together in Paris in the 20s); famed actress and teacher Stella Adler who had been married to Harold when they were young and though divorced, remained a close friend for the rest of their lives, and many more. The speakers included Roy Scheider to whom Harold had been a mentor and a number of others whose lives he had touched.

Later in the 1980s the theatre department at Hunter came up with the idea of having a faculty-staff production of the play *Inherit the Wind* by Jerome Lawrence and Robert Edwin Lee. Such a thing had never happened in Hunter's long history and has never happened since; I don't know who thought of it; it was certainly not I. In any case, the play, first performed on Broadway in 1955, was based on an actual event: the Scopes trial in a small town in east Tennessee that drew national as well as international attention. The issue was a law passed by the Tennessee legislature that evolution could not be taught in public schools. A young teacher decided to defy the law and began teaching

Darwin's theories. A lawsuit was brought that attracted the noted evangelist William Jennings Brian to take the side of literal interpreters of the Bible and an equally famous lawyer, Clarence Darrow, to serve as the attorney for Scopes. A noted journalist, H. L. Mencken, covered the trial for his newspaper. The playwrights, who gave the characters in their play fictitious names, determined that the trial could serve as a cautionary tale at the time the McCarthy hearings in Congress were taking place.

The great beauty of our production was that it brought together, in a way that had never been done before nor has been since, various segments of the Hunter family – the academic and the administrative sides of the college – in one cooperative, happy undertaking. We encouraged everyone in the school to audition: faculty members from full professors to adjuncts in every discipline, as well as staff members from vice-presidents and library chiefs to clerks in finance and admissions. People flocked to the try-outs, and Donna agreed to play a walk-on part near the end of the play. A former Chair of the theatre department, Marvin Seiger, played the evangelist and Richard Mawe, the Dean of the Science and Math Departments, played his opponent, the lawyer. I directed the production, the first time I had done any directing in 20 years and the last play I would ever direct.

Someone connected with the production knew Jerome Lawrence, one of the authors of the play, and invited him to come to rehearsals, which he did, giving us invaluable advice. It turned out to be a marvelous experience. The cast we chose was a grand mixture of individuals from all parts of the college and they worked tirelessly, learning the script, attending every rehearsal, asking dozens of questions. We played two nights in the Playhouse, which seated just over 700, and sold out both nights.

There was a marvelous post-script to the whole affair: it

turned out that Dick Mawe, the dean of science who played the lawyer, had always had a secret desire to be an actor and not too long after our production he resigned his post at Hunter to take up acting. For the next 30 years he pursued a successful career as a full-time performer, appearing constantly in plays, TV productions and films.

CHAPTER EIGHT

The American Theatre Emerges

In the early 1970s, when I began writing for the *Journal* and working on my first text book, I was writing against a background of remarkable achievements in the American theatre that was completing four decades of outstanding accomplishments. In drama there was a burst of creativity that historically competed with the flowering of modern theatre in Europe in the late 19th century in the works of Ibsen, Strindberg and Chekhov. In mid-century in the United States, beginning with Eugene O'Neill and continuing with Lillian Hellman, Arthur Miller, Tennessee Williams, Lorraine Hansberry and Edward Albee, there was an outpouring of works that startled and impressed audiences and critics world wide. Moreover, these works have stood the test of time.

It was, however, in the musical field that America could claim a unique place in theatre history. American librettists and composers did not just excel at musical theatre, they invented it. Prior to the American musical there had been opera, oratorio, operetta, and such piece-meal forms as burlesque, the revue and vaudeville, but there had never been the type of musical that appeared in the U.S. in the early and mid twentieth century. In the 1920s, composers such as Jerome Kern, George Gershwin, Richard Rodgers and lyricists like Oscar Hammerstein, Ira Gershwin, and Lorenz Hart – as well as two men who wrote both words and music,

Irving Berlin and Cole Porter – created the modern musical out of whole cloth. The first musical acknowledged as the harbinger of the ones to follow appeared in 1927 – *Showboat,* with music by Jerome Kern and book and lyrics by Oscar Hammerstein II. The songs were glorious, the story was serious and the entire piece, ranging from serious to comic, was expertly integrated. This combining of song and story, of the comic with the serious (including the subject of miscegenation – the romance of a white person and a negro), was a hallmark of the wholly new, wholly original American theatre musical.

Showboat was followed in the 1930's by George Gershwin's *Porgy and Bess* which in turn was succeeded by two musicals with songs by Rodgers and Hart and books by George Abbott, who also directed them: *On Your Toes* and *The Boys from Syracuse,* the latter being the first American musical based on a play by Shakespeare: *The Comedy of Errors.* The Rodgers and Hart musicals were significant in another way: in both of them Abbott added the final ingredient to complete the range of the American musical – ballet. In addition to the songs and the story, Abbott induced George Balanchine, the Russian born head of the NY City Ballet to choreograph dances for both works. Balanchine, having distinguished himself in his native Russia as a dancer and choreographer, had been induced by Lincoln Kirsten to come to the U.S. where the two formed the NY City Ballet. To have the most distinguished choreographer of the day join in creating a musical theatre piece on Broadway completed the components leading to a burst of creativity at mid-century that remains a hallmark of the modern theatre. An outpouring of stunning musicals followed: Cole Porter's *Kiss Me, Kate,* Irving Berlin's *Annie Get Your Gun,* followed *by Guys and Dolls, Gypsy, West Side Story, Fiddler on the Roof* – the list could go on and on.

136

This was the heritage, the legacy and the state of the American theatre when I began to write about it for the *Wall Street Journal* in 1972, and continued to until 1995, and after that, for twenty years more in my text books. Along with the continuing emergence of important new plays and musicals, several clear trends unfolded during my tenure at the *Journal*. They included the arrival and recognition of women playwrights as a significant part of the theatre scene; the transformation of choreographers into directors of musicals; the emergence of the off- and off-off-Broadway movement; the consolidation and strengthening of regional theatre; the invasion of Broadway by large-scale British musicals.

Prior to the 1970s and 80s, female playwrights in the United States had rarely been acknowledged as the equal of their male counterparts. The few women dramatists who had been recognized early in the 20th century included Rachel Crothers, Sophie Treadwell and Hallie Flanagan; in the 1930s and 40s Lillian Hellman had been widely praised, as had Lorraine Hansberry two decades later, but in every case these playwrights were the exceptions. By and large it was not until the last three decades of the 20th century that women playwrights were accorded the kind of recognition their male counterparts had received. In that later period a number of widely acclaimed female dramatists appeared on the scene including such writers as Wendy Wasserstein, Marsha Norman, Beth Henley, Maria Irene Fornes, Paula Vogel, and Tina Howe, as well as many others. Not only did these playwrights receive enthusiastic critical praise but their plays were frequently produced and awarded literary prizes.

It was my good fortune as a critic to be able to join in welcoming this important new segment of live theatre to a world long enjoyed by their male counterparts. Along with the usual reviews in which I discussed the arrival of an interesting, challenging, or provocative new play from a woman writer, every so often I had the opportunity to chronicle an unusual event involving a new play by a female writer. Such was the case with Marsha Norman's first play, *Getting Out,* a play about a young woman leaving prison. It was being presented by the Phoenix Theatre, headed by T. Edward Hambleton and Norris Houghton, and prior to its engagement at an uptown theatre, it was being shown to a group of prison inmates at a maximum-security prison in lower Manhattan known as the Metropolitan Correctional Center.

The performance had been arranged by the producers with an official of the Center who was charged with helping the inmates prepare for life outside. It was this performance that I had received permission to observe and write about. The play, which my wife and I went to the prison to see, dealt with a young woman just getting out of prison after serving several years of incarceration. One actress played the woman just about to be released while another actress played the woman's character when she was much younger; the play skillfully alternates between the views of the older woman and the younger one. The night of the performance, my wife and I arrived at a designated location just in time to join others (including the cast and crew) being led into the prison.

Here is the way I described the event:

> *The scene was the new Metropolitan Correctional Center in lower Manhattan, a federal maximum security institution. Because of the subject matter of "Getting Out," it was felt that inmates in a correctional center would have a special feeling for*

the play. With this in mind, Aaron Lewitt, who plans visits by artists and entertainers to the center, got together with the Phoenix and the performance was arranged.

As the cast, the crew, and a few observers entered the center, each was carefully searched and the hand of each one was stamped with an invisible ink that glows when put under an ultraviolet lamp. The group had to be walked in together through a series of heavily locked doors. The site of the performance was the common room. There was to be no scenery, no costumes, no lighting effects; the outlines of the stage areas-Arlene's bedroom in a boarding house and the cell and a catwalk in prison-were taped on the floor. A long wall served as the back of the "stage"; furniture consisted of two cots, a trunk and a couple of chairs.

Male inmates filed in dressed in varicolored jump suits-red, yellow, orange and Blue and sat on chairs, sofas and stair-steps. Later women inmates, in the same kind of jump suits, entered and took what seats remained. Director Jon Jory greeted the group and explained the layout of the stage. Then, under the glaring white lights of the common room, the performance began.

The first task the actors faced was to draw the audience in. At the beginning several inmates were playing pool in an adjoining room, and two men near the stage were determinedly playing chess. In a few minutes, both the pool table and the chess board were abandoned.

As the audience settled down, however, it became apparent that this would be no ordinary performance. Life in the institution continued to intersect with life in the play. More and more, the evening took on an eerie, Pirandellian quality.

A phone hung on the wall behind the stage. A dozen or more times during the performance the phone rang. Each time a guard from the center walked across the stage behind the actors to answer the phone. Once or twice he passed an actor-guard en route.

In the middle of scenes, individual inmates got up, walked along the edge of the stage and disappeared behind the back wall. One man, however, rather than skirting the stage, walked through the imaginary cell. There was nothing unusual about his movements, but the reality of an inmate walking through a make-believe cell while an actress-prisoner sat there was unsettling.

For the actors, though, the most sobering part of the experience was emotional: the vibrations they received from this audience while playing in this locale. The character of Arlene is trying desperately to establish a new life but people around her make it nearly impossible. A flamboyant pimp (Leo Burmester) from her past tells her how much money she could make as a prostitute; her mother (Madeleine Sherwood) offers nothing but criticism and a cold shoulder; a bumbling guard (Barry Corbin) who has driven her home from prison wants to take advantage of her. The only alternative Arlene sees to the pimp's proposition is a poorly paid job as a waitress or dishwasher, but she is determined to take it.

Playwright Norman has sketched Arlene's dilemma in a series of forceful, poignant scenes. According to Susan Kingsley, who plays Arlene with great authenticity and conviction, audiences usually root for the character to start a new life. In Ms. Kingsley's mind the performance at the Correctional Center was different. At the end she stood at the edge of the stage, visibly shaken. "They weren't with me," she said. The inmates, she felt, had trouble facing the harsh choices that await them when they get out.

Pamela Reed, the young Arlene, was also affected. "I've been doing these clever things as this sassy kid," she said, "but no more." Director Jon Jory says the effects of the experience in later rehearsals was unmistakable.

The center considers the performance a real success. One inmate ran across the room after it ended to congratulate Mr. Corbin as the guard. But the actors were left to wonder whether he liked the unflattering way in which the guard was portrayed, or the way the actor played the part.

When the play ended, the cast, the crew, the director, and the observers were taken as a body from room to room, through one locked door after another. In each room the group was counted again, and one by one hands were thrust under an ultraviolet

141

light. Finally, at ground level it was assumed that everyone could go, but a guard stopped them. "It'll only be 20 minutes more." he announced. "We have to do a body count inside."

When the group eventually emerged into the crisp, autumn air of Manhattan, its members had undergone their own small version of "getting out."

In turning to a discussion of the off- and off-off-Broadway movement I would like to say a word about the producers of *Getting Out*. T. Edward Hambleton (along with his partner, Norris Houghton) was in many ways the founder of off-broadway. T., as everyone called him, was the scion of a family whose presence and prominence in Baltimore go back two hundred years. Of all the people involved in the world of theatre in the second half of the 20th century, no one could match the devotion, dedication and old-word charm of T, a gentleman of the old school who nevertheless threw himself heart and soul into bringing new theatre at it's best to New York audiences.

When T. and Norris founded The Phoenix Theatre they took over the space once occupied by the Yiddish Art Theatre, a 1200 seat space at 12th Street and 2nd Avenue in lower Manhattan. There they presented classics, European imports such as the works of Bertolt Brecht, and the latest avant-garde plays featuring the finest performers Broadway had to offer as well as outstanding directors and designers. Along the way they also gave their first professional exposure to such actors as Uta Hagen and Carol Burnett as well as director Harold Prince. In 1961, the Phoenix moved uptown to a series of smaller spaces where over the next 22 years they presented the debuts of a number of young writers, not only Marsha Norman mentioned above, but such playwrights as Wendy Wasserstein and Chris Durang. In addition they also gave a start to a number of performers, including Glenn Close and Meryl Streep.

Before I leave The Phoenix and T. Hambleton, I would like to add a personal note. For nearly a quarter of a century, from 1980 to 2004, I served on the Board of TDF (the Theatre Development Fund), the not-for-profit enterprise that among other activities runs TKTS, the half-price ticket booth in Times Square. During the time that I served as Chairman, in the late 1980s, one of my proudest achievements was to bring T. Edward onto the Board of TDF, where he served for many years. Another board member at that time was Geraldine Stutz. Gerry, as she was called, was a fashion powerhouse and icon. When she was in college she thought she wanted to be an actress but fate would have it that she was a bit of a genius at merchandizing and fashion. She found herself at a relatively young age the vice president of the high-end shoe company, I. Miller.

One of her many innovations there was to give the artist Andy Warhol his first job – illustrating shoes for I. Miller advertising. Later she found herself president of Henri Bendel, an upscale company that had become moribund. In a very short time she turned the 5th Avenue store around completely, creating the modern Henri Bendel ladies store that she owned and ran for a quarter of a century. Gerry had taken a moribund enterprise, women's couture, and re-invented it, devising in the process the modern lady's apparel store with an approach – the idea of substituting for large, open sales areas, a series of discreet boutiques – that was copied world-wide. Along the way she is credited with giving a start to such later stars as Perry Ellis, Sonia Rykiel, Mary McFadden and Ralph Lauren.

Gerry, however, was not simply a brainy merchandiz-

143

er; she loved the arts, particularly theatre which she had been attracted to when she was younger. She served on the National Council of the National Endowment for the Arts and the boards of the Actors Fund and TDF. Somehow, the three of us, Gerry, T. Edward Hambleton and I found ourselves, along with serving together on the TDF Board, a strangely compatible threesome – and for 15 years beginning in the mid 80s, we had lunch together every six weeks or so at the Century Club. It was only when writing this account that I suddenly realized that each one of them, T. and Gerry, were extraordinary pioneers: T. for inventing off-Broadway and Gerry for revolutionizing couture. When Gerry died the Century Association asked me to write the tribute to her that appeared in the section on memorials in the Club's annual yearbook. In some ways, it was a nearly impossible task: covering her many innovations and achievements, describing her great love of the arts, as well as recounting her unbounded enthusiasm for everything she held dear.

Another pioneer in the off-Broadway movement was producer Joseph Papp who, in 1967, established the Public Theatre on Lafayette Street on the lower East Side in a space that had been the Astor Library. (A later venture of the Public was presenting free Shakespeare Productions each summer in Central Park.) Papp encouraged new playwrights and directors and in 1975 hit the jackpot when a musical which he had sponsored, and to which he had given free rehearsal space, became a gargantuan hit on Broadway, namely, *A Chorus Line*. Having a substantial percentage of the profits – amounting eventually to many millions of dollars – the Public was put in a strong financial position for years to come.

Other theatres emerged in the off and off-Broadway

movement, including La Mama (founded in 1961) that provided a home for a number of important playwrights of the 60s, 70, and 80s (such writers as Sam Shepard, Adrienne Kennedy, and Harvey Fierstein), the Manhattan Theatre Club (founded in 1970), The Second Stage Theatre (founded in 1979) and the Signature Theatre (founded in 1991). The contribution of this segment of the American theatre was rich in every way and incalculable in terms of new talent discovered and given an invaluable platform. Because the *Journal* was a national newspaper, in addition to covering off-Broadway, I was also able to write frequently about the burgeoning regional theatre movement, covering theatres from Boston to San Diego and Minneapolis to Montgomery, Alabama.

Another development of the final three decades of the 20th century was the emergence of former choreographers as director-choreographers. The foundation for this phenomenon had been laid in the 1930s. George Abbott began using George Balanchine during his productions in the 1930s. After that George used Jerome Robbins as his choreographer of choice as early as 1944 when he engaged him to choreograph *On the Town* which he was directing. George continued using Robbins through the next two decades for such productions as *Pajama Game* in 1954 and *A Funny Thing Happened on the Way to the Forum* in 1962.

George once told me in an interview that Robbins was his go-to man on anything having to do with movement. In *Pajama Game*, for example, the choreographer of record was Bob Fosse in one of his early attempts at Broadway choreography. "The dances were fine," George said, "but Fosse hadn't yet learned how to direct musical numbers", by which he meant the musical numbers without dancing performed solo or by several singers. A director doesn't want performers to just stand stage center and sing; the number needs to be "staged." So when George was dissatisfied with the way Fosse was handling the non-dancing musical numbers in *Pajama Game* he called on Robbins. "He knew how to stage these things," George said, "he was the best there was. When I asked Robbins, he said he would do it if he could get credit as the co-director of the show. I said 'Fine.' Titles didn't matter to me." Robbins break-through effort as both director and choreographer was *West Side Story* which opened in 1957. From then on a number of choreographers moved into the directorial ranks. Bob Fosse improved his skills following his work on *Pajama Game* and was director as well as choreographer for *Sweet Charity, Pippin* and *Chicago*. Michael Bennett did the same with *A Chorus Line* and *Dreamgirls,* as did Tommy Tune in *Nine* and *Grand Hotel*. By the 1980s the notion of the director-choreographer had become well-established in the Broadway theatre.

The final trend I will mention occurring during my years as a critic was the invasion of Broadway by the blockbuster British musical. We were accustomed to British imports on the straight play side of things, plays by John Osborne (*Look Back in Anger*), Peter Shaffer (*Equus*), Caryl Churchill (*Top Girls*), David Hare (*Plenty*), and Tom Stoppard (*Travesties, Jumpers*), but not an abundance of musicals. Except for a few lighthearted romps, the British had rarely dipped their toes into those waters. The person who began making a move in that direction some 20 years after World War II, was Andrew Lloyd Webber. He had started his career rather tentatively, sometimes collaborating with Tim Rice, in pieces that were more like oratorios than fullscale musicals. The two would try out segments of musicals at schools and other non-mainstream venues. This process resulted in full-scale pieces like *Joseph and the Technicolor Dream Coat* and *Jesus Christ, Superstar.* Eventually Lloyd Webber moved into the large-scale musical world with *Evi-*

ta in 1979 followed by *Cats* in 1982. Both were lavish to the nth degree: scenery, costumes, sensational lighting effects – all of them over-the-top. Spectacular, entertaining: yes. What they were not was the equivalent of *West Side Story, Fiddler on the Roof*, or *The Sound of Music*. Hummable melodies were in abundance as well as spectacular visuals but with *Cats*, for instance, there was no story; it was based on poems by T. S. Eliot and *Evita* was all about its heroine, Eva Peron, unable to balance her dazzling qualities with her indisputable negative side. With *Phantom of the Opera* in 1988, Lloyd Webber was able to add a narrative which is one reason it is still running so many years later.

The Brit who followed Lloyd Webber was not a musician but a producer: Cameron Mackintosh, who saw what was happening with Lloyd Webber's shows and wanted to get in on the game. He had been sent a "concept album" developed by French composer Claude-Michel Schonberg and lyricist Alain Boublil based on the Victor Hugo novel *Les Miserables*. After a considerable amount of work, including the addition to the team of British lyricist Herbert Kretzmer, *Les Miz*, as it was often called, became a full-scale musical directed by Trevor Nunn and John Caird that opened in New York in 1987 and has been playing somewhere in the world almost constantly since then.

Cheered on by the success of the Hugo novel a few years later the same French team came up with another idea: Take the story of the opera *Madam Butterfly* and adapt it to the Vietnam War. Going through the same development process (this time with American lyricist Richard Maltby) the work became *Miss Saigon* which opened in New York in the spring of 1991. This time the visual fireworks of directors Nunn and Caird were even more spectacular, culminating with the landing of a helicopter on the stage of the Broadway theatre. So important were the special effects of the helicopter rescue that the scene, which should have occurred in act one, was postponed and shown out of sequence in act two in order for it to have a greater impact. Between Andrew Lloyd Webber and Cameron Mackintosh the British invasion of Broadway had become a fait accompli.

Before I come to the final segment of my years as a reviewer I would like to take a detour to Brooklyn, specifically the Brooklyn Academy of Music that was part of my beat at the *Journal*. The Academy had begun in 1861 with a 2,000-seat opera house on Montague Street in Brooklyn Heights, in a building that unfortunately burned down in 1903. In 1906, the Academy reopened in the Fort Greene area of Brooklyn, again with 2,000-seat opera house, in a complex that also included an 875 seat theatre and two smaller spaces. Sadly, over the next 60 years, a period including two world wars, the Academy had become moribund.

In 1967, Harvey Lichtenstein was made manager of the Brooklyn Academy of Music and charged with reviving it, and revive it he did. Among other things the Academy became a favorite venue of the avant-garde and experimental projects that included presenting such luminaries as Pina Bauch, Merce Cunningham, Robert Wilson, Peter Brook and Philip Glass. By the time I began writing for the *Journal* in 1972 it had become part of the regular beat of any New York critic. One group Harvey had sponsored there was The Living Theatre, perhaps the most notorious avant-garde group of the post-war period. In a piece called *Paradise Now*, which Harvey presented periodically from 1968 to 1973 and which featured half-naked performers roaming through the audience, inviting spectators to join them in rituals and ceremonies that involved removing their garments, sometimes partially, sometimes altogether.

One of the first shows Chic and I saw at the Opera House of the Academy was one of the final performances of The Living Theatre's production of *Paradise Now*. Before the house lights dimmed, the performers left the stage and descended into the audience. A favorite bit of theirs was to walk up the aisle, spot a reserved white-haired lady, approach her and throw some outrageous or even scatological comment her way hoping to get a shocked reaction. In *Paradise Now* they dispensed with that opening and instead, with the lights still on, positioned themselves in the aisles and, following a moment of silence, very quietly began a chant: "I cannot drive without a license; I cannot drive without a license..." Continuing to repeat the phrase over and over, they increased the volume until a moment of crescendo came when they suddenly stopped, and a period of deadly calm followed. This went on through several iterations of the chant: "I cannot vote unless I register ..." "I cannot travel without a passport ..." each time followed by a protracted silence. After three or four of these, in the deadly silence that seemed to continue for some time, a man in the second balcony yelled loudly: "I could not get in without a ticket ..."

It took a moment for the audience to realize what had just happened, namely, that a sharp-pointed pin of enormous proportions had been stuck into the balloon of a pretentious performing ensemble. Once the import of the spectator's declaration sank in, the entire audience exploded in a cascade, a torrent of laughter such as I had rarely heard in a theatre, ever.

Slowly, agonizingly, the performers silently found their way back to the stage, attempting to gather themselves in order to continue, and for the next 20 minutes moving almost as automatons.

It was because of the Brooklyn Academy that Chic and I met George Oppenheimer, at that time the theatre critic of the Long Island newspaper, *Newsday*. In those days we kept a car in a garage near our apartment on the West Side and always drove to the Brooklyn Academy, taking our friend Edith Oliver, the critic of *The New Yorker* with us. Edith, in turn, suggested we begin taking her old friend George Oppenheimer with us; the two, it turned out, had known each other since childhood. Thus, it became a ritual: whenever there was an opening in Brooklyn, I would drive the four of us to Gage and Tollners, a marvelous, old-world restaurant in Brooklyn Heights where we would have dinner before proceeding on to the performance at the Academy. (The restaurant featured waiters who had stripes on the sleeves of their dark coats – one for each five years they had served, just as Pullman porters on trains used to have.)

Regardless of the quality of the performance we saw, the evening was always lively. For one thing, when we were driving home, Edith absolutely refused to talk about the show we had just seen, whereas, George could not wait to discuss it in detail. Needless to say, on one night, when we were on the Brooklyn Bridge, George began to hold forth on the play we had seen. "Stop the car," Edith shouted. "If George talks about the show, I'm getting out." "On the Brooklyn Bridge?" George asked. "Absolutely. One more word and I'm walking." We resolved that in the future there would be no more discussions of the night's events. George, however, continued to hold forth on other favorite subjects as only he could.

George was one of the most intriguing people around at a time when there was a surfeit of such individuals. Born in New York, educated at Harvard, he began his career as a co-founder of Viking Press, but soon left for Hollywood where he became a screenwriter, first for Sam Goldwyn and then for 14 years for MGM. Sometimes on his own, but mostly as a collaborator, he received writing credit on some 30 successful films including several Marx Brothers' hits. Both in Hollywood and New York George, quite literally, knew everybody and was not shy about letting others know it.

There was a famous story, repeated in his obituary, about George and the famed, acerbic Dorothy Parker. Dorothy, who lived just below George in the same Hollywood apartment house, had friends in for a small dinner party one night. Shortly after the guests arrived one of them said to Dorothy: "What is that noise coming from the apartment above?' "It's nothing," Dorothy said. When, after a few minutes the guest heard the commotion again she insisted: "Dorothy, there it was again – that noise up above – only this time louder." After a moment Dorothy said: "Pay no attention; it's only George dropping names."

After serving in World War II, George returned to New York eventually becoming the critic for *Newsday*. A bit of background: every Christmas, Chic and I received a holiday recording from Harvey Schmidt who, among other things, had written the music for *The Fantasticks*. One of the numbers on the record he sent this particular year had George listed as a co-lyricist. Shortly after receiving the record, I saw George and said to him, "George, I didn't know you were a song lyricist." "I'm not," he said. I replied "I just got a record that includes the number 'I Feel a Song Coming On,' and it says "Lyrics by Dorothy Fields and George Oppenheimer." "I'll tell you a story," George said, "One Friday afternoon I had a phone call from Dotty. "George," she said, "I'm desperate: I've got a Monday deadline. I need a song title by tonight – no lyrics, just a title. If you give me a title, I'll make you the co-lyricist." "Dotty," I said, "I feel a song coming on... After all this time I still get over two hundred dollars a month in royalties."

(I should say a word here about Dorothy Fields a lyricist who is often not given the credit she deserves. For several decades she was the clever, inventive, sophisticated lyricist for some of the best composers of the golden age: Jerome Kern ("A Fine Romance," "Just the Way You Look Tonight"); Jimmy McHugh ("On the Sunny Side of the Street," "I'm in the Mood for Love"); and Cy Coleman ("If My Friends Could See Me Now".)

Returning to George, one day sometime later, when we were scheduled in a few days to take our usual trip to Brooklyn George called me: "Ed," he said, "when we go on Thursday do you think I might bring a guest, a lady?" "Absolutely," I said, "you can sit in the front with me and the three ladies can sit in the back." "Great," he said and was about to hang up. "George," I said, "do you mind if I ask who it is?" "Oh, didn't I tell you? – Joan Fontaine." And so on the appointed night we picked up Edith, George and Joan and headed for Brooklyn Heights where we had a wonderful, low-key dinner at Gage and Tollners before heading for the theatre. After dinner, before we headed to the theatre, Chic and Joan went to the lady's room. Later Chic told me about their conversation. "Joan" Chic said, "I'm struck by the color of your hair – it's lovely." "It's nothing," Joan said, "I do it myself – a combination of topaz and moon glow."

(A brief word here about my wife, Chic. Obviously to me she was someone special: charming, vivacious, full of life. I loved her deeply, but so did everyone else – her joy in living was infectious. Along with her other abilities she had a special talent for color and design. She had her own interior design company for 40 years – practicing in southern Connecticut, Long Island and Manhattan as well as two apartments in Paris. Her comment to Joan about the color of her hair brought to mind a particularly significant talent

Chic had for gradations of color. Uniquely, in Chic's mind's eye she could see every shade of every color imaginable. It was the equivalent of a musician with perfect pitch – being able to hum an F Sharp of a B Flat without an instrument in sight. When Chic went to a paint store it was not to find a color in a sample book, it was simply to find the order number for the color that was already in her head. In this respect she was the equal of any artist you could name. To me, of course, she was not only an artist but much more.)

CHAPTER NINE

High Drama and Low Comedy

I intend to finish this account of my years writing about the theatre for the *Wall Street Journal* with a high and a low – the low not meaning worthless or inferior but meaning an account of a low comedy musical. The high is an account of an outstanding playwright. The musical will probably be unexpected because it is far from being one of the immortals, rather it is a low comedy revue that opened in 1979, named *Sugar Babies*, that starred Mickey Rooney in his first Broadway appearance along with dancer Ann Miller. It was a celebration of the halcyon days of vaudeville and burlesque and I was looking forward to seeing it not only because I had a soft spot for the material but also because it was the inspiration of two men I knew well. One was Ralph Allen, my successor at the Yale Drama School as John Gassner's assistant who went on to become a noted theatre scholar and writer. In addition to his academic credentials, Ralph had a not-so-secret passion: his inordinate love of vaudeville sketches and jokes. He was the repository of literally hundreds, perhaps even thousands, of comedic exchanges and one-liners.

Ralph's collaborator in developing the book of *Sugar Babies* was Harry Rigby, a man I had gotten to know in the 1960s when I was a would-be producer. Harry was an admirer of by-gone material, not jokes or punch lines, but shows. It was he who came up with the idea of reviving *No, No, Nanette* and persuading the wizard of comedic film blockbusters, Busby Berkeley, to come out of retirement and direct the show. (With several shows including *Nanette*, Harry was often taken advantage of by crass co-producers; not so with *Sugar Babies*, however.) In the show Mickey sang – I *Can't Give You Anything but Love, Baby* and *On the Sunny Side of the Street* – and Ann Miller, who was said in her dancing to produce more taps per minute than anyone in the business, gave it her all. (For those who are interested, you can still catch a glimpse of Mickey and Ann on YouTube giving us five and a half minutes of a routine from the show.) In addition Ann and Mickey, there were jugglers, ventriloquists, and a whole panoply of vaudeville routines.

Best of all for many was a dog act. When people first saw the animal on a table with his trainer standing by no doubt their first reaction was "what is a tired routine like that doing here?" Five minutes into the routine they found out. The trainer had a number of props: a hoop, a cane, a mirror. The idea clearly was that this was a trained dog who, when his master commanded him, would jump through a hoop, stand on his hind legs, or retrieve a walking stick. This particular dog, however, was having none of it. The trainer would carefully go through his preparation, indicate to the audience what was about to happen, give the dog a milk bone, and then attempt to do the trick. Meanwhile, the dog would not budge but rather, with a bored expression, look at the audience as if to say: "Who is this guy? What does he expect me to do – jump through a ring? Come on; we all of us know I could easily do it, but why? You've seen it a thousand times. It's boring, boring, boring. I'm comfortable where I am." Meanwhile, the audience who had begun with puzzlement and then a chuckle or two was now beginning to roar with laughter as the trainer moved from one trick to another, becoming increasingly frustrated with the extreme lethargy of his pupil.

Mickey and Ann performed the show on Broadway for three years, and after a hiatus, went on the road. During the tour I ran into Ralph, congratulated him, and asked him how things were going. "I can never let up," he said. "Mickey gets bored so easily that I have to send him two or three new jokes every week whether he's in St. Louis, Kansas City or Denver. I had to do the same in New York: provide an endless supply of jokes." "Ralph," I said, "if anybody can do it, you can: the man who knows more burlesque jokes than anyone alive."

I turn from *Sugar Babies* and my light-hearted experiences in the theatre to the serious one with which I conclude my time as a critic, namely, a profile of the person I consider the most important playwright of the late 20th century, August Wilson. August was born in 1945 and spent his early years in Pittsburgh moving in and out of schools and joining the army for one year. On his 20th birthday his sister sent him some money as a present and August promptly went out and bought an old-fashioned typewriter which he placed on the kitchen table, slowly typed out his name, and said to himself, "Now I am a writer." At the beginning he wrote short stories and poetry, which he submitted unsuccessfully to *Harpers Magazine*. When August was 23, he and a friend, Rob Penny, founded the Black Horizon Theatre in the Hill district of Pittsburgh. When the time came to appoint a director, there was no one to take the job and so August volunteered. He had never directed before, but his home away from home throughout his youth had been the Carnegie Library of Pittsburgh so his first move was to go to the library and take out a book on directing. As an off-the-radar theatre Black Horizon turned out to be a success, performing not only in Pittsburghh but being invited to perform at colleges throughout the midwest.

Three years later a mentor persuaded August to come to St. Paul, Minnesota, where he found him a job writing educational scripts for the Science Museum of Minnesota. Three years after that August was accepted into a program at the Playwrights' Center in Minneapolis for which he received a scholarship. "I walked into a room in which I joined a group of 16 playwrights," he told me, "it was one of those rare moments, like the day I bought that first typewriter and placed it on the kitchen table, I saw those 15 other playwrights and said to myself 'I guess I'm now a playwright.'" Later, there was another revealing moment he told me about. He had written two or three plays but was dissatisfied with the dialogue. Sharing his apprehension with his best friend, the friend said: "You don't write dialogue, you listen: you try to hear what they would say; how would this person speak? How would it sound? "I tried it," August said, "I listened and my characters began to speak." Teachers who had worked with August always said that he had a prodigious, almost uncanny, memory: listening to voices he had once heard, the words came back to him almost verbatim.

His lyrical, musical dialogue is one of the qualities August became famous for, along with his indelible characters, and his strong sense of situation and plot. There was also great versatility in his subject matter: some plays were family plays, some group plays, others more historical. *Ma Rainey's Black Bottom* was about an entertainer; *Fences* was a family play as was *The Piano Lesson*; *Joe Turner's Come and Gone* was about the migration of African-Americans from the South to the North. After he had written three or four plays August realized, quite by chance, that each one was set in a separate decade of the 20th century and so

158

he set himself the task of writing a different play for each decade of the 20th century: a task he completed masterfully. In October 1987, I wrote a piece about August that appeared in the *Wall Street Journal*. I never picked the headlines, an editor did that, but the title chosen was "A Great American Playwright." For the last twenty-five years of the 20th century, he was *the* great American playwright.

During the 1980s I became more and more immersed in various theatre activities in the City. In addition to teaching and writing I became active in the New York Drama Critics' Circle and other organizations. When I joined the Circle the theatre world in New York was a far different place than it is today. There were 20 of us, most of them fulltime critics appearing in a wide range of newspapers and magazines and, of course, I saw them quite often: Edith Oliver and Brendan Gill from *The New Yorker*, Walter Kerr from the *New York Times,* John Simon from *New York*, Harold Clurman from *The Nation*, Doug Watt from the *Daily News,* Marilyn Stasio from *Cue*, John Beaufort from the *Christian Science Monitor*, Jack Kroll from *Newsweek*, Ted Kalem from *Time*, Bill Glover from the AP. There was a great deal of camaraderie among us, but now, sadly, some of these publications no longer exist or if they do they no longer have full-time critics. The Circle is only a shadow of its former self. This loss is symptomatic of a much larger change in the theatre that I will take up later in the book.

In the meantime, in addition to the *Critics Circle*, I joined several boards and other groups. I have already mentioned TDF, the Theatre Development Fund, on whose Board I served for a quarter of a century, as well as other boards: the Susan Smith Blackburn Prize and the John Golden Fund which supports small theatres dedicated exclusively to producing works by new, young playwrights. I was also active with the Pulitzer Prize Drama Jury, serving on their board for a number of years and as Chairman for a time.

Academically during the 1980s I was dividing my time between Hunter College and the aforementioned CUNY Graduate Center on 43rd Street but by the end of the 80s I had moved entirely to the PhD program at 43rd Street, though I visited Hunter often and kept in close contact with my colleagues there. At the Grad Center, as I mentioned earlier I was in charge of CASTA, the Center for Advanced Studies in Theatre Arts. CASTA published theatre books and a magazine, the books being largely devoted to theatre research and collections of plays. Beginning in the late 1980s I added another component to CASTA's activities – a television interview program entitled Spotlight, produced in partnership with CUNY-TV that had studios in the same building.

Over the next three years, in a series of half hour programs I interviewed 14 actors, 22 playwrights, 13 producers and 6 directors, all of them the most prominent artists in their respective fields. In some cases, such as with well-known artists like Arthur Miller, Edward Albee, Hal Prince, Jason Robards, Claire Bloom, Neil Simon, August Wilson, Tony Randall, George Abbott, Julie Harris, Jessica and Hume Cronyn there was not one half-hour interview, but two so that I had more time to cover their careers. Harvey Schmidt recorded for us *Try to Remember,* one of the songs he had written for his musical *The Fantasticks*, as a theme to open and close each interview. The Spotlight programs were broadcast over CUNY-TV in New York and over 200 stations on PBS. (In 2017 I was standing with friends in front of the Music Box Theatre on 45th Street when a young man came up to me and inquired: "Are you Ed Wilson?" When I answered in the affirmative he said, "I thought so; I see your interviews on YouTube." I have since learned that these interviews are all over YouTube. Who knew?)

When I called Jason Robards, who then lived in Connecticut, to invite him to be interviewed, I said, "Jason, you may not remember me. I'm Ed Wilson. and I was Lew Allen's assistant on *Big Fish, Little Fish*." Jason, who early in his career had a serious alcohol problem, replied: "It's not that I don't remember you; I don't remember anything from that year." When he came on the program, however, he was a perfect guest: jovial, forthcoming and quite amusing. Among other things he told me how he got his start on the stage – in a children's play in New York when he was the rear end of a horse. When Colleen Dewhurst came on, unbeknown to me (and to virtually everyone else because she had not spoken of it) she was suffering from cancer at an advanced stage. One would never have known this, however, because she was extremely lively, amusing, and remained passionate about theatre. Four months after the interview she succumbed to the cancer. Looking back, I could not believe her forbearance and courage.

Another actress on *Spotlight*, Julie Harris, had won ten Tony awards overall, five of them as Best Actress in a Play, two more than anyone in history. The emotional moment in my interview with her did not concern statistics, however, but a scene in the play *The Member of the Wedding* in which I had seen her perform. The play opened in 1951 when she was 26 years old but playing the part of a 12 year-old. The play, a dramatic adaptation of her novel by Carson McCullers, tells the story of a lonely, awkward 12-year-old in the South whose older sister is getting married and who believes she would be less lonely herself if she could go away with the bride and groom on their honeymoon. Her only friends are her black mammy and a much younger boy who is her cousin. Previously I had heard the story of how producer Robert Whitehead had pursued the actress Ethel Waters to get her to be in the play.

Waters, who was a singing star in the 1930s and early 40s – starring in such films as *Cabin in the Sky* and becoming famous for her rendition of the song "Stormy Weather "– had fallen on hard times and was singing in a down-and-out nightclub in Detroit when Whitehead tracked her down. He watched her show one night and went back with her to her place in a shabby rooming house. She told the producer: "Mr. Whitehead, I get down on my knees by that iron bed every night and pray to God he will bring me a good booking." "Miss Waters," Bob said, "do I have a booking for you." The play was to be directed by Harold Clurman and Julie told me how supportive and protective of Miss Waters he was. In the interview I told Julie that Bob had told me there was some switch at the end of Act One initiated by Waters.

Julie explained what it was. The script called for Ethel's character to sing an English nursery rhyme at the close of the act: "Who killed Cock Robin? I, said the sparrow, I killed Cock Robin with my bow and arrow." They had been rehearsing the play with this as the closing moment of Act One, but one night after they had finished rehearsals, Ethel, Harold, Julie and Carson were sitting around, talking about one or two scenes that had raised questions, when Ethel said to the group: "That song at the end of Act One; it's not right; it should be something else." "What should it be?" asked Bob. "A song my mama taught me," Ethel answered. "Sing it for us," Bob said. And she did. The song was a spiritual called "His eye is on the Sparrow and I know He watches me," and when Ethel finished, said Julie, everyone in the room was crying." And at this point in the interview Julie herself had a catch in her throat at the memory of it. "I know how you all felt," I said; "I saw the production when I was in my early 20s and at the end of Act One every person in the theatre had tears in their eyes; I certainly did."

The only playwright of note I was not able to interview on *Spotlight* was Tennessee Williams who had died five years before the series began. I was able, however, to have a conversation with him in the late 1970s before he was in his final, sad days. The occasion was a production at the Hartford Stage Company in Connecticut of *The Glass Menagerie* that the theatre had induced Williams to attend. The morning after the opening there was a brunch attended by Williams and the press. I knew that when I spoke to him there was a need, in order to engage him, in coming up with a question other than one such as "How did you like the production?" or "Are you working on a new play?" Rather, I decided to ask him about a controversy that had surrounded *Cat on a Hot Tin Roof* when it first opened.

During preparations for the initial production of the play Williams and his director, Elia Kazan, had a serious disagreement. In his original manuscript Williams had indicated that the character of Big Daddy, the plantation owner and a major figure in the play, did not appear in the third act. Kazan had argued that Big Daddy must appear in the last act and was persistent in arguing that if this character was absent the play would never be a hit, knowing that at that point in his career Williams needed a hit. Eventually Williams capitulated and furnished a version that included the re-appearance of Big Daddy. The play was a hit but Williams never conceded the idea that the play should have been presented only as he originally wrote it. To emphasize this point, when the play was published Williams insisted that both versions, his and Kazan's, should be printed. I asked Williams if he still felt that way. "Absolutely," he said, but it did not end there. He segued into a lengthy account of

163

an incident in his childhood when, in the company of his maternal grandfather, Reverend Walter Dakin, the two of them visited an actual Mississippi plantation in the parish of his grandfather lorded over by prototypes of Big Daddy and Big Mama.

Williams had never forgotten the way the real-life Big Mama treated his grandfather. "Preacher," she yelled to him across the room, "come here." Williams and his grandfather made their way slowly across the large living room. When they arrived Big Mama pointed to the top left side of her dress on which a large diamond pin was featured. "See this brooch, Preacher; this brooch is made of 24 carat diamonds and made by 'Tiff-ah-nees'." Williams had never gotten over the demeaning way in which she had treated his beloved grandfather, calling him Preacher instead of Reverend. In short, the plantation setting and the pivotal characters of Big Daddy and Big Mama were based on an actual experience Williams had in the company of his grandfather.

His love and admiration of Reverend Dakin began early when, at a very young age, his father deserted his family. (The line Williams used to describe his father's departure from the family was spoken by the mother's character in *The Glass Menagerie* – "he was a telephone man who fell in love with long distance.") When his father had departed, young Williams and his mother and sister would end up spending more and more of their time with Rev. Dakin and his family in Mississippi. Williams' special feeling for his grandfather would remain with him for the rest of his life.

One indelible memory Williams had of his grandfather was the latter's lifelong devotion to the seminary at Sewanee where he had received his degree in divinity. It is easy to see why the Reverend Dakin had such fond memories of his alma mater. In many ways Sewanee, also known as the University of the South, is unique among colleges in the U.S.

Founded 150 years ago, its campus is gorgeous, consisting of 13,000 forested acres atop the Cumberland Plateau, a raised area in southeastern Tennessee that looks out over miles and miles of the farms and woodlands surrounding it. The school is the only one of its kind, being owned and governed by the Episcopal dioceses of the southeastern U.S. It's student body is small, only 1,700, but its reach is wide. Over 40% of its students study abroad and it has through the years produced a disproportionately large number of Rhodes Scholars.

I knew Sewanee well because a number of friends, as well as family members, had gone there. Sometime in the late 1980s or early 90s I was asked by the theatre faculty to speak there. It was on this visit that I was told by my colleagues an intriguing story about Williams and his will. Some 10 or 15 years before Williams had died the theatre faculty at Sewanee had a call from his attorney saying that because of his grandfather's deep affection for the institution Williams might leave a bequest in his will to the school in his grandfather's name; would the faculty please make a suggestion as to what might be appropriate?

The theatre department thought long and hard about what they should ask for. The one thing they did not want to do was overreach and so they came up with the idea of a named chair, the Dakins Chair, for a theatre professor. The lawyer thanked them and they never heard from him again as long as Williams lived. Not long after his death, however, the same lawyer got in touch with officials at Sewanee and stated that Harvard would decide on the fate of Williams' papers and manuscripts but that his fortune, worth $10,000,000, as well as all of the income from future royalties to his plays would go to Sewanee provided, of course, that the endowment be named for his grandfather. (I need not point out that the income from the royalties amounts to a tidy sum, which will continue until the copyrights on the plays expire.) There were numerous delays and obstructions in the execution of the will, but once those were disposed of, in 1996, Sewanee received the whole kit and caboodle. In the aftermath, the university's theatre was completely refurbished, any number of new scholarships were created and annual workshops and conferences were established – a rare fairy tale come true for an academic theatre department.

I mentioned earlier, when discussing *The Member of the Wedding*, that this was the first collaboration between the producer Robert Whitehead and the director Harold Clurman. These two were to go on to collaborate on thirteen more exceptional productions. Each man in his own way was extraordinary: a person of superior intelligence, enormous talent, great taste, seriousness of purpose, and absolute integrity. They were unquestionably the class act of the American Theatre during the quarter of a century between 1950 and 1975. I had the good fortune to work with both of them, not on one of their productions but in the classroom, on boards, as well as elsewhere. I also had an opportunity to honor them. I have already mentioned the memorial for Harold we held at the Hunter College Playhouse; in addition to that we established at Hunter, The Harold Clurman Professorship to honor him in perpetuity. Over 120 individuals and foundations helped establish the professorship: foundations such as the Shubert, John Golden Fund, and Billy Rose were extremely generous and among individuals Paul Newman and his wife Joanne Woodward were the most generous supporters of all, followed by Stella Adler, Aaron Copland, Whitehead-Stevens Productions, Sheldon Harnick and his wife, and many, many others.

As for Bob Whitehead, you may recall that my first theatre job in New York was reading scripts for his office. Later,

166

I was able to recruit him for the board of TDF and knew him there. As Bob's 80th birthday, March 3 1996, approached TDF decided to honor him with a celebratory event at the Laura Pels Theatre, at that time a 200-seat house just off Times Square. I was asked to put the tribute together, a task I happily accepted; with Bob I had come full circle. The title of the tribute was "Mister Class," a play on words of the name of a Broadway show then playing called *Master Class* which starred Bob's wife, Zoe Caldwell, and which he was producing. The play, about the opera singer Maria Callas, was written by Terrence McNally with Zoe portraying Callas. The cast from the production included the amazing Audra McDonald and opera singer Jay Hunter as pupils of Callas and David Loud as her piano accompanist, all of whom took part in the gala. The title, Mister Class, for Bob's event was altogether appropriate because if anyone in the Broadway world had "class" it was Bob.

He had been born in Canada as had his cousin the actor Hume Cronym. At the gala Hume provided a number of anecdotes about the two as youngsters who spent their summers together playing theatre games. As Hume was five years older he always played the role of the hero, while the younger Bob, Hume said, ended up in the cellar "which had a low ceiling, was dank and dimly lit." When Christopher Plummer, a fellow Canadian, learned about the event honoring Bob he volunteered to serve as Master of Ceremonies and added not only anecdotes to the proceedings but his own particular panache. Secretly, we had learned from Zoe that Bob's favorite song was a surprising one: the late night number written by Harold Arlen and Johnny Mercer which ends with the line: "So make it one for my baby, and one more for the road, that long, long road." It turned out that Audra, by chance, knew a marvelous, close harmony arrangement of the song. The event was kept secret from Bob

167

and when Audra, Jay and David began playing the song, Bob, watching with Zoe from his box, broke into the widest grin I had ever seen on his face. All told, happily, it was a joyous, fitting, and most successful occasion.

One more story about the twentieth century: on my *Spotlight* TV program one of the most meaningful interviews I conducted occurred in the early fall of 1989 when I talked for two half hours with George Abbott who, at the time, was 102 years old. Six years earlier, when he was 96, George had married Joy Valderama, a marriage that turned out to be a happy union for both of them and which lasted until George died at 107. The two of them split their time between their home in Florida, George's longtime summer place in Merriewold in the Catskills, and frequent visits to New York where they usually stayed at a hotel near the theatre district. Fortunately for me, I often saw the two of them on their visits to Manhattan.

There were many stories about George in his old age. The chief recreations for George had always been dancing and golf, the latter being a game he pursued almost to the end. There was a famous account of the time when he was playing golf with Joy in Florida at age 103 or so. Halfway through the round George fell on the ground, seemingly unconscious. Joy rushed to him, touched his shoulder and urgently asked: "George, George, are you all right?" When he did not move she continued: "George, please say something, don't just lay there." In a moment, slowly, George opened his eyes and spoke: "Lie there," he said. Another story about George, not so well known, concerned his visit to his doctor when he was 95 and who informed him that he needed a pacemaker for his heart. "How long do these things last?" he asked the doctor. "About ten years," the doctor replied. "You mean I'll have to do this again?" George asked. And he did: at 105 he had his pacemaker replaced.

In my hour-long interview with George I took him back to the days when he began, attending Harvard to be in George Pierce Baker's course, Workshop 47, which at the time was the only playwriting course in the country, as I mentioned earlier. (At this point I would like to digress briefly to say a word about that famed Baker workshop entitled Drama 47. So well known did it become that in the early 1920s philanthropist Edward Harkness – in 1918 listed as the 6th richest man in America – offered to establish a theatre department at Harvard if Baker could be in charge. The Board of Overseers at Harvard, however, insisting that Harvard should teach only the theoretical arts not the practical ones, turned the offer down, at which point Harkness made the same offer to Yale, his alma mater. Yale readily accepted it and in 1925, Prof. Baker and his wife moved to New Haven where the Yale Drama School began, making it, along with Carnegie Mellon, the first such school in the U.S. At Yale, Baker kept the same title he had used for his course at Harvard – Drama 47 – which remained the title when I taught the course at Yale in 1962-63.)

Returning to my interview with George Abbot, as we moved through the years I was astonished by the fact that whatever period or decade we discussed, George had virtually total recall of experiences and events of that time. It turned out that when George went to New York in 1913 he could not get a foothold as a playwright; he could, however, become a successful actor and director and from that springboard, he gradually moved into writing. In the meantime, in the period from 1925 to 1935, he established himself as an astute, masterful director and in the years that followed, with straight plays and the musicals of Rodgers and Hart, he became the most sought after director on Broadway.

In the meantime, by default he continued to be a playwright. When, for instance, Hal Prince and Richard Griffith, two of George's protégés, came to him saying they wanted *Pajama Game* to be their first Broadway production, he looked at the script and said, "no way." They kept insisting, however, so finally George re-wrote the entire play and it became a hit. Again, on the writing side of things, with the musical *Fiorello* I had noticed that he was the co-author with someone else. When I asked him about this he said, "The script was hopeless. I started from scratch and wrote the whole thing myself. The other man's name was on there strictly for contractual reasons." George's work on *Fiorello*, incidentally, won the Pulitzer Prize that year for a musical script.

In addition to golf, George, for recreation, loved to go dancing and would often be seen at Roseland, the dance palace on West 52nd Street, tripping the light fantastic with the latest female star of one of his musicals. When I interviewed Gwen Verdon she told me she often went dancing at Roseland with George. "He wasn't a particularly good dancer," Gwen said. Quite a surprising statement about the man who directed more successful musicals than anyone in history, and collaborated with George Balanchine and Jerome Robbins the greatest American choreographers of the 20th century. It's OK, however, if George was not particularly light on his feet, he remains the nonpareil creative force in the American musical theatre, probably for all time.

CHAPTER TEN

Theatre in the 21st Century

Thus far I have been writing about people and events in the 20th century, but we are now two decades into the 21st century and on at least two fronts I have experienced and observed a serious sea-change, one, in the case of my long-time text book publisher, a drastic, most unfortunate change; in the other, the state of the Broadway theatre, a highly questionable, but not disastrous alteration.

Turning first to my publisher, McGraw-Hill. As I suggested earlier, my relations with the company were a remarkable collaboration for many, many years. From the time my first book, *The Theatre Experience*, came out through the period when Al Goldfarb joined me as co-author on two additional text books and through numerous editions of all three books, our work together could not have gone better. Editors came and went but many things remained the same, a good example being Inge King our photo researcher. As a publishing company, McGraw-Hill had a long and honorable history. Founded in 1888, by James McGraw, the original company joined forces early in the 20th century with another company owned by McGraw's friend, John Hill, to create the company that continued throughout the 20th century. When, in 1986, McGraw-Hill bought a competitor, The Economy Company (at that time the largest text-book publisher in the country) the company founded by James

McGraw assumed leadership in the field. In 1966 the company had acquired the credit rating agency Standard and Poors and from that point on McGraw-Hill was really two companies: the publishing wing and the financial services wing.

Throughout the rest of the 20th century the publishing side of the company went along as usual and either I alone or Al and I together continued to produce new editions of our three text books with the same expert work on the part of our publisher. After the turn of the century, however – toward the end of the first decade – things began to change rapidly. Three developments occurred almost simultaneously. First, McGraw-Hill became obsessed with the notion of digital: all textbooks they felt would, in a very short time, be sold in digital form, rather than as printed books which would quickly become obsolete. I remember around 2008 or 2009, the vice president of Higher Education, Mike Ryan, told me that in three years time, the majority of their textbook sales would be digital; I demurred saying that I did not think it could possibly happen in such a short space of time. It is a conversation we would repeat once a year over the next eight years and every year the fateful takeover of digital did not occur.

To indicate their blind belief in this eventuality in 2007 McGraw-Hill began using an on-line study program called GradeGuru.Com intended to connect students via computers rather than with printed texts. Five years after they initiated the program, in 2012, they abandoned it; as I say, things did not work out as they had predicted after all. At the same time that this rush to digital was going on – perhaps as part of it – McGraw-Hill changed its management style, drastically. We no longer had editors, we had "managers" who, incidentally, knew nothing about the style or content of a book, only its salability in a new edition. Another way to put this is that they appeared to be totally uninterested in creating new material, only in preserving books they already had.

In 2012 the serious deterioration of the McGraw-Hill Higher Education division of the company was compounded enormously when the entire publishing division was sold outright to a private equity firm, Apollo Global Management. The chief officers of the overall operation had decided to cast their lot with the financial services division of the company and to cast off book publishing. As most readers will know, a private equity firm like Apollo moves in one of two ways when it acquires a property. Either it attempts to improve the financial situation of its acquisition so that it can quickly sell the asset or it runs the company into bankruptcy. At the moment the jury is still out on which path Apollo will take with McGraw-Hill publishing.

For Al and me the high point of the disastrous turn of events came during 2017 when we were preparing the 10th edition of *Theatre: The Lively Art*. Not only were we dealing with "managers" instead of editors, McGraw-Hill refused to budget any money for our photo editor, Inge King, they insisted on using someone, perhaps from India, who knew absolutely nothing about theatre in general, let alone theatre in the United States. It was a nightmare. (For the next edition of *The Theatre Experience* (the 14th) McGraw Hill, embarrassed at the disaster they had experienced in photo research, found a far more competent person in Emily Tietz from Austin, Texas.)

A further sign of their desperation was the move in 2018 not to sell books, but to rent them to students. Second-hand books had always been a serious problem for text book publishers; McGraw-Hill Higher Ed was hoping to solve this by only renting them out again and again. There was an ironic turn of events with this development. McGraw-Hill had long since begun selling our texts as paperback only. With the rental policy they discovered that the soft cover books quickly wore out and they were forced to return to hard-back covers. It is too soon to tell how this rental experiment will work out but whatever the outcome, McGraw-Hill Higher Education at this juncture is clearly in a state of flux. Further complicating matters was the announcement in May, 2019, that McGraw Hill Higher Education would merge with Cengage, one of the other two largest publishers of college text books in the U.S. Cengage, by the way, publishes the books that are Al's and my most serious competitors. What this means regarding the future of our two Intro to Theatre books is anyone's guess. Thank goodness our theatre history text, *Living Theatre*, is safely in the hands of the wonderful W. W. Norton.

Along with the serious, perhaps fatal, deterioration of McGraw-Hill higher education publishing, my second bête noir with what occurred in the opening decades of the 21st century has to do with the state of the Broadway theatre, not in terms of attendance and financial health but in terms of art, aesthetics and tradition. In the previous century the American theatre during the six decades from the mid-1920s through the mid-1980s had its own version of a "golden age." Serious theatre, comic theatre, and especially musical theatre, in which American talent created what was virtually a new genre, were astonishing.

As I have pointed out previously, no one expects a creative burst of theatrical activity to last. Artistic creation does not flow in a steady stream, it surfaces in fits and starts. Outstanding theatre, dance, opera, literature, painting, sculpture are fly-by-night activities, creations that appear, seemingly in a flash, and then lay dormant, sometimes for centuries. In what I am about to say about the current state of the Broadway theatre, in the first two decades of the 21st century, I am not asking for a continuation of what happened in the years mentioned above. There are bound to be times when a fruitful period of creation in any field takes a breather, a pause or a time out.   I have no objection to well done revivals, imports, revues, or imitative comedies and musicals. I am responding not to the lack of originality but to other aspects of the theatre experience: the way theatre is created and produced, the experience of attending a performance, and the marked change in certain aspects of content. I begin where my own exposure to theatre began, both in observing it and writing about it.

When I first covered the theatre for the *Journal* in the early 1970s, as I have said, there were 20 members of the New York Drama Critics Circle representing the print world. This included both newspapers and weeklies: there were seven daily newspapers and even more weekly publications, such as *Time, Newsweek, The Nation, Commentary* and *The Village Voice.* When people attended the theatre, men wore suits and neckties and women wore dresses. Obviously, times have changed, which is inevitable: print has given way to digital, just as formality in dress has given way to extreme informality.

Along with such matters as dress and print media there have been other drastic shifts such as the quality of dramatic offerings. To take but one example, one could look at the brief, three-year period between 1962 and 1965 on Broadway and the deterioration in quality of creativity and originality in theatre from that time to this. In doing so one can only see the drastic change that has occurred, not just in one type of theatrical offering but in all of them: musicals, light comedies, and serious drama. In 1962 Edward Albee's play *Whose Afraid of Virginia Woolf?* opened, a worthy successor to the plays of Arthur Miller and Tennessee Williams. The premiere author of light comedy at that time was Neil Simon and in the period between 1962 and 1965 two of his plays opened: *Barefoot in the Park* followed by *The Odd Couple.*

As for musicals, the classic piece, *Fiddler on the Roof*, with book and lyrics by Sheldon Harnick and music Jerry Bock opened in 1964. With the work of such artists as Stephen Sondheim in the musical field and August Wilson in drama such creativity continued through the rest of the 20th century. In the early 21st century, however, there is nothing to compare with this kind of fecundity in theatrical creation, not just in the fields of comedy, drama and musicals, but in any one of them. When we compare what was happening half a century ago to what is occurring now, the difference is not only striking, it is extremely disheartening.

As a part of this sea-change, in the theatre world other types of entertainment began to appear in place of high quality theatre. More and more revivals of past plays and musicals began to take the place of new material until such revivals represented a fairly large percentage of the plays appearing on Broadway. In addition, new types of second tier entertainment appeared, a good example being the "juke box" musical that was not drama in any shape or form but a compilation of song hits. Two good examples were *Mamma Mia* featuring the songs of the musical group ABBA and *Jersey Boys* highlighting the music performed by Frankie Valli and the Four Seasons. Still another trend invading Broadway were extravagant musicals aimed at young people. The chief producing group behind this development was the Disney Corporation that began with *The Lion King,* which happened to be a quite original musical appealing to adults as well as children and settled down for an extended run. Following this, however, Disney simply took popular cartoon films and turned them into musicals such as *Alladin* and *Frozen*. When you add to these a show brought from Britain, *Harry Potter and the Cursed Child*, on which, in 2118, the producers spent $65,000,000 not $35,000,000 on renovating the Lyric Theatre and $30,000,000 on the show itself – you get some idea of how the youth market has taken over.

Throughout the 20th century the American theatre was blessed with a series of outstanding artists: playwrights, actors, directors and designers. The Broadway theatre in particular was fortunate as well to have a series of exceptional producers. A producer first identifies the material that he or she believes will make an excellent drama or musical. It might be a novel, an older play that can be beneficially revised, or entirely new material created by a playwright or, in the case of a musical, by a writer, composer and lyricist.

Throughout most of the former century plays were produced by men and women who had given their lives to presenting plays and musicals they were passionate about. Often it is not the producer who identifies the material but a writer or a musical team that seeks out the person who might produce it. In any event, the producer agrees that the work in question has merit – the makings of a successful, worthwhile Broadway play or musical and undertakes making it a reality: hiring a director, designers for scenery, lighting and costumes and engaging a theatre in which the production can be presented. Next comes the awesome task of raising money to finance the production. Often the producer has developed a small roster of backers: people of means who love the theatre and have the wherewithal to make it happen. The result is a carefully selected play or musical and a relatively small group of wealthy investors. Such people appeared on the scene throughout the 20th century. Chiefly they were single producers, or at the most one or two additional co-producers.

Irene Selznick produced *A Streetcar Named Desire* all by herself just as Kermit Bloomgarden was the sole producer of *Death of a Salesman, The Most Happy Fella* in addition to other plays and musicals. Bob Whitehead, with his partner Roger Stevens, produced *Bus Stop, Waltz of the Toreadors, The Visit, A Man for All Seasons,* and many more. Herman Levin, on his own, produced *My Fair Lady* in addition to *Gentlemen Prefer Blonds.* Hal Prince produced or co-produced any number of high quality musicals and David Merrick produced or co-produced an astounding 88 Broadway productions. The key point here is that during most of the 20th century individual producers presented all of the outstanding dramas and musicals that arrived on Broadway.

What a difference today! The musical *American in Paris* which opened in 2015 had the names of 25 people or organizations "above the title" in the program, implying that all 25 "produced the play or musical." *Dear Evan Hansen* which opened a year later, and had only eight performers in the cast, had 35 names above the title. The musical *Tootsie,* which opened in April of 2019, had an astounding 60 plus named producers. This designation, "above the title," had in prior years indicated the person who actually produced the play: a Whitehead, a Bloomgarden, a Prince, or a Levin. Sixty people cannot produce a production, neither can 35 or 15. It is a hand-crafted business of no more than two or three people, and latter day, would-be producers do not have the stature, authority or resourcefulness of their predecessors to do this.

In the face of such ineptitude, Broadway producers of today seek out any source of money, no matter how remote or arcane. Over time they discovered there was an entire tribe of individuals and small organizations who were willing to make a deal with producers looking for financial backing. In general these so-called "producers" asked for two items: 1) that their name would be "above the title" in the theatre program and 2) that they could dress formally in tuxedos and fancy gowns so that in the case the show they backed won a Tony Award, they could appear on stage with some 25 or more so-called "producers" and have their two minutes of television fame. This exercise has the earmarks, not of a serious undertaking but a real-life farce. The Broadway League will point to the fact that at the end of the second decade of the 21st century attendance was up and revenues were up. They did not, however, have much to say about content.

The fact that revenues are up is deceptive. For some time now theater owners have been fine-tuning the way they manage ticket prices. For many years outside operators called "scalpers" were a permanent fixture on the Broadway scene. The way scalpers operated was simple: if they thought a show was going to be a hit, or even a semi-hit, they would buy a good supply of orchestra seats early on and sell them later at two to three times the original box office price. Fifteen years into the 21st century, however, producers and owners, in order to take business away from scalpers, began to engage in what they described as "dynamic pricing." What this means is that the theatres no longer charged the same price for tickets throughout the week; instead they charged more on Fridays and Saturdays than for Mondays and Tuesdays. Moreover, they moved aggressively into the territory of the scalpers. In 2018 the first eight rows or so of the center section at the Richard Rodgers Theatre where Hamilton was playing were selling at the box office for $849 per seat in the early summer of

2018. Contrast that with the super hit *A Chorus Line* that opened in July of 1975 with a top ticket price of $15. That is a whopping, almost unbelievable increase of 5,566 %. The revival in 2017 of *Hello, Dolly!* Starring Bette Midler added an even further twist: the front row seats, with a runway wrapping around them where Midler could parade by and touch their hands, sold for $989 dollars each. No wonder gross sales are up – it's certainly not because of the quality of the product on offer.

Another trend the Broadway League points to is increased attendance. Once again it has nothing to do with high-quality, first rate, innovative theatre but with the increased attendance in two categories: people from out of town and young people attending the Disney shows who continue to visit Broadway in larger numbers year by year. As I say, this has little to do with quality. Thus far, with the single exception of Lin-Manuel Miranda, the author of *Hamilton*, the 21st century has not produced a single playwright or musical team to equal the two or three dozen that could be named in the years from 1930 to 1990.

Not only is there a paucity of new first-rate dramatic offerings, the experience of theatre-going is coarser and less appealing than I can ever remember. On a recent Wednesday, just before matinee time, I took a tour through the theatre district between 1:15 and 2:00, the curtain time. Near the entrance of every theatre, ticket holders, dressed as if they were about to go on a picnic, lined up not at the entrance to the theatre but on the sidewalk, snaking a hundred feet or so in each direction from the entrance to the theatre. Once they finally entered the theatre lobby, one by one the women's pocket books were checked before they could enter. I realize that for safety reasons the handbags of women must be looked at, but surely there is a way to handle this expeditiously so that patrons can make a reasonably dignified entrance in the front door as they enter the lobby. The people I saw in these long lines did not look like people anticipating a magical, uplifting, joyous experience but rather like a group of refugees being herded into an orientation meeting in a foreign land.

It will no doubt be argued that people must move with the times and that anyone, like me, who bemoans the state of things just now is an old fuddy-duddy, unwilling to accept change and move with the times. But the changes I am criticizing are not impressions or stray opinions, they are facts: a 5,000 plus per cent increase in ticket prices is not a mirage, - it is a reality. The difference of 35 so-called producers instead of one or two is equally a cold, hard fact. The Broadway theatre has changed, there is no getting away from it, and not for the better.

I don't wish to end this book on a negative note and fortunately I do not have to. In its downward spiral McGraw-Hill Higher Education decided to de-accession volumes that they felt were not selling enough copies to warrant their keeping them on their list. Al's and my theatre history book, *Living Theatre*, was one of those and so they presented the two of us with a "Reversion Letter," returning the publishing rights to us. It was time for a new edition of the book and it was our good fortune that a person we knew from McGraw-Hill had moved a year before to another publisher: W. W. Norton. His name was Chris Freitag and we had gotten to know him well at McGraw-Hill because he was an expert on sales figures and trends. Learning of the reversion of *Living Theatre,* Chris agreed to introduce us to an editor at his new employer, Peter Simon. It was our good fortune that although Norton had a very successful two volume anthology of dramatic works, they had no theatre history volume. They had history books in other arts such as music and art and this would add to their portfolio. They agreed, therefore, to publish what would be the 7th edition of L*iving Theatre*. It was one of the luckiest things that happened to us in the 35 years since the first edition appeared.

Working on the book was a joy from start to finish. Norton, we soon learned, was an exceptionally good publisher, highly respected by everyone, ethical, enlightened and with the added fact that the company was owned by its employees, a rarity in today's world. Peter and his assistant Gerra Goff proved to be extremely knowledgeable and invariably helpful. The company allowed us to bring Inge King out of retirement to become the photo editor, which had the added value that she knew the book inside out and had always been a joy to work with. The final product, which came out in the summer of 2017, may well have been the handsomest volume of all our 31 different editions.

In 2018 another fortuitous event came out of the blue. In order to tell this story I must go back 50 years. Some time in late 1968, when I was happily teaching at Hunter College, a young man I had never seen before named Harry Wiland sought me out. How he found me I will never know but he seemed to know a great deal about me, particularly the fact that I had done a bit of theatre producing and that I was from Nashville, Tennessee. Harry began by telling me that in filmmaking, documentaries were the coming thing: especially documentaries of music festivals and other live events that were already taking place. In such cases, you avoided the expense of commissioning a screenplay, hiring talent and a staff, and orchestrating a series of events. You merely piggybacked onto an event that was already occurring. You simply had to come to terms with the producers and the talent involved and pay them a little extra in order to film the event.

"What is this leading to," I asked.

"I'm coming to that," Harry said, "I have friends who are planning something like this for an event coming up next summer at Woodstock, New York."

"Never heard of it," I said.

"You will," Harry assured me.

"Anyway, what does this have to do with me?"

"Ah, hah," said Harry, "You won't believe this but I know something that will easily be the equal of Woodstock."

"Which is?"

"The annual Disk Jockey convention in Nashville, Tennessee."

"The What?"

"One week every fall, country music stars – no matter how famous or important, no matter how far away they are – return for one week to perform at the Grand Ole Opry as well as for their fan clubs who congregate at the same time. Sometime during the week radio and TV disk jockeys from around the country – from Maine to Arizona, Oregon to Georgia, Minnesota to Mississippi – congregate in strategic locations while the stars move through the melee stopping to be interviewed by one disk jockey after another in a five minute conversation. The next week the disk jockey returns home and announces on the air: 'I was just in Nashville talking to Johnny Cash...' or Loretta Lynn, or Dolly Parton, or whomever."

"Where does this plan of yours come in?"

"Those performances are going to be taking place all week with or without us – all we have to do is be there to be included."

"I still don't see what this has to do with me?"

"I've got everything set up. A film-maker, Amram Nowak, who will arrange the mechanics: cameramen, lighting and sound technicians, editing facilities, the works."

"So why don't you go ahead?"

"Only one thing missing."

"Which is?"

"Backing – the money."

"So that's what this is about."

"You can raise it, everybody says you can."

"Everybody?"

"Well, two people."

"Who?"

"Well, one person actually, and I promised not to use his name. But look," he continued, "you have raised money for theatre productions, you are from Nashville. At least give it a try."

"What kind of money are we talking about?"

"$75,000 dollars."

"To make a film?"

"Amram says that's all he needs – that is, if we can get the talent for almost nothing and I think we can."

I told Harry I would think about it but for all intents and purposes to count me out. That night I told Chic about this odd conversation. "You're a theatre person; You've never produced a film in your life."

"That's what I said," We both agreed it was the most far-fetched thing imaginable, and to me that was the end of the conversation. Much later that night, out of the blue, Chic observed: "I just remembered: We're already going to Nashville in a couple of weeks," she said, "to visit your family."

"So?"

"Nothing – just pointing it out"

A week later a message was left on my phone: "The first person to see in Nashville," the voice of Harry said, "is Jo Walker, the head of the Country Music Association."

We did go to Nashville and I did contact Jo Walker, who turned out to be an astute, extremely pleasant lady. When we met I told her what these people were thinking about and to my surprise she observed that this might be a good way to advertise country music. We talked about ways we might get permission from performers and rights from music publishers. Always eager to get funds for CMA, she suggested the idea of a meaningful contribution to the Country Music Association in return for which she would help us get rights, both from singers and music publishers. While in Nashville I learned that a new business in town that wanted to ingratiate itself with the country music industry and I got in touch with them.

In the end we contributed $25,000 to CMA and raised the other $50,000 and Harry and Amram moved ahead. They arranged for all the technicians; thanks to Jo I was able to get 300 performers to sign a one-page release for one dollar each and to make a deal with some 25 music publishers. We did film that week and got a lucky break when a member of the sound crew ran into a young would-be composer from Augusta, Georgia in the parking lot of their motel who had come to Nashville that week hoping to break into the music business. Named Herbie Howell, we wove his story into the fabric of the film. In the end we filmed all the stars, singing their most famous songs, and a great deal more. In the editing room Amram and his colleagues brought forth a quite respectable 90-minute documentary.

Then, out of the blue, a sucker punch – a totally unexpected body blow – hit me full force. A reality about movie making, I learned (lesson number one in financing a film) suddenly struck: namely, that when you raise money for a film you raise a certain amount – no matter how many thousands or millions – for the making of the film and an equal amount for advertising and distribution. Harry and Amram had never mentioned this to me – a major deception. There was no question that I was in no way supposed to raise money for this part; they were. I suppose they reasoned that if they could end up with an appealing film they could find a way to get funds for selling it. In any event they were unable to do that and, sadly, the only thing that happened was a premier – if you could call it that – eventually arranged by Amram in a small, backwater town in southern Louisiana.

And so I ended up with a quite decent film but with no way to sell or distribute it. During the height of Blockbuster and the DVD business, an earnest young man name Josh Tager from from Ashville, North Carolina made a decent DVD version from which I received a few thousand dollars a year for several years. Sometime later a nephew of mine who lives in Connecticut became interested in selling it and we made a deal with a man in Los Angeles who cost us a ton of legal fees for a contract that resulted in no money whatsoever. And so, I had a decent film from which I had managed to acquire far more debts than assets, languishing for 50 years in the damp basement of our home on Long Island.

Then in the winter of 2018, a strange thing happened. I had a phone call from the Vanderbilt University Alumni office; someone wanted to get in touch with me but their office did not give out email addresses or phone numbers without getting permission. I asked them who was trying to reach me and they replied, "Some man named Ken Burns's." I said yes, that Mr. Burns could call me. The person in question, of course, was the renowned documentary film maker responsible for such documentary series as *The Roosevelts, The Vietnam War, Baseball, Jazz, Mark Twain* and many more. A day or two later I had a call, not from Mr. Burns but from Katy Haas, his chief assistant. She informed me that Mr. Burns was planning a documentary on country music and wanted to use three short segments from *The Nashville Sound* for a total of two minutes and thirty seconds and that they would pay me so much per second. I had to explain that the film might not be in good enough condition for them, that cans of 35-millimeter film had been sitting in the basement of a home on Long Island for many years and a separate sound track was in a closet in our apartment in New York. She said they would be the judge of whether they could use them or not; could I have everything sent to a lab in Maryland that they used. I said certainly, and off the film and sound track went.

The lab, it turned out, not only rescued the film but turned out two different forms of a High Definition version of the film (Quick Time / Wave files & DPX files) which Florentine forwarded to me. All I needed to do to have a version I could try to market to high-end distributors was to have the film "color corrected," a process I had never heard of but seems standard with old films. It simply means that a film lab goes through the film scene by scene and makes the grass greener, the sky bluer, and a person's face more natural, all to match what the film looked like originally – and perhaps just a shade better. When we got to this point I had a call from Burn's company, Florentine, that they would like to use twice as much footage as they had originally asked for if that was all right. I had no trouble in replying that it was.

I said at the beginning of the book that this was probably my last effort of working on my textbooks. Following the publishing of the history book in the summer of 2018 and of the two introduction to theatre books, one in January 2018 and the other in January 2019, I felt it was time to bow out. When, however, I told my long-time colleague and collaborator Al Goldfarb of my plans, he strenuously objected, arguing that there was no reason for me to drop out, and that, in fact, he felt I could make a significant contribution to another round of revisions. He pointed out that while I might be reluctant to do much original writing – feeling a bit out of touch with the current trends and pedagogy – there was still much that I could and should do.

There were two areas in particular he explained where I could contribute. One was in the selection of pictures. Each of our books is heavily illustrated with color photographs: the history book has over 250 such illustrations and each one of the introductory volumes has over 200. From the beginning – along with Inge King – over a period of 40 years I have selected all of the photographs for the books, a total of literally thousands of photographs. For each new edition, seventy per cent or so have been reprints from previous editions, but over time new photographs have appeared in significant numbers. I agreed with Al that this was an area in which I could easily and happily continue.

There were other areas. Without our being conscious of it, I had become our chief editor, reading over and hopefully improving both old and new material and making corrections or revisions. Also, often along with Al I saw where we might improve our work by moving with the times and responding to the wishes of teachers. For example, in the latest version of my original book, *The Theatre Experience*, I reduced the final three chapters to two in a way that I feel made the book more timely. Thus, both in editing and conceptual areas, I felt I could be of help. And so it was determined that at least for the upcoming round of revisions – all three books are scheduled for a new edition in the next three years – I could be helpful.

Toward the end of February, 2019, I walked the two blocks from my apartment to the Mitzi Newhouse Theatre at Lincoln Center to see a preview of John Guare's new play *Nantucket Sleigh Ride* which was going to open shortly. The title refers to the term used by whaling fishermen in the 1800s when they speared a whale while in a small boat and the whale took off, leading the sailors on a wild ride until the whale eventually became exhausted. As usual, John's play was itself a wild ride, intellectually and artistically. I thought it was ingenious as well as being extremely witty and entertaining.

Walking home I realized that it had been exactly 56 years since John had been in a playwriting class I was teaching at Yale. It was the year I was teaching the classes usually taught by Professor John Gassner who was on a sabbatical. I would like to take credit for recognizing the unique talent and inventiveness of John, but to anyone aware of theatrical artistry and imagination it was quite obvious that he was a true original, a dramatic maverick of a very high order. The only thing I can take credit for is recognizing his artistry and flair and encouraging him to pursue his instincts to the limit. Apparently the teachers he had previously had failed to realize how inventive and imaginative he was and he welcomed someone who did.

Though not close friends John and I have stayed in touch through the years as he has carved out a remarkable career of writing arresting, challenging, highly amusing plays. On my walk home, the idea suddenly occurred to me that the evening formed a rather reassuring, comforting close to the parenthesis of my own long teaching career. In years past I had never really thought about that career. I began teaching at Yale in the 1957-58 school year, over 60 years ago. I have no idea how many students I have faced over those six decades. As for writing theatre text books – again, an area I had never contemplated – my two introduction to theatre books have cumulatively sold hundreds of thousands of copies, and the history book Al and I wrote has been the number one seller in its field for some time now. As I say, it has never occurred to think about these things, and I probably will not again. But on that walk home from Lincoln

Center and for a couple of days afterwards I realized that the production of John's play was a proper bookend, or the close of a parenthesis, to my academic career.

I do, however, seem not to have given up writing altogether.

SELECTED REVIEWS

THE WALL STREET JOURNAL

Plays

Equus	11/28/1974
Same Time Next Year	3/17/1975
A Letter for Queen Victoria	3/28/1975
The Elephant Man	1/26/1979
Bedroom Farce	4/3/1979
Nicholas Nickleby	9/9/1981
M/ Butterfly	3/22/1988

Musicals

Grease	6/14/1972
Pippin	10/24/1972
A Little Night Music	2/27/1973
A Chorus Line	5/22/1975
Chicago	6/5/1975
The Enchanting Lena Horne	5/15/1981
Nine	5/11/1982
City of Angels	12/15/1989

Revivals

Mourning Becomes Electra	11/21/1972
Scapino	5/21/1974
Ah, Wilderness	9/1/1975
Fiddler on the Roof	12/31/1976
The Iceman Cometh	10/4/1985

PROFILES AND INTERVIEWS

Richard Rodgers	1/4/1980
Wilie Ruff and Dwike Mitchell	8/17/1984
George Abbott	1/15/1987
Jerome Robbins	2/28/1989
Richard Malby	2/23/1990

SPECIAL PIECES

The Frogs	5/24/1974
Japanese Theatre	11/10/1978
Theatre of the Arts, Winston Salem	8/31/1979
Yves Montand	9/9/1982
Forbidden Broadway	11/9/1988

PLAYS

CONFLICTING ELEMENTS IN A HUMAN SOUL

Monday, October 28, 1974

New York

Theater is the art of bringing different worlds together: The audience comes together with the actors, the words of the playwright merge with the voices of the performers, characters on stage confront one another, and the vision of a director joins forces with the ideas of a playwright. When these elements strike one another with the proper force they set off sparks that light up the sky and illuminate the soul.

Playwright Peter Shaffer understands this well, for in his new play *Equus*, that has just opened at the Plymouth Theatre, he has brilliantly brought together several elemental forces of the theater. Though rare, there are plays that move us to tears and affect us deeply; they appeal to our emotions. There are other plays, equally rare, which provoke thought and appeal to our intellect.

Rarer than either, however, are plays which combine the two: which strike a body blow to the gut at the same time that they set the wheels of thought spinning in our brain. Mr. Shaffer's *Equus* is just such a play.

On one level the play is a psychiatric detective story. A seventeen-year-old boy has blinded six horses one night in a stable and no one knows why. He is sent to a hospital to be treated by a child psychiatrist, and during the course of the play — through a series of agonizing recollections and reenactments with his parents and at the stable where he worked — we gradually learn why. It is a fascinating discovery.

On another level the play is symbolic. The horse is a symbol to the boy of a god; he sees in his horse the crucified Christ who will save him. Every three weeks, in the dark of night, he rides forth secretly on the horse in ecstasy and then falls down before him in worship. The boy with his worship of the horse-god is, in turn, a symbol to the psychiatrist of the primitive passions which the world has lost and which his own profession continually sanitizes and washes away.

There are other levels to the play. Grand designs are set beside small human touches. In one therapy session the psychiatrist gives the boy a "truth" pill — it is actually harmless although the boy believes it to be a powerful drug. It is the psychiatrist, however, on whom the pill works first, for he unconsciously begins in to tell his truth before the boy can tell his. The play has many levels, therefore, but Mr. Shafer has not set his ideas spinning on separate reels that never strike a common note. He has joined the heart to the mind and the symbolic to the real. The levels of his play bounce off one another; they collide, combine, and coalesce to form a texture of immense complexity. That alone is a significant achievement.

In the theater, however, words are not enough. In the preface to the printed version of *Equus*, Mr. Shafter has written "rehearsing the play is making the word flesh," and it is in the union of Shaffer's words with the staging of director John Dexter that *Equus* achieves its final alchemy.

Mr. Dexter staged the play in London and has staged it again here. With the exception of the two leads, who are English, the entire cast is American, but so complete is Mr. Dexter's vision of the play that one loses all thought of where it started or who is participating. He has struck just the right balance between theatricality and simplicity. The stage is a circle on which rests a square platform partially enclosed by a railing with three benches resting against them. Overhead, exposed spotlights hang on bare pipes. By invoking the power of our imaginations the platform becomes the psychiatrist's office, the boy's home, or the stable. In costuming too, the same effect is at work. The horses are not stage horses but men who wear metal masks shaped like horse's heads, and they do not walk on all fours, but stand upright. In short, they suggest horses rather than imitate them.

The same judicious use of theater magic is employed for the action of the play. The reenactment of the boy's gallop on his horse through the fields at night is as spare and economical as it is possible for a stage event to be. As strange sounds envelope them, the boy sits astride his man-horse in the center of the platform which is spun ever faster in a circle. The two figures do not move from the center of the stage but the effect is more thrilling than a thousand wild rides in the moonlight. Later, when the boy finally blinds the horses, the scene is terrifying in its ghastly carnage, and yet not a drop of blood is spilled.

In praising the production one should not fail to mention individual actors. Anthony Hopkins is an exemplary psychiatrist and Peter Firth is unforgettable as the boy. The image of Firth nestled against the chest of his horse, or staring in terror at his god, will be indelibly burned into the eyes of anyone who sees it. The American performers — Francis Sternhagen, Roberta Maxwell, Marian Seldes, and Michael Higgins — are also caught up in the enterprise and equal to the task. One doubts that they have ever acted better in their lives.

With the collaboration of Mr. Dexter and his actors, Mr. Shafer's words do become flesh. We do not merely hear about passion and worship; we are shown passion and worship as it unfolds before us on stage, and we take part in it ourselves. Mr. Shaffer's play is about many things — the Nietzchean conflict between the

Dionysian and Apollonian impulses, the problems of normalcy and the attributes of insanity, the need we have to worship a god — and these ideas will be analyzed and criticized for some time to come. But like any exciting work in the theater, initially it should not be dissected; it should be seen and experienced. By combining so skillfully the primal elements of theater by saying so much on the one hand and leaving so much to our imaginations on the other, *Equus* becomes one of the most powerful and provocative theatrical experiences of our time.

THE REDEEMING QUALITIES OF AN AFFAIR

Monday, October 28, 1974

New York

First things first, anyone planning on being in New York in the next year or so should make arrangements now to get tickets to *Same Time, Next Year*. It is the best comedy of the season and if the present law of averages prevails, may be the best one of next season, too.

There are comedies, which seem certain to be commercial successes but have little else to recommend them. *Same Time, Next Year*, playing at the Brooks Atkinson Theater, is not one of these, for in addition to laughs it has unusual warmth, two engaging characters, and a beguiling story.

Doris and George, both married to other people, find themselves together in a guest cottage at a country inn in northern California. He is a CPA who has a big account in the area and he stays there every year. She is headed for a religious retreat that she attends every year at this time because it is the weekend when her husband takes the children to visit his mother, and Doris and her mother-in-law don't get along very well.

Doris and George — heretofore faithful to their respective spouses, spend the night together and find that they enjoy it tremendously, so much so that they vow to repeat the rendezvous at the same time and place the following year. They do, and continue the same practice for the next twenty-five years. In the play we see them in a series of six scenes, at five-year intervals, moving from 1951 to the present.

In the last segment, when George says to Doris, "I grew up with you," he speaks not only for himself but for everyone in the audience because we grow up with both of them. On one level the play is a cavalcade of the last quarter century. Between scenes the sound system plays the songs and voices at each of the five-year intervals. We move from Senator McCarthy to Milton Berle to Edward R. Murrow to Bob Hope entertaining the troops in Vietnam to Muhammad Ali before his last fight.

More important than the parade of familiar voices, though, is what happens on stage with Doris and George. They change as individuals and they also reflect the changing attitudes and mores of men and women in America through the years. George begins as an uptight, neurotic accountant, attracted to Doris but suffering unconscionable guilt feelings about his wife and three children at home. As the years pass he becomes increasingly stuffy as he becomes more self-assured, but then he decides to give it all up and go into analysis and join encounter groups.

Doris begins as an awkward, uneducated girl who never finished high school and as time goes by she too moves through various stages: the restless young housewife, a student returning to college at Berkeley to finish her education and take a fling as an over-aged flower child, a career woman with a successful catering business and finally, a settled matron.

There is always amusement as each person passes from one stage to the next. At one point George decries the sloppy dress of the young but five years later he is wearing jeans and a denim jacket himself. And there is further humor in that as they change these two are always a little out of sync: when George is at his most square, Doris is in her hip period and vice versa; the year he is most anxious for sex she turns up eight months pregnant.

But the play is more than the saga of two individuals, or even their life together. More than anything it is a love story. This couple who remain married to other partners and who see each other only once a year are closer than many married couples. It is an odd feeling to watch this unusual kind of love grow and to become so involved in it

The author Bernard Slade, who is making his Broadway debut with *Same Time, Next Year* has provided an ingenious framework and a number or funny lines and anecdotes but the production is fortunate also in having exceptional performances by Ellen Burstyn and Charles Grodin. Not only do they carry the whole play, they are providing two of the most solid pieces of acting New York has seen in a comedy in some time. Together with director Gene Saks they have avoided going for the easy laugh, instead they have gone for depth and dimension in the characters and they have found that (as is so often the case when performers find truth in a situation) the laughs take care of themselves.

Ellen Burstyn's transitions from shy young mother to free spirit to career woman are models of acting skills. She adopts a new lilt in her voice and a loose-limbed walk for one, and a resolute squareness in the shoulders for the other. In her last scene as the matron you would swear that she is older, her face and body beginning to sag just a touch and a tinge of weariness appearing in her voice. With Charles Grodin too, we see George transformed before our eyes, slowly, subtly, from an anxiety ridden young man to a mellow, middle-aged one.

Same Time, Next Year is a production where it has all come together. The writer, director, and actors have listened to one another and heard the same song; a song with resonance, feeling and depth. It is a song of humor and unstrained laughter, of human fallibility and human need for other people. As the evening ends we wish that George and Doris would go on meeting in their bungalow year after year and that we could meet with them each year, too, at the same time, in the same place.

THEATERGOING AS AN ADVENTURE — OR AN ORDEAL

Friday, March 28, 1975

New York

As the first act of *A Letter for Queen Victoria* ends at the Anta Theater, a young man comes on stage for the entire act. Tall and erect, he wears a black suit with a white shirt and tie — for all the world like a lawyer or a young bank executive, possibly one who has just been promoted, from cashier to assistant vice president. His conservative appearance to the contrary, this young man is considered by many to be the most interesting figure in today's theatrical avant-garde.

His name is Robert Wilson and his has been an incredible story. Born in Texas, he came to New York to paint and study architecture. He also began working with emotionally disturbed people, retarded children and the aged, with whom he displayed extraordinary powers. Finally, he abandoned painting altogether. In his words

"the images in my head were so much richer than I could get on canvas." To bring his new images to life he turned to a new form, involving theatrical performances that defy description in traditional terms. Several members of his troupe have suffered serious mental problems in the past and one of the most remarkable performers of all is a young man who is autistic.

Deafman Glance, first performed five years ago, featured a deaf-mute; a black youth from Alabama who previously had been in trouble frequently with the police but whom Wilson discovered to be incredibly imaginative. For a drama festival to which he was invited in Iran, Wilson presented *KA MOUNTAIN AND GAUARDENIA TERRACE*, which was staged mostly on a mountainside and ran for seven days - 168 hours in all-without stopping. Last year he presented *The Life and Times of Joseph Stalin* at the Brooklyn Academy for several performances. Each lasted 12 hours, from 7:00 p.m. to 7:00 a.m. and some who stayed throughout the entire performance swear they felt thoroughly refreshed at the end.

Those who have followed Wilson's other pieces say that *A Letter for Queen Victoria* is more verbal and has less humor than his earlier works. Even so, it is an arresting example of his unique art form, which, like other theater innovations of the last two decades, puts emphasis on ritual, body movement of the performers and environmental stage settings. Judging from *A Letter for Queen Victoria* he has fused the arts of painting, theater, dance and music in a way no one else has. This is not to say the synthesis is complete. Some spectators will be bored out of their minds. But he points the way to intriguing possibilities and just possibly is on the brink of important discoveries.

A Letter for Queen Victoria has four acts, with an introduction and two entire acts. Each act begins with a tableau. The first features two women: a white woman, Cindy Lubar, standing in profile, wrapped in white cloth, and a black woman, Sheryl Sutton, completely in black. The two women exchange non-sequitur dialog, with references to such disparate things as washing dishes, the Civil War and prospecting in the Far West. Later they step out of their cloth wraps and the white woman is wearing black and the black woman white. They go through the complete, dialog three times, each time with a different set of accompanying actions and gestures.

The second tableau begins with a group of four figures wearing army fatigues and World War I pilots' helmets with goggles. There is a strong cross light that casts deep shadows on the stage. The four figures range themselves in a striking pose. The lights go out and then come on again and the four are arrayed differently. Once again, and the four are on the floor. Again the dialog follows no discernible pattern and it is repeated several times.

The third act opens on a scene with a backdrop on which the words "chitter chatter" are written over and over again. Five couples are seated at cafe tables. They are dressed elegantly in white. The entire scene is gray and white except for a single red or yellow tulip in a vase on each table. The couples chitter and chatter. Occasionally someone strikes a wine glass for silence and is shot by a pistol, but soon recovers and the talk goes on.

Along with the visual elements and the action in each section there is dancing and a musical score. The music is anything but avant-garde. Composed or arranged by Alan Lloyd, most frequently it sounds like melodic chamber music and it serves to underline, heighten or contrast with what is going on.

Two dancers, Andrew De-Gros and Julia Busto, twirl in place, literally, for hours on end. It is a wonder how they did it; they have been compared in all seriousness to the whirling dervishes. They dance alongside the action and sometimes in their motion setting up a subconscious rhythm which insinuates itself into the performance.

What does it all mean? "Chitter Chatter" possibly can be taken as a satire or aimless conversation which belies the grandeur of the setting in which it take place. And the tableaus with the military figures suggest air raids, wartime photographs and a holocaust. But to search for meaning is to come at *A Letter for Queen Victoria* the wrong way. One cannot attend this production with the same preconceptions and expectations with which one goes to a play, a concert or a museum. To do so will only lead to impatience and frustration.

We need time. We need

to learn to keep ourselves open, to receive visual images, music, sounds, kaleidoscopic movements, and to let these form in our minds and imaginations of their own accord. The results are sometimes astonishing. To hear the same nonsense dialog repeated over and over again would appear to be the most boring exercise imaginable. But if you simply accept it putting aside anger and a frantic search for meaning, quite possibly the third time around certain ideas and emotions or a long-buried memory will present themselves to you. It will be your own private vision and can fill you with wonder and amazement.

This can happen at *A Letter for Queen Victoria* because the elements that Wilson has put before us have been carefully selected, with the insight, intuition and rigor of an artist. In the world of new art forms it is never easy to tell fraudulent poseurs from true artists. Wilson is sailing uncharted seas and there is always room for doubt, but his work seems to have the ring of authenticity about it. At the very least, it is work worth following and holding out great hope for.

One final note. A regular member of Wilson's troupe for the past few years has been his 88-year-old grandmother from Texas, Alma Hamilton. It is she who plays Queen Victoria.

DRAMAS THAT ILLUMINATE OUR VIEW OF WHAT'S NORMAL

Friday, January 26, 1979

New York

In the theater the abnormal has often served as a device to illuminate what most people think of as normal. The latest examples are two plays currently playing off-Broadway.

The Elephant Man, now at the Theater of St. Peter's Church, is based on the true story of John Merrick, a grotesque figure who lived in England in the late 18th Century. Grossly misshapen, Merrick had unsightly protuberances of flesh on his head and much of his body — hence the name Elephant Man. The present production quite wisely does not attempt to show an actor made up like Merrick. Actor Philip Anglim, who plays Merrick, confines himself to hiding his body in a twisted posture and speaking with great difficulty.

The emphasis in author Bernard Pomerance's play is not on Merrick's deformity but on the mirror he provides for "normal" people around him. In a series of sharply etched scenes *The Elephant Man* depicts the way in which Merrick is rescued from a freak show existence by Dr. Frederick Treves (Kevin Conway) and given a home in the London Hospital. A famous actress, Mrs. Kendal (Carole Shelley) befriends him, and in due time Merrick becomes a pet of London society, including members of the royal family.

Gifts of silver-headed canes and silver combs and brushes are showered on him, and his bulbous body is dressed in striped trousers and morning coat. To all appearances, he has found a group of selfless benefactors, but the incisive writing of author Pomerance shows that virtually every act of charity cuts two ways and raises serious questions about the value-system and compassion of his patrons.

Dr Treves's idea of a normal life for Merrick is that of an upper-class English gentleman, who adheres to a strict code of behavior. Though Merrick has been rescued from a life of brutal harshness, he has been thrust into a social prison that is all the more frustrating because everyone pretends he is now free.

An official of the hospital sees in Merrick the opportunity to tap charities for gifts to the hospital. The money that comes pouring in provides for Merrick's care, but it also represents a tidy sum for the institution. The society figures that take Merrick on as a cause see a direct relation between the enormity of his malformation and their own generosity; by helping this one man they can atone for a multitude of sins to others.

Mrs. Kendal, the most warmhearted of all, responds to an overture of love in a way that can never be fulfilled and that only hastens Merrick's eventual realization of isolation and betrayal.

In the last few scenes of the play Mr. Pomerance abandons the hard-edged logic of the first part and chases philosophical phantoms but through most of the evening his astute treatment of this unlikely subject makes *The Elephant Man* one of the best new plays of the season.

Also, the play is helped immeasurably by the accomplished playing of the principal actors and by the crisp, clear, tasteful direction of Jack Hofsiss.

British to the Core — and Common to Us All

Tuesday, April 3, 1979

New York

Any actor interested in learning how to play comedy should hasten to the Brooks Atkinson Theatre to see Michael Gough, Joan Hickson, Stephen Moore and their colleagues in action. These exemplary performers are currently displaying their incomparable comic technique in Alan Ayckbourn's *Bedroom Farce*. The play, imported from Britain's National Theatre, opened last week.

In the past Mr. Ayckbourn's comedies that attempted to cross the Atlantic, *Absurd Person Singular* and *The Norman Conquests* — have fared only moderately well. By contrast, *Bedroom Farce* should be a solid success. This is partly because of the play itself, one of the funniest to arrive on Broadway in some time, and partly because of the performers. *Bedroom Farce* is the first of Mr. Ayckbourn's plays to be presented with its original British cast virtually intact, and it makes a difference.

Bedroom Farce takes place over the course of one night in three bedrooms seen on stage simultaneously. One bedroom belongs to an older couple, Ernest and Delia. It is the night of their anniversary and they have gone to the restaurant where they go once a year to celebrate. When they return, Michael Gough who plays the husband, notes that the restaurant has definitely "gone off." Mr. Gough pronounces such judgments with the complete assurance of a British gentleman who goes to his club every day and is quick to notice that this year's cigars are not up to last year's.

Deciding that they need more food, Mr. Gough suggests that his wife get in her pajamas while he goes for a snack. His words are: "get in your jams while I fetch the sardines," and he delivers the line with a combination of schoolboy enthusiasm and utter urbanity that is second nature to the British.

It is not only the Britishisms that Mr. Gough and his colleagues handle with complete aplomb it is just plain comic timing. Joan Hickson, who plays his wife, is not certain they should be eating in bed. Mr. Gough, fish on toast held in his hand, pauses a long time —Mr. Gough is a master of the long pause. Finally he has made up his mind. "What the hell" he proclaims with abandon, "you only live once," as he gleefully bites into his toast.

By dwelling on Mr. Gough it should not be inferred that his fellow performers are any less adept than he. Miss Hickson, Stephen Moore as the couple's son Trevor, Delia Lindsay as their distraught daughter-in-law, Susan Littler and Derek Newark as a young couple who have just moved to a new house, Polly Adams as Trevor's former girlfriend, and Michael Stroud as Miss Adams's husband confined to his bed with an excruciating back pain are, almost without exception, superb. The direction of Mr. Ayckbourn and Peter Hall is also first-rate.

If the acting is a model of comic technique, Mr. Ayckbourn's script also offers a textbook lesson in writing contemporary comedy. In *Bedroom Farce*, Mr. Ayckbourn is both exploiting and gently mocking the genre whose name he has taken for his title.

By setting up *three* bedrooms instead of one he can have more doors for people to open unexpectedly. But it is not really the breakneck pace of farce that Mr. Ayckbourn is after. His comedy comes less from people caught in closets than from the foibles of characters trapped in very human situations.

Mr. Ayckbourn's chief plot device is the character of Trevor. Brilliantly played by

Stephen Moore, Trevor wanders through the play like a combination of a bad penny and a tornado. He turns up everywhere and wreaks havoc wherever he goes.

The couple in the new home is having a housewarming party. Trevor arrives and in short order has a fight with his wife, tumbling over beds and lampshades. Next he is in the arms of his former girl friend. (Their single kiss is the only unchaste act in this bedroom farce.) Thanks to Trevor's behavior the guests flee the party before the hostess has the food on the buffet.

Trevor's most exasperating habit, though, is his insistence on offering profuse apologies whenever he does something wrong. Rather than making things better, his apologies invariably create a situation for absolute disaster.

Just as Mr. Ayckbourn does not rely heavily on the usual revolving-door plot devices, neither does he rely solely on comic one-liners for his dialog. The funniest moments in Bedroom Farce derive from situations and characters. After their guests have prematurely departed, the couple in the new home is in their bedroom. Derek Newark, the husband, is on the floor fiercely concentrating on assembling a wooden desk from a kit. Susan Littler as his wife, is kneeling on the bed deep in thought. She ponders the fact that she is not as strange and unpredictable as Trevor's wife. Thinking he is reassuring her, Mr. Newark casually comments: "Mrs. Normal, that's you."

Miss Littler does not reply. She stares ahead with a troubled look on her face. It slowly dawns on the audience that this is just what she is worrying about: perhaps she is too normal. Miss Littler continues to look troubled. Without a word, the laughter grows and grows.

The characters and milieu of Bedroom Farce are British to the core, but the situations that lead to the laughter are common to us all.

Along with the comedy in the play it becomes apparent during the evening that in dealing with his couples Mr. Ayckbourn makes a number of astute observations about the institution of marriage. The point of the evening is not philosophy, however; it is to see marvelous performers in a very funny play. In this regard, a word of warning: the British cast is only scheduled to remain for the first two or three months.

NICKLEBY: MARVELOUS MELODRAMA AT $100 A SEAT

Friday, October 9, 1981

New York

First things first. Anyone interested in taking part in one of the rare theater experiences of our time should plan to be in New York before Jan. 3. That's the last day he can immerse himself in *The Life and Adventures of Nicholas Nickelby*, the dramatization of Charles Dickens's novel by the Royal Shakespeare Company.

Immerse is the proper word. The production is in two parts and altogether takes over nine and half hours. On Wednesdays, Saturdays and Sundays, it begins at 2:00 p.m., except for one intermission in the afternoon, an hour's break for dinner and two short intermissions in the evening, it lasts until 11:40 p.m. People bring apples and chocolate bars to eat during intermissions and by the end of the evening they and their neighbors have become old friends.

Seeing *Nicholas Nickleby* is different from attending an ordinary show not only because of the time factor, but more because during the evening everyone present is transported to England in the 1830s. As the audience comes into the Plymouth Theater, they are greeted by catwalks and scaffolding of rough timbers ropes and wrought iron. The set, designed by John Napier and Dermot Hayes, is the stage.

Performers — the women in bonnets and long dresses, the men in knee breeches and waistcoats, stroll through the theater talking to members of the audience. The 14-piece offstage orchestra sounds a fanfare, the 39 cast members assemble on stage in a tableau, and the play begins.

During the journey the cast wearing 375 costumes will portray 137 characters.

With an imaginative use of props they will create stage-coaches, taverns, schools, offices and drawing rooms that look as if they had come to life from prints of the period.

In the story, when their father dies, young Nicholas Nickleby (Roger Bees) and his sister Kate (Emily Richard) are left in poverty with their mother (Priscilla Morgan) a foolish loquacious woman. Their uncle Ralph (John Woodvine), a rich, heartless moneylender, sends Nicholas to teach at a boys' school in Yorkshire that is a prison-like institution for misfits. Soon Nicholas turns on the headmaster and leaves, taking with him Smike (David Threlfall), a half-witted boy who has known nothing but cruelty.

The rest of the play is taken up with the adventures of Nicholas — as a member of a theatrical troupe, in confrontations with his uncle and other sinister characters, in his oft thwarted pursuit of the lovely Madeline Bray (Lucy Gutteridge). Finally, he finds success working in the firm of the Cheeryble brothers (David Lloyd Meredith and Hubert Rees). Meanwhile, his sister Kate undergoes her own adventures in a dress shop and is the victim of two degenerate noblemen.

Dickens wrote *Nicholas Nickleby* in 1838, when he was 26. It is a sprawling novel that succeeds on several levels. On one, it is a vivid depiction of life in London and the provinces. On another level, it is an incredible gallery of idiosyncratic but all-too-human characters: Mr. and Mrs. Wackford Squeers, a sadistic schoolmaster and his equally sadistic wife; Mr. and Mrs. Crummles, managers of a provincial theater, company; Newman Noggs, a down-at-the-heels but kindly office clerk; Mrs. Mantalini, a dress shop owner who falls prey again and again to the false protestations of her profligate husband.

On a third level, *Nicholas Nickleby* is a marvelous melodrama, with a complex plot that pushes us ever forward to the next episode and a full complement of good and evil characters. The good suffer and the wicked prosper, but in the end all comes right.

Scene after scene cries out to be dramatized, and probably the best company in the world to answer the cry is the Royal Shakespeare. Formed in 1960, it plays at Stratford and London, and has sent 29 productions to the U.S. Through the years it has developed a fluid style for Shakespeare and the classics that make full use of suggestive staging. With a gesture from an actor, a prop (a wicker hamper or a Regency chair) or a sound effect (the clopping of horses' hoofs) a complete world is created in the audience's imagination. At the same time, the acting is extraordinary. In *Nicholas Nickleby* most actors play many roles, each with conviction and style.

Audience members may quarrel with individual scenes or characterizations. For those not familiar with the novel, for instance, a fleeting appearance by a minor character may only prove confusing. Roger Rees in the title role though admirable in his stamina and determination is given to abrupt, staccato gestures and a punctuated vocal delivery that emphasize too heavily the melodrama in Dickens. By contrast, David Threlfall's portrayal of the crippled half-wit Smike is brilliant in its sincerity and understatement.

Such inconsistencies, however, are forgotten as one is swept along in the rush of events. Throughout, adaptor David Edgar and directors Trevor Nunn and John Caird have preserved Dickens's superb comic touch on the one hand and his biting commentary on wretchedness and injustice on the other. So masterful is the overall effect that many will regard seeing *Nicholas Nickleby* as one of the highlights of a lifetime of theatergoing.

One last thought. There has been much discussion, about federal funding for the arts, with some arguing that such funding should be eliminated or sharply curtailed. In this regard, it is worth noting certain facts about *Nicholas Nickleby*. The cost of a single ticket for Parts I and II is $100. Even at that, the production is so expensive that U.S. producers will barely break even. As for originating *Nicholas Nickleby*, it would be impossible for any private management. Were it not for the RSC, a subsidized non-profit organization, this unforgettable production would not exist.

THEATER: OF RELATIONS EROTIC AND DIPLOMATIC

Tuesday, March 22, 1988

New York

Playwright David Henry Hwang has something to say and an original, audacious way of saying it. Right away that makes him a rarity on Broadway. In his new play M. *Butterfly*, which just opened at the Eugene O'Neill Theater he ingeniously has woven together a real-life story and events from Puccini's opera *Madame Butterfly*.

The true story is one of the most bizarre of recent history. In the mid-1960's a French diplomat assigned to a post in Beijing fell in love with and began a long term affair with an actress in the Chinese opera. Nearly 20 years later, after he had returned to Paris, his mistress followed him with an infant she claimed was their son. French authorities quickly seized her and charged her with being a spy. Both the diplomat and his paramour were convicted of espionage.

The most incredible twist of the story, however, was that at the trial it emerged that the diplomat's mistress of 20 years was actually a man. The diplomat, professing total ignorance of this fact, stated that he was "shocked."

In M. *Butterfly*, Mr. Hwang makes no attempt to recreate factual history; rather, he uses the story as the basis for a provocative look at the way men view Asian women and the West views the East. It is his contention that there is a close parallel between the two, and this is where *Madame Butterfly* comes in.

The opera Mr. Hwang claims, is written entirely from a Western, chauvinist position; from the Asian point of view, it is patently absurd. "What would you say," a character in M. *Butterfly* asks, "if a blond homecoming queen fell in love with a short Japanese businessman?" He treats her cruelly, and then goes home for three years, during which time she prays to his picture and turns down marriage from a young Kennedy. Then, when she learns he has remarried, she kills herself. Now, I believe you would consider this girl to be a deranged idiot, correct? This is exactly, however, what Lt. Pinkerton of the opera expects of his bride Cho Cho San. The leading character of M. *Butterfly*, whom Mr. Hwang calls Gallimard, looks at Asian women just as Lt. Pinkerton did.

The play begins with Gallimard in prison, looking back on the events of his life with Song, the opera star. We see Gallimard when he first encounters Song as a performer in the Chinese opera. Watching her delicate movements and modest demeanor as she glides gracefully across the floor Gallimard is smitten. Gradually the two see more and more of each other. Gallimard has a wife, Helga (Rose Gregorio) but he becomes increasingly infatuated with Song. Her shyness in refusing to make love or remove her clothes only adds to her appeal. Mostly, though, it is the way she flatters him and feeds his male ego. Gallimard, who is unprepossessing looking, always has been awkward with women. Song makes him feel confident — and superior. They take an apartment where they meet regularly. Eventually he divorces Helga and marries Song.

Throughout the play, events from *Madame Butterfly* are cleverly interspersed with scenes from Gallimard's life; Gallimard even calls Song his "butterfly." All the while, Song is deceiving Gallimard, not only with regard to her sex, but in her work as a spy, as we learn when we see her routinely interrogated by Comrade Chin (Lori Tan Chinn).

Mr. Hwang's tale is made all the more electrifying thanks to key elements in the production. Among these are the stunning scenery and costume designs of

Eiko Ishioka. Ms. Ishioka who, like Mr. Hwang, is making her Broadway debut, has fashioned a vivid Chinese-red backdrop that envelops the entire stage. Three *kurogo* (the black clad invisible stagehands of Asian theater), move Chinese screens and curtain embroidered with lotus flowers across the stage to change scenes. The kimonos and dresses Ms. Ishioka has created for Song are as exquisite as any female impersonator could wish for.

Another plus is the performance of the two principals. As Gallimard, John Lithgow is giving his finest stage performance to date. In the past Mr. Lithgow has played everything from a newspaper reporter to a heavyweight boxer but here he is required to embody a wide range in one role. One moment he is an awkward schoolboy, the next an ambitious diplomat, and then an enraptured lover. With agile gestures and an expressive face, he mirrors joy and torment, pain and self-delusion with equal effectiveness.

Matching Mr. Lithgow's performance is B.D. Wong's portrayal of Song. As a star of Chinese opera or a shy seductress, he moves with grace and dignity. Then in a scene where he ritualistically removes his female makeup he is transformed before our eyes into an unrepentant male spy.

The production is not without flaws. One is director John Dexter's tendency to give way to excess theatricality. As an example, several secondary characters such as Gallimard's old school chum, a sexually liberated French woman and Comrade Chin, are played as broad stereotypes which work against the subtlety and sincerity evinced by the principals and there are times, too, when Mr. Hwang's story goes astray. The difficulty for everyone — both in the true story and the play — is accepting the idea that a man could have a long-term love affair with someone who he thought was a woman but was actually a man. Mr. Hwang's attempts to provide explanations are not always convincing.

Fortunately, the main thrust of his argument — and the thesis of his whole play — is that some people live largely in fantasies and dreams. Gallimard lived in such a fantasy. The idea is that Asian women, and indeed Asian nations, are inferior and readily accept the subordinate position to the Westerners they flatter and serve. When those fantasies come face to face with a quite different reality, one view must give way. In a striking and unexpected finale Mr. Hwang shows that given the choice between his fantasy and the true state of affairs Gallimard must cling to the former, even if it means sacrificing his life.

MUSICALS

Grease: A Memoir of '50's Youth

Wednesday, June 14, 1972

New York

The 1980s was a transitional period for growing up in this country. The time just after World War II was not too different from that just before. Values had been held in suspense during the war, and when it was over people wanted to reassert them and pick up where they had left off. In the 1950s, however, there was a stirring among young people, a restlessness of more than seasonal proportions. They were standing on a threshold just before starting on the road that eventually led to hippies, the counter-culture, and the new freedom.

No one knew that at the time, of course, especially the young themselves. They felt the desires, confusions, and frustrations all teenagers feel, not realizing they were poised so precipitously between the old and new. It is this tension that has been caught so remarkably well in *Grease*, a musical that played downtown and has just moved to Broadway's Broadhurst Theatre.

One of its many virtues is that it is firmly rooted in a specific time and place. It deals with a high school class of 1959. It is a public school and the students are largely Catholic, clean-cut kids who edit the yearbook or go out for sports. The boys — members of a gang who call themselves the Burger Boys — are interested in girls and cars, the latter as souped up as possible. The girls, called the Pink Ladies, are interested in boys and the latest hairstyle. This is the group which feels most strongly the tug of the daring and defiant and hence is caught most strongly in the cross current.

The authors have not simply looked at them from the outside — the boys in black jackets, the girls in pleated skirts just below the knees, using terms like "groovy" — they have gone inside. They show us a world in which boys speak of school in the most profane and vulgar terms imaginable, but become the model of respectfulness the moment their teacher, Miss Lynch, appears on the scene. School and its attendant institutions are still important.

It is a world in which no matter how convulsive the dancing becomes — with the snapping and jerking inspired by Elvis the Pelvis — the boys and girls still dance together and hold on to one another. The boys let their hair grow long in outrageous ducktails but it is not unruly. It is slicked down with vast quantities of grease, and they stand with combs always at the ready.

The tension between old and new is retained even in the humor, of which there is a great deal and which is handled with just the right note of self-mockery. The song,

"Look At Me, I'm Sandra Dee," satirizes the saccharin, sweet purity of Miss Dee and Doris Day, and the effect is enhanced when it is sung by the most obviously promiscuous girl in school. Another girl, an empty-headed number who leaves school and then beauty school, is visited by an angel — Elvis Presley dressed in white — who tells her in song that she is a Beauty School Dropout and should go back. We forget how recently it is that young people did not drop out. Time and again we are reminded how much has happened in a few, short years. A boy on a picnic is told he will have to go to Confession because, he is reminded, it is Friday and he is eating a cheeseburger.

It is the insight into the period undoubtedly, which accounts for the success of the show. The music is infectious, the actors perform with verve and energy and it has marvelous pace, but these alone would not explain why it should have caught on to the point where it has been given new life on Broadway. Rather, it is the straightforward unsentimental look it affords us of the beginning of everything that happened to young people in the Sixties and has persisted into the Seventies. It pin-points it beautifully, and it is all there; the vulgarity, the letting down the bars, the open rebellion but still only as a glimmer in the eyes of the young and under the watchful eye of the home-room teacher.

CHARLEMAGNE, MAGIC AND MUSIC

Tuesday, October 24, 1972

New York

The American musical is alive and well and living in the eighth century, A.D. That is the period of *Pippin* which opened last night at the Imperial Theater and was seen by this reviewer at a preview. Pippin, played by John Rubinstein, is the oldest son of Charlemagne, and in the musical he is trying to find himself. Successively he tries being scholar, soldier, libertine, and even ruler of the Holy Roman Empire. As he fails or becomes bored with each one, he continues his search: he wishes to be extraordinary, and will not settle for anything less. In the end, however, he does settle for the ordinary, in the persons of a wife and child, and perhaps lives happily ever after.

At the same time Pippin is Charlemagne's son, he is also a modern young man, and while the play is set in the eighth century, it invokes modern times as well. Modern in this case means pre-World War II, particularly the show business of that era: vaudeville, burlesque and radio.

The production is conceived as a magic show. The curtain rises on a sheet of smoke through which we see illuminated white hands — no bodies or faces — but stark white hands suspended in a black void. The effect is startling, but it is only the beginning. An M.C., or Leading Player as he is called, stuffs a red handkerchief into his fist. It disappears and he displays his empty hand. He goes to a crack in the floor, and pulls out the handkerchief; it opens into swags of red silk and arches of rope that rise to the ceiling across the entire stage, framing the court of Charlemagne. It is a spectacular feat. But the magic of *Pippin* is more than handkerchief tricks; it is theater magic of a kind we have not seen for a long time.

Most American musicals follow trends: shows made from movies, for example, such as *Sugar*, *Zorba*, and *Promises*; or nostalgia musicals (*No, No, Nanette*, et al.). When someone comes along with a period as unlikely as the eighth century or a hero as unlikely as Pippin, we know they are leading and not following; and we are grateful for their originality, especially when they make it work.

And *Pippin* does work. The juxtaposition between medieval history and modern show business is often brilliant. Pippin's stepmother, Fastada, wants the throne for her own son, Louis. As played by Leland Palmer, Fastada is a burlesque queen of a very high order, like the women in the audience. Her musical number plotting Pippin's downfall is the best bump and grinding routine to be seen in New York since Mayor LaGuardia closed down burlesque.

After his failures Pippin is taken in by a young widow who has a small son and a large estate. When he tells her he is in despair, she answers by telling him her tale of woe. As she begins, organ music — a theme from quintessential soap opera — swells in the background. There is even an audience sing-along led by Charlemagne's mother with a bouncing ball moving over the words on a large medieval scroll.

The most chilling counterpoint though, occurs when Pippin goes to war. The battle is a minstrel show with an interlocutor and end men: as soldiers die in tableau in the background, three dancers with straw hats and canes do a superb soft shoe down front. It is quite possibly the most original and telling anti-war number the American musical has produced.

Pippin is not a perfect show: one or two numbers are overlong, and it gets a bit coy at times, particularly toward the end when the M.C. calls an actress by her real name. But it is close enough for now. This is what the American musical should be: using the vast resources of dance, music, scenery, and lighting we have developed to serve an original idea.

The parts of *Pippin* are exceptional — the fresh music and lyrics of Stephen Schwartz: the stained glass figures on Tony Walton's scenery; the commedia dell'arte costumes with their false noses and half masks; the strutting choreography of Bob Fosse; and the superior performances. But more than that, the parts fit the whole; no matter how far the show goes toward fantasy, it always returns to Pippin's simple story.

What other recent musicals — *Follies*, to name one — have tried to do, *Pippin* has succeeded in doing, and we can breathes a brief sigh of relief. Though no one wishes to say it out loud, the American musical has been suffering a serious decline. *Pippin* cannot turn that around single-handed, but its taste, imagination, and discipline point us in the right direction. In the meantime, like the boy Pippin himself, we have found happiness for a while.

A Musical Show with Elegance

Tuesday, February 27, 1978

New York

As the second act of *A Little Night Music* begins we see the green lawn of a country estate, surrounded by graceful white birch trees, with a handsome chateau in the background. Madame Armfeldt, the owner, is sitting at tea while her family plays croquet, the women in large hats and long dresses. It is pastoral and elegant. What makes the tableau breathtaking is that everyone is dressed in pure white, with only a touch of pale color here and there.

Refinement, beauty and romance: these are the hallmarks of this new musical which just opened at the Shubert Theatre. There are many, no doubt, who will welcome these qualities back like long lost friends.

In recent times it often looked as if earthiness and seediness had won the day completely in the Broadway musical. We have had *Hair*, *Grease*, and any number of other musicals celebrating youth and untidiness. Even the ones with style carried a downbeat message: *Company* presented the sour side of marriage and *Follies*, the disillusionment of glamour.

Ironically, the very men who brought us *Company* and *Follies*, Harold Prince, the director and producer, and Stephen Sondheim, the composer and lyricist, are the ones pushing the pendulum back again in *A Little Night Music*. Sociologists can make it what they will, but romance and the finer things have made their way back to Broadway.

* * *

All those qualities we look for in such musicals are here: tasteful scenery, gorgeous costumes, handsome actors, beautiful actresses and in the case of Glynis Johns, the heroine, an enchanting woman. The play is set in Sweden at the turn of the century. The people live well and have servants; they entertain properly and best of all fall madly in love. As befits the genre, there are several romances which after the proper amount of confusion and indecision fall happily in place.

No small part of the tone of the evening is due to Stephen Sondheim's music and lyrics. Many of the songs are in three-quarter time. The waltz after all is the music of romance. It is in the lyrics, however, that Sondheim once more comes into his own. He is the cleverest lyricists working today, and *A Little Night Music* will do nothing to dim his record. From *West Side Story* and *Gypsy* straight through, he has brought a freshness and vigor to his words which few can match.

Who else would think of rhyming "cigar butt" with "he was bizarre but . . . " or let a woman tell us that following an affair with a noble-man she did not leave empty-handed: she had acquired position "plus a tiny Titian." He brings his full talent to bear on two or three songs which make for near-perfect musical numbers. There is one where a man sings to his mistress. "You must meet my wife," while she sings words which counterpoint his in more ways than one.

* * *

Alas, as often happens at *soigné* affairs, there are moments where the fun runs down and the champagne goes a trifle flat. *A Little Night Music* is based on Ingmar Bergman's film classic, *Smiles of a Summer Night*. (The current predilection for using films as source material for Broadway musicals is a phenomenon in itself.) In structure and finesse the musical cannot touch the original film. The latter had four couples held apart in fascinating suspension for most of the action who came together at the finish in a brilliant unraveling. The musical needlessly short circuits some of the connections and telescopes others taking away both mystery and surprise.

There are minor problems too, such as an opening ballet which presages the action of the play: it is superfluous for those who know the story, and means nothing to those who don't.

These problems should not deter anyone however, who has been awaiting the return of elegance to Broadway. What if the book falls short of the film, or one or two moments are less than magical? It is still the handsomest show in town, lovely to look at and a pleasure to hear. A song in the show extols the benefits of "A Weekend in the Country." A *Little Night Music* offers us the same: a chance to get away, to taste the good life and even to toy with romance. Who can argue with that?

Bring on the Dancing Girls

Thursday, May 22, 1975

New York

Whenever people in show business write about themselves, there is always the danger that they will be too self-indulgent, or to egomaniacal, or just plain dull. When such an enterprise succeeds, however — as in the case of *Kiss Me, Kate,* for instance — the results can be doubly rewarding for those responsible to know the subject inside out. The most recent example in the latter category is *A Chorus Line,* a new musical which opened last night at the New York Shakespeare Festival's Newman Theater and which this reviewer saw at a preview.

The show concerns exactly what its title suggests — a chorus line. It opens with a group of dancers auditioning for a Broadway show. The stage is bare except at the back we see a series of gigantic mirrors in which are reflected not only the danc-ers but the audience. We are all in on the process. The director-choreographer who is to pick eight dancers from the 24 on hand begins to put them through their paces. The dancers let us know how much they want the job, expressing in song what is on their minds but what they would never say out loud — "I Hope I Get It."

The director moves to the rear of the rehearsal hall and asks the dancers to a line up on a white line which runs across the stage near the footlights. One by one they step forward to give their names, their agents (sometimes reluctantly), and their home towns. Thus begins the process by which we come to know most of these 24 individuals intimately.

One of the signal achievements of *A Chorus Line* is to give a face to those faceless people whose artistry depends on losing themselves in a crowd, on moving in step with everyone else. The group is a genuine cross-section of dancers and we discover that each has a story to tell: the girls who went into ballet because when they danced they felt beautiful or forgot a miserable home life; the young man from an upper middle class home who never conformed to his father's idea of a son — he was terrible at sports and his father, not knowing how to explain this aberration to his friends, told them that the boy had polio; the girl from the Midwest who never aspired to ballet but did long to be a Rockette at Radio City Music Hall.

As the evening progresses we dig deeper into the careers of several dancers. One is Cassie, played by Donna McKechnie, a woman who had once been in love with the director and lived with him. He wanted her to be a star so she left him and went to Hollywood, but she failed and now she wants only to be back in a chorus line. The director thinks she is too good for this and so he doesn't want to hire her, but she pleads with him; she needs the job desperately and besides, she is happiest when she dances. To prove it she starts to dance and at this point Miss McKechnie gives us a solo routine which ranks with the best of them, including Gwen Verdon's better work through the years. It's a number to remember, in show biz parlance, a smasharoo.

Toward the end the director asks the dancers what they will do when they must stop dancing, and they cannot answer. Though the future is uncertain, perhaps even bleak, they love what they are doing too much to worry about that — and perhaps in its own way that is an answer to the future because at least one can then look back on life with joy rather than regret.

And so we have the life of the Broadway show dance — past, present, and future.

But we have more; we have appearance and reality, the façade and what goes on behind it. In musicals we see the facile slick performance. In A *Chorus Line* we see that too because, needless to say the dancing is superb. But we see more. We get a glimpse of the rigor, the discipline, the training, the dedication behind every step. We see how steps are learned and how the dancing part of musicals is put together.

We get to know the dancers so well that toward the close when the losers are eliminated we suffer with them just as we rejoice with the winners. But all is not lost because at the very end the entire cast comes back for a grand finale, one that both they and we have earned. And it does not let us down. In fact, it's so sensational that it's bound to go down in show business annals as one of the most exciting finishes in modern musicals.

A *Chorus Line* could be called a Michael Bennett production because it was conceived, directed, and choreographed by him, but there are others in addition to Bennett and the performers who deserve mention. Marvin Hamlisch has written an excellent score including several quite hummable tunes; Robin Wagner has designed a clever set of louvered mirrors at the rear of the stage; and Tharon Musser has created some extraordinary lighting effects — at times the dancers move through pools of light which change colors and shapes as they change positions, and at other times, lights beam horizontally across the stage just above floor level, giving the dancers a sculptured look.

Naturally, A *Chorus Line* will have special appeal for those who love dancing or who are fascinated by what goes on behind the scenes in the theater, but it has qualities which should prove attractive to many more. A few reservations: in the early stages the pre-pubescent and adolescent confessions go on too long and become a trifle tiresome. Also, toward the end a couple of moments veer toward the sentimental. These are minor quibbles, though. The important thing is that A *Chorus Line* is the best integrated, the most original, and in some ways, the most exciting musical of the season. Recently people have been asking where the new musicals are; for the time being they can stop asking and take a trip down to Lafayette Street for a visit to the Newman Theater.

Show Biz with a Sharp Edge

Thursday, June 5, 1975

New York

It is difficult to determine whether *Chicago*, the new musical which just opened at the 46th Street Theatre, is the last big show of this season or the first big show of next season. The confusion comes because June 1 is traditionally the cut-off point for the theater season. But new shows keep opening with little regard for the time of year. A *Chorus Line*, the biggest musical hit of the year — or of several years, for that matter — opened only a week or so ago, and now we have *Chicago*.

Chicago is based on a 1936 play about the jazz age which in turn was made into a silent movie and then into *Roxie Hart*, a 1942 film starring Ginger Rogers and Adolph Menjou. All versions, including the latest, tell of Roxie, a Chicago murderess who meets up with a clever lawyer while in jail.

She feigns pregnancy, and that, together with the help of her attorney's wiles, wins her an acquittal. The previous versions have been lighthearted spoofs of the Roaring Twenties and the world of gangsters and speakeasies. The current version has all of that but has considerable bite as well.

This is due, no doubt, to Bob Fosse, the director, choreographer, and co-author of *Chicago*. Those familiar with Mr. Fosse's previous work — particularly the film version of *Cabaret* and the musical *Pippin* — know that he is fond of seeing show business as a metaphor for various aspects of life. Here he has carried the notion further: murder, bribery, law and justice are all seen as facets of the entertainment world; and criminals, lawyers, judges and jurors are characters in a play. Building a case is like writing a script: appearing on a witness stand is like acting in one.

Mr. Fosse makes his image obvious at the start. A band plays Chicago-style jazz on a high platform enclosed by an art deco railing. In front of the band is an old-fashioned microphone with a center piece suspended from wires in a large circle. Lights on the translucent scenery illuminate figures looking like those from a John Held cartoon, and every segment of the story is seen as a song and dance routine. An announcer says, "And now, ladies and gentleman, a tap dance," and we see a scene with Roxie persuading her hapless husband to raise money for the lawyer while in the background, four men in bowler hats do a tap routine.

The same husband later dons the costume of a pathetic baggy-pants comedian, including gloves with no fingers and oversized, floppy shoes, to sing a touching number telling us he is the cellophane man whom no one sees — and in the middle of the number he has a scene with the lawyer which proves the truth of his assertion. A woman in prison with Roxie who is to be hanged is presented as a high-wire performer in the circus. Just before her limp body is seen hanging from a rope in silhouette, she takes off her prison garb to reveal an acrobat's spangled outfit and proceeds to climb a rope ladder to a high wire where she will "perform" her act.

Some numbers are stunning. The lawyer, who cares only about money, sings a marvelously ironic song, "All I Care About is Love," backed by six statuesque girls wafting huge fans more deftly than Sally Rand ever could. Later, when the lawyer is coaching Roxie in her statement, he becomes a ventriloquist and she a dummy mouthing his words. With every number there is a chorus of dancers in the background commenting on the action, sometimes in slow-motion, at other times with enormous energy. There are cakewalks, Charlestons, and soft shoes: all bearing the Fosse trademark of hard-edged, angular movement executed with verve and precision.

Of great assistance to Mr. Fosse are three veteran performers who have show business in their blood and know how to sell a song or dance as few can: Gwen Verdon as Roxie, Chita Rivera as one of her prison mates, and Jerry Orbach as the lawyer. Worth mentioning, too, are the stylish, incisive songs of Fred Ebb and John Kander, the sets of Tony Walton and the highly imaginative costumes of Patricia Zipprodt.

Unfortunately individual numbers in Chicago are better than the whole. Mr. Fosse's energy does not falter but his invention does, and banality creeps into several scenes. Also, many will feel that the show is too reminiscent of Mr. Fosse's earlier work. In spite of these lapses, however, and the show's uneven-ness, Chicago makes its point. The number summing up its meaning is "Razzle Dazzle," in which the lawyer insists of his trade that "It's all a circus, it's all a show." If you make enough noise, he says, "how can they hear the truth above the roar?"

Mr. Fosse is saying that three elements in our society — the media, trial law and show business — have much in common. In their theatricality, their desire for sensationalism, and their emphasis on razzle dazzle they are inextricably intertwined. In our world we turn criminals into heroes and heroines and dramatize their deeds to the point where we cannot tell fact from fiction. Crime becomes glamorous, no matter how rotten.

Director-choreographers like Mr. Fosse and Michael Bennett of A Chorus Line increasingly are finding ways to combine genuine entertainment — with all the appeal of the song and dance — with trenchant comments about our life and times. Slowly

— by fits and starts — the American musical is coming of age and entering a new era. Despite a few faults *Chicago* is moving in that mainstream. Besides, it follows its own dictum and absolutely bedazzles the eyes.

THE ENCHANTING LENA HORNE

Friday, May 15, 1981

New York

Singer Lena Horne in her new musical revue on Broadway speaks about the mishaps in her career: "my timing was notoriously bad."

In times past, when she just missed a role given to a white woman, her timing might have been off, but just now it is perfect. Her show, "Lena Horne: The Lady and Her Music," which opened this week at the Nederlander Theatre, is a triumph in every way.

First of all, it is a victory over the past. The show consists almost entirely of Ms. Horne singing songs identified with her career. The only other performers — aside from a superb on-stage band — are three singers and dancers who back her up occasionally in a routine from Cotton Club days.

From time to time Ms. Horne interpolates autobiographical details and makes it clear that she experienced rough times during her career. There were days in Hollywood, for example, when no one knew what to do about her color. Max Factor even invented a make-up called "Light Egyptian," to make her darker, but then the part was given to Ava Gardner and the make-up was used on her. Another time Ms. Horne reminds us that she went for 22 years between movie roles, until recently when she had a small part in *The Wiz*.

Through her early years Ms. Horne had to look pretty and remain quiet about how it felt to be trapped by her color. Now she is throwing off the restraints of the past and speaking frankly about her experiences. She has not forgotten them. In songs like "Life Goes On," she exalts in the fact that she has endured and remained an energetic woman.

And what a woman! With

242

her shining eyes, sparkling teeth, sculptured features and slender figure, she is one of the truly beautiful women of the world. At 63 she looks 29 years younger. She also sings like someone 20 years younger, and that is what brings the audience to its feet, not once but several times.

Unlike most singers as the years pass, her voice has not gone husky or lost its force and timbre. In fact, she has never sounded better. The control, the infinitely varied tones, the impeccable phrase and the telling hand gestures, perfectly matched to the lyrics, are the marks of a singer at the height of her powers.

In some love songs, such as "I'm Glad There is You," Ms. Horne turns introspective; she appears to forget the audience and loses herself in the intensity of the moment. At other times she reaches out, quite literally, making contact with the audience in a way that only a performer with her assurance and magnetism can.

There are plenty of expected moments — Cole Porter songs like "From this Moment On" and "Just One of Those Things" — but there are unexpected ones too. She sings a straightforward "The Surrey with the Fringe on Top," and gives every phrase a fresh meaning.

Part of Ms. Horne's secret is her ability to be a lady and low-down at the same time. She sings all the sexy — and usually omitted — lyrics to "Bewitched, Bothered and Bewildered," and makes their meaning unmistakable. When she sings "The Lady is a Tramp," she does not hold back on the bumps and grinds of the tramp part. But no matter how suggestive she becomes, she remains always a lady.

Twice during the night, she sings, as no one else can, her theme song, "Stormy Weather." Ms. Horne has been through her share of storms but in the months ahead on Broadway there will be nothing but fair skies for her — and her unceasing applause.

In the Musical *Nine*, the Women Rate a Ten

Tuesday, May 11, 1982

New York

As *Nine*, the new musical at the 46th Street Theatre, begins to unfold it has the look of a musical that can't go wrong. The curtain rises on a set that is stunning in its simplicity and grandeur — a vast space of white tiles designed by Lawrence Miller that looks as if it is a high-tech spa, which is what it later turns out to be. The spa is in Venice and when the hero decides to go there, a backdrop rises behind the tall, open windows at the rear to reveal a glorious panorama of Venice across the water. The city glows in the distance and the spa's white tiles turn silver blue and deep red.

The action at the start is no less breathtaking. *Nine* is based on 8 ½, Federico Fellini's autobiographical film about a filmmaker who must come up with a new movie but has run out of ideas. He goes to a spa to try to collect his thoughts and while there his fantasy world and the real world, his past and present, continually collide.

In *Nine*, actor Raul Julia plays the filmmaker Guido Contini who has some of the same experiences. Central to his problems is his attachment to many women at the same time: his wife Luisa (Karen Akers) Carla, a creature of pure sex and Claudia, a film actress.

It is the ingenuous conceit of director-choreographer Tommy Tune to have 21 women as the principal performers in the musical; they enact the many fantasies of Guido's life including his frequent returns to childhood. At the opening Guido is sitting center stage on a cube of white tile, but gradually the women in his life enter, each one dressed in a striking black outfit designed by William Ivey Long. When they are assembled, Guido raises a baton and conducts them like an orchestra. It is a show-stopping number almost before the show has begun.

The music and the lyrics for Nine are by Maury Yeston, a professor of music at Yale, who began writing this score, appropriately enough, nine years ago. Its numerous lovely melodies give the music a complexity and sophistication many notches above the usual Broadway score. Mario Fratti adapted the Fellini movie from the Italian which Arthur Kopit then developed into a libretto. To take us in and out of the past, in and out of reality, Mr. Kopit and Mr. Tune have created a fluid, seamless form that seems the ultimate in a modern Broadway musical. We move from one musical metaphor to another. Mr. Tune has an unfailing eye for movement and pictorialization: as a result the first act is as stylish and exciting as anything on Broadway.

Guido has come to Venice to rest, but his mistress Carla has followed him there and calls, asking him to come see her. (Guido tells his wife the call is from the Vatican.) When she arrives, she wears a dress made entirely of see-through black lace and writhes her way through the sexiest, most suggestive dance number seen in many years.

Later, Guido's film producer, Liliane, (Liliane Montevecchi) questions him about the film he is supposed to be making. He says he plans to make an art film, but she insists she wants only entertainment, tosses off her black fur hat and jacket and proceeds to show what she means in a sensational number called "Folies Bergeres."

In the second act Guido begins making his movie — the story of Casanova — but he has run out of ideas and so he tries to overwhelm his viewers with effects: The women trade in their black outfits for green and white ones, pink and white ones and 17th century ball gowns. And at this point, it becomes clear that the creators of *Nine* are having the same problems with their musical that Guido is with his film. They also substitute effects for ideas.

Throughout we have witnessed not only Guido's entanglements with women, but his conflict between his sexual desires and his strict upbringing in the Catholic Church, his struggle between being a grown-up and remaining a boy (the only males in the show other than Mr. Julia are a young Guido played by Cameron Johann, and three school chums the same age), and Guido's fear that he has lost his creative talent.

What is the root of his trouble? Will he be able to work his way through it? Does his story have any significance for the rest of us? Implicitly these are questions the play raises, but for which it has no answers. At the end of *Nine*, Guido's movie fails and his women all leave him, but what does this mean? Rather than answer the question, *Nine* provides us with one final striking effect: the women reappear on stage once more but this time in dazzling white rather than in black.

If, with its failure to come to grips with its subject, *Nine* turns out not to be the revelation we are looking for in new musicals, it provides a great deal to enjoy: the stylish music of Mr. Yeston, the daring form of Mr. Kopit's book, a number of strong performances, including Mr. Julia's and the indelible stage picture of Mr. Tune.

BROADWAY GETS BITCHY

Monday, December 18, 1989

New York

There is a great moment at the end of act one of *City of Angels* that brings the modern American musical slam-bang against Pirandello, the Italian playwright who was fascinated with the relationship of reality to fiction and of life to art.

In *City of Angels*, which opened recently at the Virginia Theatre, Stine (Gregg Edelman), a young novelist turned screen writer, has created a hard-boiled private eye named Stone (James Naughton), the hero of a detective movie in the Raymond Chandler mold. The character is giving Stine trouble, and at the close of the first act when both men — the real and the reel one — are on stage, an angry Stine turns to Stone and sings, "You're nothing without me, without me you're nothing at all." Of course this is true: Stone is a fictional creation of Stine's and would not exist without him. But then the film detective turns on his creator and sings the same lyrics to him: "you're nothing without me, without me you're nothing at all." Suddenly we realize that this is equally true: in a very real way, a writer has his truest existence in the characters he creates. Seeing the two performers on stage, hurling these truths at each other in song, brings this Pirandellian idea home in a way even the master himself would have approved.

This unexpected revelation is only one of many surprises in *City of Angels*. The time of the story is the late 1940s. Stine has written a novel that a Hollywood mogul, Buddy Fidler (Rene Auberjonois), plans to direct as a movie. The novelist's wife (Kay McClelland) accuses him of selling out, and quickly beats a retreat back to her job in

New York. Stine, however, is convinced he can retain his integrity as he turns his detective story into a screenplay.

The script concerns a tough-guy private eye who is hired by the sexy wife of a millionaire to find his missing daughter Mallory (Rachel York). No sooner has Stone taken the job than two tough guys in broad-brimmed fedoras, one towering (Herschel Sparber) and the other tiny (Raymond Xifo), accost him in his bungalow and give him the beating of his life. Naturally he survives, just the way Sam Spade and Philip Marlow always did.

In *City of Angels* all the scenes from the movie are shown in black and white, exactly like the films of the '30s and '40s. It is here that the designers — Robin Wagner (sets), Florence Kiotz (costumes) and Paul Gallo (lighting) — have wrought a miracle. As we move from the real-life scenes to the ones in the movie, a mansion, an office, a seedy bedroom suddenly appear from nowhere and just as quickly disappear. These movie scenes are stunning in their various shades of black, white and gray, the women's clothes fancy white silk or slinky black satin. Just as smooth as the scene changes is director Michael Blakemore's blending of the multilayered action.

The music for *City of Angels* is by Cy Coleman and the lyrics are by David Zippel. There are very few boffo numbers, one exception being "You Can Always Count on Me" delivered by Randy Graff who plays the hard-luck secretary who loses her man in both the movie and real life. But Mr. Coleman's movie-style underscoring is sensation, with wailing saxophones, blaring trumpets and soaring violins. There's even a Bing Crosby-type crooner (Scott Waara) and four doo-wop backup singers.

In the end the film mogul, Buddy Fidler, does completely take over the movie, and Stine realizes he has been both corrupted and betrayed.

But he recovers his integrity just in time. Meanwhile Hollywood is held up to hilarious ridicule by author Larry Gelbart. *City of Angels* is a writer's revenge on Hollywood — and what sweet revenge it is. Mr. Gelbart, one of the cleverest wordsmiths working today, not only captures the spirit of the film-noir, he delivers one knock-out punch line after another. The material is familiar, but served with such relish you may think you're seeing it for the first time.

* * *

Revivals

A Well-Handled O'Neill Classic

Tuesday, November 21, 1979

New York

The opening last week of a new production of Eugene O'Neill's *Mourning Becomes Electra* provided two landmarks, one new and fairly minor and the other somewhat older and more substantial. The new one is the theater itself: The Circle in the Square Joseph E. Levine Theatre situated in the basement of the new Uris Building. Although located in the Broadway area, the new theater is not the usual house; it seats 650 people, about half the customary number, and is in the shape of a "U" — the same shape as the old Circle in the Square in Greenwich Village.

It has elements, in other words, of both Broadway and off-Broadway. The intention is to offer revivals of important plays with good casts for limited runs. (There is an "Uncle Vanya" starring George C. Scott and directed by Mike Nichols promised for later this season.)

With this production of O'Neill's trilogy in the Circle in the Square is off to a strong start in its new home. The production is an honest, straightforward one which allows us to see the play for what it is, and that is a real service, for it too is a landmark. Written over 40 years ago, it has been the subject of controversy ever since. The present production, together with the perspective of four decades, let us view it more clearly than has been possible before.

* * *

Mourning Becomes Electra concerns the Mannons, a New England family consisting of the father, Ezra, an office with Grant just returned from the Civil War, his wife, Christine, who has been having an affair with his cousin, his daughter, Lavinia, who loves her father and hates her mother, and his son, Orin, who loves his mother and hates his father. During the course of the three plays, the mother poisons her husband, the son shoots her lover, and then, in turn, the mother and the son commit suicide. Strong medicine indeed.

From the beginning, O'Neill contributed to the controversy by modeling the play on the *Oresteian Trilogy* of Aeschylus: to draw even more attention to its Greek heritage, in the title he called the heroine Electra rather than Lavinia as she is called in the play. In short, he invited comparison with Greek tragedy.

But the play is not Greek, it is American; and in coming to grips with his subject O'Neill leans more to the Gothic than the tragic. As drama it probes the New England Puritan soul in the way William Faulkner in his prose probed the Southern soul: both men study the landscape on the dark side of the moon, ruthlessly and relentlessly. When we understand this we realize that all these years the argument over *Mourning Becomes Electra*, the bases on which it has been attacked and defended, the wrong one.

By any standard it has faults: such devices as a chorus of townspeople which open each of the three plays, or the recurring references to South Sea Islands as the antithesis of Puritan rigidity are too obvious; several scenes are overly melodramatic; and the play's literary merit is dubious.

When the worst has been said, though, the power of the play remains. Every drama has both a literary and an emotional curve, and the latter is far more important than the former. Library shelves are full of attempts at drama by men of unquestioned literary ability, from Lord Byron to Henry James to John O'Hara, which do not hold up two minutes on the stage. *Mourning Becomes Electra* plays for almost four hours. In spite of wanting to turn away, we cannot; we are held by its sheer drama.

***

With the exception of Strindberg, no dramatist of the past century has been able to string together a series of two-character confrontations so filled with raw passion as O'Neill has in this play. In scene after scene, mother faces daughter, son faces mother, sister faces brother, their souls stripped bare. The cumulative effect is terrifying, an anguished primal scream, to use the current term, prolonged interminably.

Here a word must be said about the acting. Colleen Dewhurst as the mother is giving perhaps the best performance of her life. She has just the right combination of sensuality, strength, and vulnerability. And Pamela Payton-Wright is not far behind as the embittered Lavinia, determined to exact revenge.

O'Neill wrote some great scenes for actors. When the son, Orin, comes home from the war he expects to find his mother standing on the wide-columned porch, but she is not there. Later, after he has killed her lover, he returns and she is standing there. The tableau is indelible. So too is the visual image of Lavinia wearing her mother's clothes after the mother is gone.

It is time we became more aware of our dramatic heritage, its strengths as well as its weaknesses. O'Neill's work has plenty of both, and the only way we will be able to judge it truly is in productions such as this. A rough-hewn landmark, *Mourning Becomes Electra* may be, but no more to be dismissed than many another imperfect but enduring testament to the human struggle.

THE PLEASURES OF A KNOCKABOUT FARCE

Tuesday, May 21, 1974

New York

Nothing could attest to the universality of theater better than *Scapino*, the delightful romp which just opened at the Circle in the Square Joseph E. Levine Theater. Based on an Italian model — the commedia dell'arte — it was written by Moliere, a Frenchman, and is now being presented by an English company, The Young Vic, in the United States.

But it is not only the way it cuts across national lines which marks it as universal; it is also the play's wide appeal to different age groups. At the matinee performance attended by this reviewer there were quite a few children present, and they were having as much fun as if they had been at Ringling Brothers Circus currently in residence a few blocks away. Young and old joined together to laugh, applaud, and even to take part. At the

urging of Jim Dale, the ingratiating and talented young man playing the part of Scapino, we stamped our feet to form an invisible marching army then played imaginary trombones and mandolins as part of an Italian orchestra. Obviously *Scapino* strikes a responsive chord to people of all kinds.

The secret of the production's success goes back to the original source; commedia dell'arte was quintessential comic theater. It flourished in Italy in the 16th and 17th Centuries and was adapted by Molière in his play *The Deceits of Scapino*. It featured stock characters, classic plot intrigues, and knockabout farce — all of which are freshly reinterpreted in the present version. One of the staples of commedia was the clever servant who outsmarted his dim-witted master, and that is precisely the story of Scapino for he is an ingenious rogue if there ever was one.

The high point of his skullduggery comes in the second act when he maneuvers his master inside a large sack by convincing him that his enemies are after him. Once he has his master trapped Scapino proceeds to beat him unmercifully with a large rubber sausage, pretending in turn to be a pirate, a Kung Fu fighter ("What is in this sack?" he asks), and an entire army, which is where the audience gets into the act. The scene must have been played many thousands of times since Molière first wrote it, but it is doubtful that it has ever played with more verve or invention.

Invention is a key. Commedia always allowed for improvisation: The scenario was posted on the wall backstage and the actors were supposed to fill in the details. But this is the danger of the form — left to their own devices, most performers do not know when to stop.

Happily, The Young Vic has risen to the challenge. They throw in plenty of contemporary references — to Baskin Robbins ice cream, gangster films, and the like — and they are not shy about taking pratfalls, including one by Scapino where he drops off a second story platform only to catch himself on a rope and hang by his heels above the ground, but it is still done with finesse and taste.

There is a wide variety of comic business, such as waiters clearing a table where two men have been eating spaghetti. (The play is set in Italy, in case you hadn't figured that out.) The waiters form a long distance bucket brigade in which they throw articles from the table to one another; first comes an empty wine glass, then a roll, then a butter plate — and all the while we watch a full plate of spaghetti on the table. Will the waiter throw that too, and if he does, won't spaghetti fly in all directions? Finally he does throw it, and no, it does not spill — but as you might expect it is a close call.

The entire company is accomplished, but chief credit must go to director Frank Dunlop and to the star Jim Dale. Mr. Dunlop has pulled the whole thing together with great care: updating just enough, allowing for the right amount of horseplay, and keeping the spirit alive throughout. And Mr. Dale is one of the freshest and most engaging talents to come along recently. He induced audience participation without coercion, he is mischievous without being malicious, and his comic moments appear absolutely effortless.

All in all, this is a tasty bit of Italian pastry — an evening of sheer, unadulterated delight which sadly, is a rare commodity these days.

THE PAST AS IT PERHAPS NEVER WAS

Friday, September 19, 1975

New York

Ah, Wilderness! is the play Eugene O'Neill wrote for the Bicentennial. Not literally, of course, because it first appeared in 1988, but it seems that way when you see the revival which opened last night at the Circle in the Square Theatre. The action takes place mostly on the 4th of July, in a world of picnics on the beach, fireworks displays and band concerts. The time is 1908, and the family is as All-American as they come: mother, father, three children, spinster aunt, and a reprobate uncle. They could have stepped from the pages of a Booth Tarkington novel or out of a Normal Rockwell cover for the *Saturday Evening Post.*

Nat, the father, publishes the town newspaper and is a perfect blend of parental authority and good-natured understanding and forgiveness. His wife, Essie, is the kind of mother we have in mind when we speak of motherhood and apple pie: she sees nothing inconsistent in continually ordering her children to sit up straight and mind their manners and at the same time in intervening on their behalf when they face punishment from their father.

The issue of the play, as befits its light-hearted tone, is a decidedly minor one: the crisis of a young man discovering love and having his first encounter with cigarettes, whiskey, and wild women. He survives all three temptations with nothing worse than a hangover and youthful remorse, and the play ends affirming the virtues of purity, chastity and family love.

The new production — first presented last spring at the Long Wharf Theatre in New Haven and seen here in a preview — underlines the sentimental appeal of the play. The details are carefully chosen: women in long skirts with Gibson Girl coiffures, chairs with antimacassars, a front porch filled with geraniums, and songs between the scenes like "Goodbye, My Lady Love" and "Paddlin' Madeline Home." Director Arvin Brown may have let Uncle Sid get a little too drunk and the young hero Richard moon more than necessary, but by and large he has achieved an admirable ensemble effect with the cast. And there are fine individual performances, particularly William Swetland as the father and Geraldine Fitzgerald as the mother.

The play and the production work together to produce what appears to be an affectionate recreation of an America that used to be, but a question hovers over the evening. Is it all that simple? Is this what American life was really like in 1906? We know it was not like that for O'Neill. Superficially his life bears similarities to young Richard's but basically it was quite different, as he has shown us in the ruthless, devastating family portrait he painted in *Long Day's Journey Into Night*. Even if we assume that picture to be shaded toward darkness and despair, external facts confirm that it is closer to the truth than *Ah, Wilderness!* As O'Neill himself said, the latter depicted his youth not as it was, but as he longed for it to be.

If the Miller family in *Ah, Wilderness!* does not closely resemble the O'Neills, it does resemble another family he knew well and on whom he partially modeled the Millers. The family was named McGinley: a large, close-knit group with whom O'Neill had grown up in New London, Conn., and whose relaxed family life O'Neill envied.

Critic Walter Kerr wrote recently that you cannot be nostalgic about what you have never known because you can only long for those things you actually experienced. Technically he may be correct but in practice it does not work that way. Nostalgia is based on what we wish we had been as much as on what actually was. One definition of nostalgia reads, "Homesickness, a wistful or excessively sentimental sometimes abnormal yearning for a return to some past period or irrecoverable condition." The past in *Ah, Wilderness!* is irrecoverable for O'Neill because it never happened. And the same is true for many of us; our growing up was never like the Millers', whether it happened in 1906, 1926, 1946, or whenever.

We define ourselves, however, by our dreams and fantasies as much as by our lives and *Ah, Wilderness!* shows once again how deeply rooted in the American psyche is the desire for a strong, sympathetic family and for an adolescence in which awkwardness and growing pains are assuaged in the embrace of friendly arms. In O'Neill's case the point is even more strongly made because his work is suffused with cynicism and despair few American writers can equal.

Ah, Wilderness! Is O'Neill's only comedy, and if it is excessively sentimental — which it is — this is because once he let the pendulum swing, it was bound to swing wide. But O'Neill did not linger there. Having acknowledged his longing for happy, uncomplicated childhood, he turned with new vision and vigor to his original purposes. *Ah, Wilderness!* represents a turning point of sorts for him. Afterwards he abandoned many of his expressionistic experiments with masks, etc., and the reshaping of Greek myths to produce the straightforward realistic plays of his late period — *Long Day's Journey Into Night, A Moon for the Misbegotten,* etc. — which represents his finest work. *Ah, Wilderness!* may have been salutary in another way. In his later plays, O'Neill employed more and more humor, adding an important dimension to them.

Perhaps this was the secret O'Neill discovered about nostalgia: to look back but not to linger.

FIDDLER, A SMASH, POINTS UP BROADWAY PROBLEM

Friday, December 31, 1976

New York

The newest hit in town is really an old hit which raises questions about what is happening to the Broadway theater. First, however, a look at the new show: a revival of *Fiddler on the Roof* starring Zero Mostel which opened at the Winter Garden Theatre after a six-month tour.

Fiddler opened in 1964, and went on to play 3,242 performances, making it the longest running show in Broadway history. In addition, it has played innumerable times in community and resident professional theaters.

It is easy to see why it has been so successful. It is one of the last of a long line of musicals which began with Rodgers and Hammerstein and continued through *My Fair Lady* and others by men like Frank Loesser, Cole Porter, and Irving Berlin. These were book musicals with a solid story and songs integrated into the plot. *Fiddler* fits the mold extremely well.

The story in *Fiddler* concerns Tevye, a Jewish milk peddler in a small town in Russia in 1905. Tevye has two serious problems: he is poor and he has five unmarried daughters. The first problem makes him fantasize in song about wealth — "If I were a Rich Man" — and the second makes his daughters fantasize about marriage — "Matchmaker, Matchmaker, Make Me a Match."

Several familiar but always appealing themes run through the play. One is the conflict between the old and the new, between the elders who want to maintain "Tradition" — the title of the song — and the young who want to change things. Another is the plight of the Jews, particularly in Europe. The Jews in Tevye's tiny town of Anatevka are harassed and finally driven from their homes.

A third theme concerns Tevye's shrewish wife. He must constantly invent dreams or go through other charades to avoid her wrath and win her approval for his behavior.

Along with the appeal of its story and the beauty of its music, another secret of the success of *Fiddler on the Roof* is the manner in which the elements are kept in balance: the story with the songs, the serious parts with the comic, and the borrowed elements with the invented ones. There is often something eclectic about the best American musicals and it in no way detracts from the originality of Boris Aronson's masterful settings for *Fiddler* point out that they have strong echoes of the paintings of Chagall's work evokes the same time and place as *Fiddler*. Also, choreographer Jerome Robbins quite properly has incorporated the Russian folk dances made popular by the Moiseyev Dancers in the foot stomping numbers of his men.

It is in blending the sentimental with the humorous that the star Zero Mostel comes to the fore. A consummate comedian but also a forceful actor, Mr. Mostel has from the beginning made the part of Tevye his own. He can be extremely funny as when a small, prospective son-in-law Mostel wheels in different directions only to find each time that the young man has disappeared behind his back. And no one else talks to God quite the way Mr. Mostel does, demanding, cajoling, joking, all with appropriate gestures. Also, there is the dance he has developed: with hands held high, he does a vibrant shimmy which sends the tassels on the religious garment at his waist whirling in the air.

The new production is in excellent shape. It has the advantages of the first production — including the original scenery and costumes as well as Mr. Mostel — and a fine new supporting cast. The young people are particularly able. Also, Mr. Robbins who directed and choreographed the original production came in just before the New York opening to polish things up, so the dances and ensemble work are fine tuned.

Fiddler is another revival, however, and that points to a serious problem underlying that prosperity.

There can be no question that financially the season so far as has been a huge success. We are a few weeks past the halfway mark in the 1975-77 season and grosses on Broadway are over $50 million, up nearly 40% from a year ago. Nor is this increase all due to inflationary ticket prices: *Variety*, the show business trade paper, keeps tabs on how many people attend the theater each week. Its figures indicated that the number of theater-goers is up a hefty 30% from the same time last year.

This financial health is deceptive, however, and serves to mask a genuine poverty where new work is concerned. Several worthwhile plays have opened on Broadway this fall but none has been outstanding and the general level has been disappointing. A close look at what is producing long lines at the box office shows that there is a preponderance of revivals or hold-overs from the past. *Fiddler on the Roof* is only the latest of several successful revivals including *My Fair Lady*, *Guys and Dolls*, and *Three Penny Opera*.

Aside from the revivals, the hottest tickets in town mostly are for shows from two or three years ago: *A Chorus Line*, *The Wiz*, *Chicago*, *Bubbling Brown Sugar*, and *Equus*. Some are even hold-overs from four or five years ago like *Grease* and *Pippin*.

The only recent shows to score at the box office are *Sly Fox*, which has established itself as the newest hit, and *For Colored Girls Who Have Contemplated Suicide* . . . the moving dance-drama at the Booth.

There is, therefore, a paucity of new work. In the past the Broadway theater seemed reluctant to include first-class revivals among its fare and that was a mistake which fortunately has been remedied in recent seasons, but now the pendulum seems to have swung too far in the other direction. New plays are in short supply. The saddest part is that among the crop of new playwrights, several show real talent but few hold out the promise of producing major work. Not only serious plays are missing, but comedies and musicals too. Unless new work comes along soon. Broadway, which now seems so solvent, seems headed for it's own recession.

Friday, October 4, 1985

New York

Occasionally in the theater a performer makes such an indelible impression in a role that he or she becomes synonymous with it. One thinks of Marlon Brando as Stanley Kowalski in *A Streetcar Named Desire* or Ethel Merman as Rose in *Gypsy*. Ranking alongside such definitive portrayals of recent times is Jason Robards as Hickey in Eugene O'Neill's *The Iceman Cometh*.

In 1956, Mr. Robards played the role in a Circle in the Square production directed by Jose Quintero. The production catapulted Mr. Robards to fame and restored O'Neill to prominence after the playwright had been in eclipse for 20 years. On the strength of that production, O'Neill's widow Carlotta allowed Mr. Quintero a short time later to mount *Long Day's Journey into Night*. Mr. Robard's portrayal of Jamie in that production further solidified his reputation as an interpreter of O'Neill. Now, nearly 20 years after the first *Iceman*, Mr. Robards and Mr. Quintero are reunited in a new production that played first at the Kennedy Center in Washington and has now opened here at the Lunt-Fontanne Theatre.

Mr. Robards is a better Hickey than ever and in the new production he has strong support from other cast members, especially Donald Moffat as a one-time anarchist. *Iceman* takes place in New York in 1912. The setting is Harry Hope's bar, a gin mill that serves as home to a group of derelicts. Once men with some chance of having a family and a career they now sit besotted with their booze and their "pipe dreams." Each man tells himself that tomorrow he will pull himself together, get his old job back, and resume an active life, but tomorrow never comes.

Into this world twice a year comes Hickey, a hardware salesman, or "drummer" as he calls himself, who stakes everyone to drinks. Except this time there is a difference. Instead of joining in the drinking, Hickey remains sober, and instead of peddling hardware, he is selling his own brand of religion. Convinced that he can bring peace to these men by stripping them of their illusions, he succeeds only in making them hate themselves, and each other, more than ever. It is a bleak play, illuminated by O'Neill's relentless pursuit of the truth and the rich glow of the acting and directing.

Mr. Robard's Hickey is no carbon copy of his earlier portrayal. He retains the infectious bonhomie of the perpetual salesman, cocking his boater straw hat and snapping his fingers. Some of the most effective moments in the play are when Mr. Robards throws cold water on the expectations of the group only to raise them an instant later with a joke or a flashing smile. We watch transfixed as the emotions of the men are whipsawed time and again between hope and despair.

But along with the effervescence of the salesman, Mr. Robards also conveys the underlying sense of the toll that life takes and of impending death — the iceman of the title who is on his way. This dimension Mr. Robards invests with tremendous insight and conviction, a result, no doubt, of his own experience and maturity.

O'Neill remains our most demanding playwright, demanding on himself as well as his audiences. *Iceman* lasts almost five hours, and Hickey does not even make an appearance for more than an hour. But the waiting is worth it, both for the cumulative power of the play and the incandescence of Mr. Robard's performance. For those who admire challenging drama brought to life by superb performances, *The Iceman Cometh* affords a rare opportunity.

PROFILES AND INTERVIEWS

THE LEGACY OF RICHARD RODGERS

Friday, January 4, 1980

New York

"Without music," Nietzsche wrote, "life would be a mistake." Without the music of Richard Rodgers, one might add, life would be a mistake.

As a modern theater composer, Richard Rodgers, who died Sunday night at 77, was *sui generis*, truly one of a kind. His career spanned more than 50 years, from *The Garrick Gaieties* in 1925 to *I Remember Mama* last spring. Altogether he wrote the music for 39 Broadway shows from which came literally hundreds of songs: "Manhattan," "My Heart Stood Still," "Blue Room," "My Funny Valentine," "Spring is Here," "This Can't be Love," "Oh, What a Beautiful Morning," "Some Enchanted Evening." The list could go on for several columns.

Nor did Rodgers go unrewarded for his compositions. In addition to numerous honors he earned more than $100 million.

But it is not merely his longevity or his earnings that set him apart; it is the special quality of his talent. One aspect was his adaptability. For the first 22 years of his professional life, from 1920 to 1942, he collaborated with Lorenz Hart. With Hart, Rodgers always wrote the music first, spinning out a waltz, a ballad or a patter song, and Hart would add his intricate, urban lyrics: "we'll go to Greenwich, where modern men itch to be free."

When Hart, due to personal problems, could no longer serve as his lyricist, Rodgers turned to Oscar Hammerstein II, and began a second remarkable collaboration. (One collaboration would have been sufficient for most composers.) Beginning with *Oklahoma!* In 1943, Rodgers and Hammerstein turned out hit shows year after year: *Carousel, South Pacific, The King and I, The Sound of Music.*

Where Hart's lyrics had been sophisticated, often bittersweet, Hammerstein's were sincere, straightforward, and sometimes even overly sentimental. But Rodgers adjusted: his music took on a warmer, down-to-earth quality. He even changed his composing habits; instead of writing the music first, he set his tunes to Hammerstein's completed lyrics.

After Hammerstein died in 1960, Rodgers wrote on his own ("No Strings") or with other collaborators for nearly 20 years more.

He could write love songs, comic numbers, ballets — you name it. He could also capture the mood or the geographic location of a play, from the turn-of-the-century American West in *Oklahoma,* to the Siamese world of the *The King and I.*

It has been said that the musical comedy is one art form indigenous to America.

If so, Rodgers was one of the people who created it. With *Slaughter on Tenth Avenue* in *On Your Toes* (1936) he wrote the first ballet in a musical. *Pal Joey* (1940) was the first musical with a heel as a hero. And the Rodgers and Hammerstein musicals achieved a new high in the integration of book, songs and dances.

Through all of these changes one thing remained constant: Rodger's great gift for melody and his solid musicianship. Alec Wilder, whose book *American Popular Song* is probably the definitive study of composers like Jerome Kern, Cole Porter, Irving Berlin and Rodgers, made detailed analysis of more than a hundred Rodgers tunes. Afterwards he wrote: "I am more than impressed and respectful: I am astonished." Over the years, Mr. Wilder concluded, Rodger's songs "revealed a higher degree of excellence, inventiveness and sophistication than any other writer I have studied."

Sir Thomas Beecham once

remarked, "if an opera cannot be played by an organ grinder, it is not going to achieve immortality." Richard Rodgers's songs have been played by organ-grinders, sung by Ella Fitzgerald, and performed by a thousand dance bands. They have more than met the test and have achieved their own form of immortality.

THE JAZZMEN WAILED AND EVERYONE CRIED

Friday, August 17, 1984

New York

Every year hundreds of new books are launched by New York publishers. Frequently this takes the form of a cocktail party. On one table, the obligatory white wine will be served, and on another, cheese and stalks of broccoli and cauliflower surround a pale-green dip. The editor praises the author; the author praises the editor: and after a brief period of chit-chat, the group disperses.

A recent publisher's party I attended began like all the rest. Held on the 11th floor at the Harper and Row offices, its purpose was to introduce *Willie and Dwike* by William Zinsser. A company official delivered a few perfunctory and self congratulatory remarks, and then introduced Mr. Zinsser. The subjects of Mr. Zinsser's book are two black musicians, Willie Ruff and Dwike Mitchell, who have played together as a jazz

duo for nearly 30 years. Both men were present, and after talking briefly about the book Mr. Zinsser said that they would play for us, explaining that they had played the night before with the Boston Pops orchestra.

Mr. Ruff, who is a professor of music at the Yale Music School, went to a canvas case and pulled out his French horn, an unusual instrument for jazz. Mr. Mitchell, who ordinarily plays a concert grand Baldwin, sat down at an upright Yamaha.

Mr. Ruff announced that they would begin by playing "St. Louis Blues." It was an appropriate choice because the song's composer, W.C. Handy, was born in a log cabin only a few miles from where Mr. Ruff himself was born in Northern Alabama. Mr. Mitchell began a tango rhythm, and the two played an inventive and evocative

274

version of the famous blues. After a few phrases, everyone stopped eating and drinking, and sat on the carpet to listen.

Next, Mr. Ruff said they would play Billy Strayhorn's "Lush Life," a quiet, sensual number whose serenity was counterpointed by sharp cracks of thunder from a summer storm outside. Following that they played "Lazy Afternoon," and John Hammond, the dean of jazz record producers who was sitting along a side wall, wrinkled his face into a broad smile as first Mr. Ruff and then Mr. Mitchell improvised around the familiar tune.

For their finale the two men played a medley from *Porgy and Bess*. When they reached "I Love You, Porgy," I felt my eyes fill with tears. The lyrical beauty of Gershwin's melody, the resonance and purity of Mr. Ruff's French horn and the delicate, mystical quality of Mr. Mitchell's piano affected me in a way I was not prepared for.

When they finished playing, I discovered that almost everyone present had been affected in the same way. The publishing official, who previously had spoken perfunctorily, stood to thank the musicians but his voice broke, and he said simply that he could not remember when he'd last been moved in this way. People were astonished not only that they had been deeply touched, but that it had happened so quickly and in so unlikely and unpromising a place.

The one person who was not surprised was the author, Mr. Zinsser. Since he first met Messrs. Ruff and Mitchell at Yale in 1973, Mr. Zinsser has followed their careers and traveled with them on a number of their tours, where he saw them play — for homefolks in Muscle Shoals, Ala., for employees at John Deere headquarters outside Moline, Ill., or for a group of restrained, bewildered music students in China — Mr. Zinsser observed their uncanny ability to communicate with audiences.

One reason is their superb musicianship, another is their incredible rapport with each other, and still another is that they are both born teachers. Mr. Ruff always does the talking, and in order to reach foreign audiences he has become a first-class linguist. In 1959, the Ruff-Mitchell duo played in the Soviet Union and Mr. Ruff taught himself Russian. He is now fluent in eight languages, the most recent being Mandarin Chinese, which he learned for their trip to Shanghai in 1981.

In *Willie and Dwike*, Mr. Zinsser chronicles the trips and the lives of these two remarkable men. He does so in a clear, spare prose that is good as any reportage being written today. Mr. Zinsser obviously admires his subjects and has a sense of wonder at the way they have combined lowbrow and highbrow, stern intellectual discipline with joyful emotion, and humble origins with astonishing achievements.

Though temperamentally quite different, the two men have much in common. Both were born into poor families in the South, Mr. Mitchell in Florida and Mr. Ruff in Alabama; both came from broken homes and suffered their share of prejudice and poverty. They also showed prodigious musical talent that led them boy by circuitous routes to Lockbourne Air Force based outside Columbus, Ohio, in 1947.

Following World War II, military installations were still segregated and returning black heroes found themselves unable to visit such places as officer's clubs. The embarrassed War Department solved the problem by establishing Lockbourne as an elite black base. It was distinguished by having more college graduates per capita than any base in the country and the best music program, with a 160-piece orchestra and two jazz bands. The older musicians at Lockbourne taught the younger, and that's where both Mr. Ruff and Mr. Mitchell got their start.

After Lockbourne they separated, with Mr. Ruff going to Yale to study with Paul Hindemith and Mr. Mitchell moving to Philadelphia to study classical piano at the Musical Academy. In 1954, Mr. Mitchell was playing with Lionel Hampton's orchestra when Mr. Ruff saw him on television and got in touch with him. The two have been playing together ever since.

The subtitle of Mr. Zinsser's book is *An American Profile*, and it is appropriate because Messrs. Ruff, and Mitchell's story is uniquely American. Throughout their early careers both men were befriended by a series of teachers, many of them white, who took a keen interest in their careers. They, in turn, have taught literally thousands of others in private classes, at colleges and universities, and on concert tours. Now, thanks to Mr. Zinsser's book, the rest of us have a chance to learn from them too.

GEORGE ABBOTT: THE 100-YEAR-OLD MAN

Monday, June 15, 1987

Cleveland

For three days a group of the most important figures in the history of the American musical gathered here recently to discuss the work of director George Abbott, who will turn 100 next week. Mr. Abbott himself was on hand and was the liveliest person in whatever room he entered.

Most of the discussions centered on Mr. Abbott's successes, but Mr. Abbott himself brought up a few failures. When someone asked him if he'd worked with Rodgers and Hammerstein, he said, "yes, on 'Me and Juliet,' and it was failure. I'll tell you why, it was the first time Hammerstein wrote the lyrics after the tunes instead of before, and they were too pompous and artificial. The big song was 'No Other Love Have I.' Now there's a comment you hear on the street every day."

At a Saturday-night gala, following two arduous days of seminars and productions, Mr. Abbott put aside his cane.

It was Gerald Freedman, artistic director of the Great Lakes Theater Festival, who had the bright idea to celebrate the Abbott centennial by letting Mr. Abbott do what he enjoys most, namely, go to work. The highlight of the three-day event here was revivals of *The Boys from Syracuse* and *Broadway*. Mr. Abbott adapted the first from Shakespeare's *Comedy of Errors* and directed it in 1938. The second Mr. Abbott co-authored and directed in 1926. For the Great Lakes Festival, Mr. Freedman directed and Donald Saddler choreographed *The Boys from Syracuse*, and Mr. Abbott, 61 years later, directed *Broadway*.

Broadway takes place back-

278

stage at a New York speakeasy during Prohibition and won fame as the first play to present a realistic picture of gangsters. The story concerns the bootleggers who kill each other and the chorus girls they pursue.

Mr. Abbott arrived here in early April, and after two grueling days of auditions set to work with the 20-member cast. At first the actors were put off by Mr. Abbott's practice of telling performers exactly how to say a line and where to move. "When I say he was specific," notes Eugene Anthony, who played Porky in *Broadway*, "I mean specific: 'say the first two words, take one step to your left, say the next three words, then look right.'"

"In the beginning it drove us crazy," remarks Richard Poe, who plays chief mobster Steve Crandell, "but we came to realize that he was providing a grid within which we could grow and develop."

"His concentration and attention to detail are amazing," adds Janet Aldrich, who plays Ruby, a chorus girl. "In the opening scene I'm supposed to light a cigarette while we're rehearsing and I didn't know how to do it. He watched the scene for five days and then told me exactly when to move to the piano and light up. It was the perfect moment."

The play holds up amazingly well, better than many other comedy-melodramas of the period that have been revived lately. It doesn't hurt, either, that the Abbott touch is there: the crisp, clear, fast-paced direction that points up each laugh and elicits every emotion. Matching the fun and authenticity of *Broadway* is the revival of *The Boys from Syracuse*, in which Mr. Freedman and Mr. Saddler wisely did not try to update the material but presented it with impressive integrity and imagination.

Several themes emerged during three-day conference. One is the great number of people Mr. Abbott started on their careers: not only most of the well-known figures here, but dozens of other performers, writers, directors and choreographers who were given their first job by him. The comic Nancy Walker told of her initial audition with Mr. Abbott. "I was 19 when I went to tryouts for *Best Foot Forward*. The last thing in the world I wanted to be was funny; no girl 19 wants to be funny. But Mr. Abbott listened to me sing and later cast me. In his response to my singing those 32 bars he told me who I was. Beginning right there he defined my career and, in fact, my whole life. And I am eternally grateful . . . Mr. Abbott's genius is that he never let me know I was funny."

"The bottom line," added Garson Kanin, "is that George treats comedy seriously."

After the performance of *The Boys from Syracuse*, Eddie Albert, who was in the original production, mused: "I sat there tonight thinking how lucky I was. The first three shows I played in were directed by George, and they were

all hits. I remember a scene in *Brother Rat*. It was a love scene between a shy boy and girl and was funny when we opened. But gradually I added schoolboy stuff: a tug at the forelock, digging my shoe in the carpet. Three weeks into the run the laughs were gone, and George said to me: Just say the lines flat without those curlicues. I decided to try it, just to prove he was wrong, and the laughs came cascading back. It's a lesson I never forgot."

By this time Mr. Abbott is a phenomenon, a force of nature, but he doesn't think in those terms, and that's maybe his biggest secret. As his actors will attest, he lives totally in the here and now, preoccupied with his schedule for the next few weeks, his many current projects, never with something vague and restful such as retirement or next fall. When I asked about his plans for the future, he said: "after this we go to our place in Miami, then come to New York for that party thing (a gala in

his honor on June 22), then
to our summer place in the
Catskills." Then I said, I suppose you'll return to Miami.
"Oh, no." he replied, "we
go back to New York. I'm
working on this pop opera:
all singing without any dialogue. You know, that's the
way they do it now."

Jerome Robbins: Back on Broadway

Tuesday, February 28, 1989

Cleveland

When the 1962 musical *A Funny Thing Happened on the Way to the Forum* opened out of town it was deep in trouble. A cry of help went out to Jerome Robbins, who came to the rescue by adding a brilliantly choreographed opening number, "Comedy Tonight," which set the tone fore the whole show and turned disaster into triumph. Mr. Robbins's contribution to the show, however, remained anonymous and his name never appeared in the program.

It's another story this time around. Mr. Robbins gets full credit and not only his name in the program, it's on the marquee. *Jerome Robbins' Broadway* is one of those dream shows that gets talked about year after year and never happens, except this time it has. A supportive group of producers gave Mr. Robbins 22 weeks of rehearsal and an additional seven weeks of previews: an unprecedented period of preparation for a Broadway musical. The show also has an unheard of 62 performers and a full orchestra of 28.

The result is a unique event in Broadway musical history, a retrospective of dances choreographed by Mr. Robbins in the 20 years between 1944 and 1964. The production, which opened this week at the Imperial Theatre, offers a rare opportunity to see some of the most memorable and exhilarating numbers in the American musical theater, created afresh by the artist who thought them up in the first place.

First comes "Comedy Tonight," with classical allusions cleverly turned on their head by composer Stephen Sondheim. It was meant to set the stage for a Roman farce, and there is farce aplenty in Mr. Robbins's madcap shenanigans. Then, from *The King and I*, we have *The Small House of Uncle Thomas*, an Asian comic version of *Uncle Tom's Cabin* presented before the King of Siam. From *Gypsy* comes "You Gotta Have a Gimmick," in which three striptease artists indoctrinate young Gypsy Rose Lee in their trade.

And on and on: the sailor's ballet from *On the Town*, the first show Mr. Robbins choreographed for Broadway in 1944; the flying scene made famous by Mary Martin from *Peter Pan*; numbers from *West Side Story* and *Fiddler on the Roof*; and the absolutely hilarious bathing beach scene from *High Button Shoes*.

The last was inspired by Mack Sennett film comedies and the Keystone Kops, and features con men, lifeguards, bathing beauties and crooks in a nonstop chase scene in and out of bathhouses on the beach at Atlantic City. It has to be one of the wildest, most amusing scenes ever created for the musical stage

and is alone worth the price of admission. That is saying a lot because *Jerome Robbins' Broadway*, at $55 a ticket, sets a new high for Broadway prices.

The material is expertly strung together by an affable, engaging narrator, Jason Alexander, who also is the star of several segments. One of them is a delightful rendition of "I Still Get Jealous" from *High Button Shoes*, in which he sings a duet and dances a soft-shoe with Faith Prince. The singing is not an exception, since *Jerome Robbins' Broadway* is by no means just a dance show. Many segments are complete scenes that include extensive singing and a good deal of dialogue as well.

Seeing the numbers unfold side by side brings home several noteworthy points about Mr. Robbins's work in Broadway musicals. One is his sparkling sense of humor, which is apparent not only in the obvious numbers like "Comedy Tonight" and the bathhouse ballet, but

283

throughout the evening. In "Charleston," for example, from the 1945 production *Billion Dollar Baby*, he has cleverly exploited every cliché accumulate during the 1920s. The result is not just another Charleston number but a pastiche of character types and physical attitudes that is continually amusing.

For me the least satisfactory part of the evening is an extended section from *West Side Story*, which closes the first act. Perhaps this is because the material is so deadly serious: the one segment in which Mr. Robbins' comic sensibility does not shine through.

Another striking point that emerges is Mr. Robbins's strong narrative drive. Virtually every number tells a story that pulses with life. This is the case with straight dance numbers, such as an Irving Berlin number, "Mr. Monotony," which was cut from two shows out of town; and with extended tales such as Tevye's mock dream in *Fiddler on the Roof*, in which he is warned not to let his daughter marry the butcher.

This gift for narrative is a reminder that Mr. Robbins is the man most responsible for the emergence of the director-choreographer. In his first three shows he was responsible only for the dance numbers and the overall director was George Abbott. By the time he ended his Broadway career, with shows such as *West Side Story*, *Gypsy*, and *Fiddler*, Mr. Robbins was the director and the choreographer, a twin role that set the pattern for a whole generation of directors who started out as choreographers: notably Bob Fosse, Michael Bennett and Tommy Tune.

In the last segment of *Jerome Robbins' Broadway*, three sailors on shore leave and their girls perform an appealing but little-known song from *On the Town* called "Some Other Time." The three couples sing about having to part, postponing the things they want to do to some other time. Those interested in seeing Broadway musical numbers at their best had better not wait for some other time; the time is now.

THEATER: THE MAN WHO MAKES LYRICS SING

Tuesday, February 13, 1990

New York

Closer Than Ever is an intimate musical at New York's Cherry Lane Theatre, with four performers, two musicians, and a virtually bare stage in a theater with less than 200 seats. By contrast, *Miss Saigon* is a blockbuster musical in London: 40 cast members, an orchestra of 30, myriad special effects, including a helicopter that lands on stage for the final rescue of Americans in Saigon, and all of this at the mammoth Drury Lane Theatre, which seats 2,700, far more than any Broadway theater.

Given their differences in size, subject matter and the rest, these two musicals would appear to have absolutely nothing in common, but they do. Both have the same lyricist: Richard Maltby Jr. Not exactly a household word for the ordinary theater-goer, Mr. Maltby has been moving quietly but suc-

cessfully through the minefield of the American musical for more than 30 years. His father, who began as a musical arranger for people such as Andre Kostelanetz, became the leader of a well-known dance band. In addition to that musical influence, Mr. Maltby was taken by his parents to see *Carousel* when he was eight and soon thereafter realized he wanted musicals to be his career.

Rather than following his father into the musical side of musicals, Mr. Maltby decided that lyrics would be his forte. While at Yale he found his collaborator, classmate David Shire, the leader of a popular jazz quintet. In 1958, they wrote a musical version of *Cyrano* and the next year *Grand Tour*. Both shows were produced by the Yale undergraduate theater club, the Dramat, and included in the casts were a number of people who would go on to fame on their own: Dick Cavett, Austin Pendleton, Peter Hunt, Gretchen Cryer and Nancy Ford.

Mr. Maltby and Mr. Shire, whose most recent work is "Closer than Ever," have been working together for 32 years, which in itself is some kind of record. Rodgers and Hart were together for 21 years, and Rodgers and Hammerstein for 16. When Messrs. Maltby and Shire left Yale, they were hopeful that they could step into the mainstream of American musicals, but the mainstream was drying up. *Fiddler on the Roof* (1964) was the last musical of the "golden age" that many think ended official with the 1967 rock musical *Hair.*

In 1977, not having had a Broadway musical success, Mr. Malby collected songs from their numerous shows into a musical revue, *Starting Here, Starting Now,* which had a lengthy off-Broadway run and subsequently has had close to 500 produc-

tions in the U.S and around the world. Long before this, however, the two men had begun to move into other directions. Mr. Shire answered the siren call of Hollywood, where he began to write film scores. So far he has been responsible for the music for 40 feature films, including *All the President's Men, Farewell, My Lovely* and *2010.*

For his part, Mr. Maltby in the year 1970s began thinking of directing rather than writing. It was not only that the musical field was changing, Mr. Maltby says he was missing something: "When I was working on a production, everyone else seemed to be more involved than I was — the performers, the director, the designers, even the composer who was working with the orchestra. But as a lyricist, I was usually off in a corner reworking the words of a song, agonizing over a phrase or a rhyme. So I set out to become a director."

"I realized," Mr. Maltby continues, "that I always saw a scene visually; even when working on a lyric, I saw the number being staged. I knew no one would hire me as a director, though, so during the 70s I directed a little bit of everything: night-club acts, cabaret acts, and benefits." This activity culminated in *Ain't Misbehavin'*, a musical revue based on the music of Fats Waller that Mr. Maltby created and directed. The show, which opened in May 1978, ran for nearly four years and won numerous Tony Awards, including one for Mr. Maltby as best director.

Mr. Maltby has continued directing. He's even branched out into successful productions of non-musical plays by such heavyweights as Eugene O'Neill and Tennessee Williams. Having proved himself in that field, however, Mr. Maltby was ready once more to throw himself wholeheartedly into lyric writing. "Creating lyrics," Mr. Maltby says, "is the technical manipulation of language. The musical line tells you where the accents are, which beats must be em-phasized. My job is to fit the words into that line to make it sound like natural speech: as if that's the way the phrase *has* to sound."

This kind of thing is Mr. Maltby's meat. His way with words has not only made him a master of song lyrics but also a cult figure for crossword puzzlers. For many years now, first for *New York Magazine* and more recently for *Harpers*, he has fashioned a series of punning, English-style puzzles that challenge the most expert solvers. But Mr. Maltby's heart belongs to the theater, where he lavishes his wordsmanship on lyrics that are adroit and affecting at the same time.

In "Doors," the opening song of *Closer Than Ever*, Mr. Maltby sardonically hymns the modern city:

What's in the skies from Boston to Florida

High rises rising, each being horrider

What hits your eyes as you hit a corridor?

Nothing but a wall of doors . . .

288

Closer Than Ever is the latest in what might be called the Shire-Maltby Second Act. In the early 1980s, after Mr. Shire's foray into Hollywood and Mr. Maltby's into directing, the two men began collaborating again in earnest and the result was *Baby*, a musical that, as the name suggests, is about the trauma and excitement of parenthood. *Baby* opened on Broadway in late 1983, and though not a blockbuster, had more than its share of champions as well as a respectable six-month run.

Closer Than Ever is also a revue about modern life, about the alternating angst and joy of urban dwellers roughly between the ages of 30 and 50. "I really like to do in a song what a writer does in a short story," Mr. Maltby says, "trace the life of one, two or three people through a memorable moment or a significant turning point in their lives." And this is exactly what the songs in *Closer Than Ever* accomplish; they provide not just witty lyrics but a series of vignettes portraying what it means to be left in the lurch, to get divorced, to see an old friend after a separation of 10 or 20 years,

As for *Miss Saigon*, Mr. Maltby first worked with its producer, Cameron Mackintosh, on *Song and Dance*, a 1985 Andrew Lloyd Webber piece that Mr. Maltby adapted for America and for which he provided additional lyrics. When Mr. Mackintosh, who had produced *Les Miserables*, decided to use the same two Frenchmen who had written that play to create a latter-day *Madame Butterfly* he asked Mr. Maltby to collaborate on the lyrics. He says he worked on all the show's lyrics, "every single one of them." Since the entire show is sung, that meant a lot of work.

While waiting for *Miss Saigon* to make its appearance on Broadway, Mr. Maltby is working on several new projects: another musical with Mr. Shire as well as a musical version of the Thin Man stories called *Nick and Nora*. Meanwhile, he is celebrating a milestone. Tomorrow, cast albums of both his current shows, *Closer Than Ever* (on RCA Victor) and *Miss Saigon* (Geffen), will be released in the U.S on the same day, the first time this has happened to anyone: Cole Porter, Irving Berlin, Richard Rodgers or any other of Mr. Maltby's illustrious predecessors.

SPECIAL PIECES

ABSORBING CULTURE IN A BIG POOLROOM

Friday, May 24, 1974

New Haven, Conn.

Unquestionably the high point of theatrical novelty this season — or should we say the high water mark — is the production of a classical Greek play, *The Frogs*, at the Yale University swimming pool. The pool has an indoor amphitheater with seats rising in steep banks on all sides, and even with one end blocked off for a stage, there are 1,600 seats roughly approximating the shape of the original Greek theaters: an apt setting for this Aristophanes comedy written in 405 B.C.

Yale has many honored traditions but none more fascinating than its longstanding relationship with *The Frogs*. Research indicates that in the 1890s it became the custom for Greek scholars at Yale to gather in the spring under the windows of their professors to sing the chorus from *The Frogs*,

a catchy chant which went "Brekekekex Coax Coax." So taken were the undergraduates with the words that they incorporated them in a Yale football cheer which remains in use to this day. In 1921, there was a production of the play at Yale directed by none other than Monty Woolley with the chorus coached by Stephen Vincent Benet.

In 1941, Burt Shevelove, then a young man directing the Yale Dramatic Society, had the inspired idea of presenting *The Frogs* at the exhibition pool. The production became a legend, and Mr. Shevelove went on to become well-known as the writer of *A Funny Thing Happened on the Way to the Forum* and the director of such musicals as *No, No, Nanette*. With this background it was a natural, therefore, for the Yale Repertory Theatre to present Mr. Shevelove's new

293

version some 33 years after his first one.

* * *

This is surely the most elaborate production of all; one end of the pool serves as a stage and has a huge orange and yellow cloth draped from ceiling to floor for a good part of the Yale band, 24 frogmen in the pool, dancers, singers, and actors making a total cast of close to 90. The evening begins most promisingly: Larry Blyden as Dionysus comes to the edge of the pool to sing a song of welcome, admonishing the audience how to behave: "Please don't swim," he says, "this is a temple, not a gym." Songs for the new production were written by Stephen Sondheim, who provided music and lyrics for A Little Night Music, and the opening number, especially, is up to his usual standards.

In Mr. Shevelove's adaptation Dionysus decides he must go to Hades to bring George Bernard Shaw back to earth because we are in need of such a writer now.

He departs for Hades across the River Styx — in this case in a small rowboat in the pool paddled by Charon. As he and Charon move across the pool the croaking frogs appear: members of the Yale swimming team covered in green splotches with green rubber flippers on their feet. The Frogs wish to prevent Dionysus from bringing culture back to earth and so they try to interrupt his journey. They cavort about the pool displaying all manner of aquatic acrobatics while jumping over one another. ("Look," exclaims Dionysus, "they're playing leap frog.")

* * *

The activities in the pool go swimmingly, not to say splashingly, but eventually Dionysus reaches the other side and that's where the trouble begins. Dionysus had warned us that the second part of the evening would be serious, but he failed to warn us that it would also be banal. In Aristophanes' original play Dionysus went to Hades to bring back Euripides, and when he arrived he found Euripides debating with Aeschylus over which was the greater tragic dramatist. At the time *The Frogs* first appeared Euripides had just died and the debate was timely as well as witty. It was also pointed and provides practically the first dramatic criticism of which we have a record.

Beyond that, Aristophanes tied his literary criticism to a political discussion. Aristophanes was personally conservative and opposed the liberal drift in Greek politics in his day. Thus when he had Aeschylus finally win the contest, it made his point both about literature and politics. There is no such subtlety or complexity in the new version. Mr. Shevelove has substituted Shaw and Shakespeare for the Greeks hoping to update the play, but a debate between Shaw and the Bard seems as dated today as one between two Greek dramatists. Besides, the lines Michael Feingold, who assisted Shevelove, has gleaned from Shaw and Shakespeare for their debate are little more than recitations of the obvious.

As a result the production is long on novelty but short on originality. Still, it has its bright moments, plus the fun of seeing a tradition continued. It is worth seeing if only because we are not likely to see its like again — at least not for another 20 or 30 years until some bright Yale man decides it is time to push Aristophanes in the pool again.

THEATER IN JAPAN: STRUGGLING WITH TRADITION

Friday, November 10, 1978

Tokyo

It is nighttime in Tokyo, and in Aoyama Park a steady stream of young people makes its way in the dark along a roadway and through bushes to a tent pitched on a bare spot of ground. As they enter the tent the people remove their shoes — the Japanese custom when entering a house — and sit crowded together on straw tatami mats. They have come to see *Kappa*, the latest production of Juro Kara, a young writer-director whose work is among the most exciting in the Japanese avant-garde theater.

Just west of the park, on the top floor of the Parco department store, is the Seibu Theater — a 400-seat ultramodern theater with purple, plush seats. Here another audience gathers to see Kobo Abe's *The Crime of Mr. S. Karuma*. Mr. Abe, a well-known novelist and play-wright, now directs his own experimental theater group. His new play, based on one of his short stories is about a man who has forgotten his own name. The man looks across a desk at a woman, who disappears. Then he is examined by a doctor and found to have no heart: instead, he has a desert in his chest, and the woman is discovered to be trapped in the desert inside him.

Above a coffee shop, on the north side of Tokyo, another avant-garde production is taking place. Tadashi Suzuki's company is inaugurating a small, new theater with a production of Mr. Suzuki's *Salome*. Based on an unlikely combination of Oscar Wilde's *Salome* and Samuel Beckett's *Endgame*, it has been transformed into a contemporary Japanese play. The modern themes and language of Mr. Suzuki's work are combined with an acting style inspired by Noh and Kabuki.

Nearer the center of Tokyo, in an 800-seat theater, an attentive audience, largely middle class and middle-age, is watching the Mingel Company production of *Mountain Range*. Written by Junji Kinoshita just after World War II, *Mountain Range* is the story of a city family evacuated near the end of the war to live with a farm family. It touches on several themes important to the Japanese in the modern era: Hiroshima, the conflict between city and country life, and a love that defies tradition (both hero and heroine are married to someone else). This is the first revival of the play since its original production 29 years ago, and the audience is deeply affected by it.

In a commercial vein, there is a revival of the Toho Company's version of *Fiddler on the Roof*, with a large orchestra and cast. Hisaya Morishige plays a lively but very human Tevye. In Japan, all theater events have short runs — rarely more than a month — but so popular is the Japanese *Fiddler* that this is its sixth revival. Playing in the 1,800-seat Imperial Theater in downtown Tokyo, *Fiddler* will soon set a Japanese record for total performances of a musical.

When Westerners think of theater in Japan they invariably think of the ancient stylized forms: Noh, Kabuki and the adult puppet theater called Bunraku. These striking, traditional forms — still flourishing in Japan — have completely eclipsed modern Japanese theater in the Western consciousness. The five examples above, however, attest to Japan's active, varied modern theater. Part of a cross section seen in a two-week period, the five are only part of the offerings recently on view in Tokyo.

Shuji Tereyama presented an avant-garde production in a large exhibition hall at Tokyo's International Trade Center: two companies performed plays by Kunio Shimizu and Misoru Betsuyaku, two of Japan's finest young playwrights: and there were a score of other productions by Tokyo's equivalent of off-off-Broadway.

When the modern theater movement began in Japan in the early part of this century, the initial debate was whether the theater should modernize or westernize. As in so many areas of Japanese life where a similar debate was held, it appeared impossible to accomplish one without the other. As a result the Shingeki ("new theater") movement of the 1920's and '30's comprised translations of Western plays — Chekhov, Ibsen and French writers — and Japanese plays written in an imitative style. Several successful troupes continue the Shingeki movement: the Mingei (producers of *Mountain Range*), the Shiki headed by Keita Asari and the Subaru directed by Tetsuo Arakawa.

Some Japanese, however, feel that Shingeki drama is too old and too Western. In the 1960's, amid political ferment that opposed further Japan-U.S. defense-pact treaties, an avant-garde theater movement was born. Writer-directors like Mr. Juro, Mr. Suzuki and Mr. Terayama and writers like Mr. Shimizu and Mr. Betsuyaku came out of the movement. Today Japan's avant-garde theater is less political than 10 years ago. Now it is using theater to pose a direct challenge to the country's traditional precepts and moral values. But though their goals are the same, Japan's theater artists are pursuing this in different ways.

Mr. Abe combines his own writer's vision-symbolic and intellectual with the acrobatic, physical acting style of this troupe. Mr. Terayama uses striking stage devices as a vehicle for social criticism. Mr. Suzuki attempts to dress modern ideas in the cloak of traditional. Japanese acting styles. Mr. Kara has developed a brand of theater different from them all.

In *Kappa*, Mr. Kara's latest play, a man with a ventriloquist's dummy dressed as a musketeer and a young woman who delivers food for a caterer set out on personal quests that take them through a series of hilarious, often heartbreaking adventures. The play is satiric and mock heroic, and the acting is charged with energy.

If modern Japanese theater is fragmented, so is the general theater audience. The avant-garde audience is mostly young, with a large female contingent: the Shingeki audience is a mainly middle-aged: still a third audience, also middle-aged, attends Kabuki and Noh. Unfortunately, these different audiences almost never attend the others' performances, unlike in the West, where a very successful or popular work will receive support from disparate audiences. Thus, it is very difficult in Japan for a theater group to build up an audience to support a sustained run.

The most serious problem facing the modern Japanese theater, however, is one that haunts all of Japanese life: the trauma of new versus old, and East versus West. Probably no nation in history has absorbed so much outside culture while holding firmly to much of its own, though it handles the situation astonishingly well. Japan inescapably suffers an ongoing identity crisis.

Keita Asari of the Shiki Company explains it this way: "Japan is caught between two contrary tides, the Oyashio, of cold current, that lashes our western shore, and the Kuroshio, or warm current that sweeps the east. In the theater it is the same way. Japanese theater artists have studied the western theater diligently, but they still do not understand it, any more than Westerners comprehend the essence of our theater. At the same time, we have not discovered a modern theater of our own. Writers and directors pursue their different paths, each hoping to find the answer."

THE ARTS PROVIDE AN OLD CITY'S FOUNDATION

Friday, August 31, 1979

Winston-Salem, N.C.

The Trade Street Mall, a pedestrian walkway in midtown Winston-Salem, is typical of the efforts made a few years ago to attract shoppers to downtown areas. Unfortunately the mall has not lived up to expectations. If you walk down Trade Street today you will see store after store boarded up for lack of customers. There is so little business in the area that Chamber of Commerce President Richard Stockton says his family's store now opens early in the morning and closes at 4:00 p.m.

Like most American cities in the last two decades, Winston-Salem has been fighting the flight of the middle class to the suburbs. A town of 145,000 on the western edge of the Piedmont section of North Carolina, Winston-Salem has already taken several significant steps to reverse the move away from

midtown. It has persuaded some of the corporate giants located in the area to place headquarters buildings in the center of town. The Wachovia Bank Corp. already occupies a large building there, Integon Insurance Corp. is building another and R.J. Reynolds Industries Inc. has just begun a $34 million structure for R.J. Reynolds, its largest subsidiary.

Besides workers, a downtown also needs people who live nearby. In the past the city has attacked blighted neighborhoods with the familiar technique of tearing down old houses and erecting housing projects. A few years ago a young man named Jon DeVries, now an alderman, joined others to convince the city that neighborhoods would improve if Winston-Salem's old houses, were restored and lived in by people who owned them. As a result, condemned houses have been sold to new owners for $1 and condemned lots for another $1. Today one sees neighborhoods downtown with beautifully restored 1890s homes, complete with stained-glass windows and wooden filigree. The percentage of owner occupancy has jumped form 20% to more than 70%.

The people in these homes include artists, faculty members from Winston-Salem's four colleges and blue-collar workers. The area is racially mixed, with some sections 30% black. (Winston-Salem enjoys strong black leadership in key posts, two good examples being Walter Farabee, Director of Economic Development for the city, and Virginia Newell, an alderwoman, member of the arts council board and chairperson of mathematics at Winston-Salem State University.)

These steps are crucial: without daytime office workers in the downtown area and healthy neighborhoods, urban renewal is almost impossible. But for Winston-Salem, as for other cities, this has not been enough; stores are still closed for lack of shoppers. What was needed, the local leadership decided, was a "critical mass": an explosive material at the center that would pull everything together. To provide this, Winston-Salem has come up with a plan many might consider unorthodox: a $13-million arts complex in the center of town to serve as the foundation of the city's economic recovery.

Of the $13 million, a little over $6 million is needed for the conversion of the Carolina Theater — an abandoned 1920s movie theater and vaudeville house — to a modern 1,400-seat theater to be called the Roger L. Stevens Performing Arts Center. The theater will serve as a performing space for various units, including professional troupes, of the North Carolina School of the Arts, and also for the local symphony and traveling Broadway shows.

The balance of the funds will be used to create Winston Square: a complex of art galleries, cabaret theaters, art exhibitions, artists' studios, as well as an outdoor park and theater on two blocks adjacent to the Stevens Center. One notable feature of the plan is that no new structures will be built: every space will be created by converting existing buildings, such as an old YMCA and an abandoned textile mill.

That Winston-Salem should be the first city in the country to make the arts the cornerstone of downtown revitalization is not surprising in view of its record in the arts. The first arts council in America — the prototype for other state and local arts councils — was founded here in 1949. In 1956, the Southeastern Center for Contemporary Art, known as SECCA, was created. A gallery for the promotion and exhibition of the work of artist from 11 Southeastern states, SECCA is still the only regional museum of its kind in

the U.S. Winston-Salem has other important museums in Reynolda House, which features American art, the Old Salem Restoration, and the Museum of Early Southern Decorative Arts.

In 1965, the North Carolina School of the Arts, the nation's first residential high school and college for the performing arts, was founded. Thoroughly professional, the school has placed an extraordinary percentage of its graduates with the country's top symphonies, dance companies and professional theaters.

What chance does a town of less than 150,000 have to raise $13 million for an arts complex? Given Winston-Salem's record, the odds look good. When the School of the Arts was created by the state government in 1965, it was sought by every city in the state, with many promises of future funding. However, shortly before the arrival of the site selection panel, Winston-Salem raised $1 million in 48 hours from

5,000 donors. It got the school.

A recent study showed that Winston-Salem raises more money for the arts per capita than any city in the U.S., and local corporations, private foundations and individual donors who have proved generous in the past have pledged their support of the new project. This latest undertaking, however, is far beyond the usual arts campaign and will require additional help from the outside.

R. Philip Hanes Jr., longtime worker for the arts in Winston-Salem, is convinced that the arts are good business. He has visions of downtown theaters, restaurants, galleries and boutiques aglow every night and of streets filled with people. His view of the economic possibilities of the arts is supported in part by the study earlier this year by the Joint Economic Committee of Congress, which concluded that in determining what attracted businesses to a given locality, the "quality of life," including cultural attractions, was more important than "business-related factors."

The Economic Development Administration of the Department of Commerce also feels strongly about the potential the arts have to mobilize other economic factors. Winston-Salem has applied to the EDA for a $2,140,000 grant to help with the Stevens Center. In commenting on the application, which is near a decision, a spokesman for the EDA said that if approved, the grant would "provide a catalytic effect to Winston-Salem to realize its dream for downtown: a renovation that will enhance the economic environment and improve the human environment."

Winston-Salem's mayor, Wayne A. Corpening, feels certain that the EDA will be proved correct. He already has indications that once the $13 million is in hand, other sources will invest $100 million in additional downtown projects. As he lists the projects — a new coliseum, an old mill converted to private stores — he punctuates each item with the phrase, "The Lord willing." But there is another expression South-erners are fond of using: "The Lord helps those who help themselves." In terms of the arts, the people of Win-ston-Salem seem to be doing their best to hold up their part of the bargain.

Mr. Wilson is the Journal's theater critic.

Yves Montand at the Met: Superb Entertainment

Thursday, September 9, 1982

New York

In 1950-51, when I was studying at the University of Edinburgh, I went to Paris several times during the year. I would sit up all night on the coach train to London and take the boat from New Haven to Dieppe, which was the longest but cheapest crossing. Once in Paris I would head for the Left Bank, the area around St. Germaine de Pres. There were still a number of Americans there after the war and their favorite night spot was a tiny club called L'Abbaye. It was run by two ex-GIs, one of whom played the guitar and sang, and it was so small that at the end of a song the customers snapped their fingers instead of applauding. It seemed the height of sophistication.

Even more sophisticated was the song that one heard everywhere that year — the record of "Les Feuilles Mortes" ("Autumn Leaves") sung by Yves Montand. Thirty years later Mr. Montand is still singing the song, this time in person standing alone on the stage of the Metropolitan Opera.

Some things in life endure; the song has endured, but more to the point, so has Mr. Montand. He is, in fact, a stronger performer than ever. Son of a working man who had to begin working himself at 11, Mr. Montand began in supper clubs in Paris, made records, and later turned to films where he has starred in 55 pictures, including *State of Siege*, *Z*, and *Is Paris Burning?*

After a 13-year absence from music hall stages, he returned on this sixtieth birthday in a triumphant one-man show at the Olympia Theater in Paris. It was this performance that prompted the Metropolitan Opera to present him for a week as

305

the first popular entertainer offered by the Met in its 96-year history.

Backed by an eight piece orchestra — without blaring trumpets or saxophones — Mr. Montand stands on stage for an hour and forty minutes singing nearly 30 songs. (Mr. Montand sings in French, and the Met helpfully provides concertgoers with printed translations of the songs.)

Watching him sing, and occasionally strut and dance, one gets intimations of many of the masters of the 20th century. When he dons tails and conducts an orchestra — in a song about a conductor who falls in love with a woman who likes only Viennese waltzes — he evokes Danny Kaye. When he opens the show with a number about sauntering in Paris, he puts his knees together and sways from side to side or stylishly extends one foot while raising an arm in the air, and one would swear that Fred Astaire had stepped on stage. Another time Ray Bolger is

dancing there.

Despite fleeting images of others, it is Mr. Montand himself who stands alone, a performer supreme. His rich baritone can by turns caress a love song, capture the infectious rhythms of jazz in a song about Duke Ellington, explode joyously in "Old Time Song," and invoke instant nostalgia in his version of "Roses of Picardy."

As an actor in his songs, Mr. Montand plays many parts, each completely convincing. In white tie and tails he is the ultra-sophisticate; in an open-necked black shirt he is a laborer just come from his job. It helps, of course, that he is an expert pantomimist: he can become a cat, punch-drunk boxer, a Western film hero. In one number about a jealous bellboy who kills a woman and her boyfriend at the hotel, he reenacts the entire story. Suddenly the light changes and he is slouched in a chair, one wrist folded across the other. The image is instantaneous: the bellboy is in jail. In another number

— about a worker on a coffee plantation — we never see his face; he stands absolutely still while a light shines down on the wide-brimmed hat he wears.

The lighting, designed by Mr. Montand, is a work of art in itself. In some scenes it is all angular: an amber or blue light striking him from the side or behind. In others, strutting in a bowler or a top hat, he is in black silhouette.

After New York, Mr. Montand takes his show to Washington, D.C., Quebec, Montreal, Ottawa, San Francisco and Los Angeles. Wherever he goes he raises music hall entertainment to a high art.

ROASTING THE PHANTOM

Wednesday, November 9, 1988

New York

The fun at *Forbidden Broadway 1988* begins when you enter the door of the theater and are handed a program. Instead of the usual Playbill, you are given "Playkill," which is a tipoff to the theatrical mayhem about to ensue. A satirical review that has been skewering Broadway shows for some years in a second-story cabaret on Manhattan's Upper West Side, *Forbidden Broadway* has recently moved across town and down two flights to the basement of the refurbished Theatre East.

The setting is still a cabaret: audience members crowd around tiny tables the size of a dinner plate that are supposed to hold six cups of cappuccino plus a platter of fruit and cookies. The stage is not much larger, but what counts is the amount of entertainment packed onto it. The entire cast — which at times seems to number thousands — consists of four performers: Toni DiBuono, Roxie Lucas, David B. McDonald and Michael McGrath. The sole musical accompaniment is pianist Philip Fortenberry.

One reason the success of *Forbidden Broadway* is the performers' ability to capture the mannerisms and voices of the people they are impersonating, from Ethel Merman to Patti LuPone. Toni DiBuono, for example as Ms. LuPone in "Anything Goes," imitates not only the latter's knife-edged nasality but her self-infatuation in "I Get a Kick Out of Me."

Forbidden Broadway is the inspiration of Gerard Alessandrini, who writes the parodies of well-known shoes and provides the direction. Fortunately for Mr. Alessandrini, in the last year and a half several large-scale musicals have opened that provide perfect subjects for satire. The new edition opens on a high note — literally. A performer is belting out a number with ear-splitting amplification, which underlines right away the pervasive electronic sound enhancement that has infected Broadway musicals like the bubonic plague.

In the past *Forbidden Broadway* has concentrated on musicals, but this time around two plays proved irresistible. One is M. *Butterfly*, about the French diplomat involved with a Chinese opera star that he discovers some years later is actually a man, and a spy to boot. Dressed in a Chinese kimono, Mr. McGrath makes fun of this far-fetched fable with biting lyrics set to the music of "Poor Butterfly."

The other non-musical subject to Mr. Alessandrini's scalpel is David Mamet's *Speed the Plow*. Here the target is Madonna, a commercial pop star who was cast in a play that claimed to be decrying crass commercialism.

The two male stars (one of them resembling Mr. Mamet) engage in a *My Fair Lady* attempt to teach Madonna to act when they sing, "I Strain in Vain to Train Madonna's Brain."

When *Forbidden Broadway* turns to the recent blockbuster musicals, it unleashes the full force of its satire. Producer Cameron MacIntosh, dressed as Napoleon, is kidded for this penchant for selling all manner of souvenirs, including "Les Miz' chocolates shaped like orphans." The Phantom figures from *Phantom of the Opera* is composer Andrew Lloyd Webber, whose wife, Sarah Brightman, sings, "I'll be at the center of the Phantom craze; and I needn't show up for my matinees." When Ms. Brightman rips the mask from the Lloyd Webber figure he turns out to be — well, I won't reveal what cartoon character he is underneath. Mr. Lloyd Webber has his revenge, however: once unmasked, he drops a tiny chandelier from the ceiling on Ms. Brightman.

By far the most extensive, as well as the most devastating, sequence is reserved for *Les Miserables*. Three characters dressed in rags and torn revolutionary uniforms come on stage twirling, imitating the turntable that spins incessantly in the show. Then Ms. DiBuono steps forward and sings:

There was a time when shows were fun
And they used bright lighting
And the shows weren't so long
And the songs weren't so biting
There was time, then it all went wrong.
I dreamed a show in days gone by
When all the scenery looked so pretty.
I didn't sing one song, and then die,
And all my costumes weren't so gritty.

Following this number, the *Les Miserables* scene builds and builds, with tricolored flags, rag dolls dressed as French orphaned, and more twirls of the turntable to a stirring mock anthem that ends Act One.

Because there is a wealth of new material in *Forbidden Broadway*, we are not as bothered as we might be in the chestnuts that Mr. Alessandrini trots out: Mary Martin and Ethel Merman in a dueling duet, *Cats*, Joel Gray in *Cabaret*. Several of the oldies, however, definitely should be retired, one in particular being a duet between Liza Minelli and her mother, Judy Garland, which misfires entirely.

The old stuff does remind us of one thing, however. At the opening of Act Two, Mr. McGrath appears on stage in the persona of George M. Cohan and, to the tune of "Give My Regards to Broadway," sings, "Give My Regrets to Broadway." It is a not-too-subtle reminder of the perilous state Broadway is in. When we look past the big musicals that *Forbidden Broadway* makes fun of, we become painfully aware of the dearth of new material.

During the past three months, only three productions have opened on Broadway. All three were revivals, and only one, *Ain't Misbehavin*, is still running. The

total absence of anything
new at the time of year when
Broadway used to be bursting at the seams makes the
title *Forbidden Broadway* sadly
prophetic.